SOURCES FOR IRISH FAMILY HISTORY

Sources for Irish Family History

A LISTING OF BOOKS AND ARTICLES ON THE
HISTORY OF IRISH FAMILIES

Compiled by

James G. Ryan

First published in 2001
Flyleaf Press
4 Spencer Villas
Glenageary, Co. Dublin
Ireland
www.flyleaf.ie

© 2001 Flyleaf Press

British Library cataloguing in Publication Data available

ISBN 0 9539974-2-1

The information in this book is subject to change without notice.

Design by Cathy Henderson

Contents

Acknowledgements 6

Introduction 7

Abbreviations and Sources 11

Listing of Family Sources 17

Placename Index 156

Acknowledgements

I am happy to acknowledge the authors Edward McLysaght and Brian De Breffni who have compiled previous bibliographies of Irish family history.

Thanks are also due to Brian Smith for his encouragement, and for his assistance in sourcing and checking references.

Introduction

This volume contains a list of books. monographs and periodical papers dealing with specific Irish families. The references cited are mainly accounts of particular family lines and vary from fond and emotional accounts of families and their ancestral homes to dispassionate, well-researched and fully documented family studies and pedigrees. The greater value of the material contained in these references is to put some human dimension to the barren facts that may be obtained from the usual range of records. No church or civil record will inform us that our ancestors were wonderful singers or dancers; or of the details of their travels or their occupation; nor whether their recorded marriages were the culminations of great romances, or of family arrangements. Such information can, however, be occasionally found in the memoirs and letters detailed in the articles and books listed here.

In terms of scale, the referenced material varies from a few lines to several volumes. In attempting to compile the list, some decisions had to be made on what to include. It would be gratifying to be able to set down exact criteria which by which it was determined how material was rejected or included. However, the only guides were usefulness and practicality. As researchers of family history will know, the information critical to research may just as easily be found in 2 stray lines of information, as in large works of reference. I have therefore erred on the side of inclusion in all cases of doubt. Some biographies, for instance, have been included where they include more than just references to the immediate family. In addition, there are references to manuscripts in various archives. However, the list does not attempt to be comprehensive on this source.

A few points to be noted by readers are:

❑ Names beginning with O' or Mc' are listed by the letter following the prefix, i.e. 'O'Connor' is listed under 'Connor' and 'McBride' under 'Bride'.

❑ The references cited are generally accounts of a particular family line and none attempt to deal with all holders of a particular surname. Some optimistic readers may be turning these pages hoping that the research on their family has already been done. Not many will be satisfied on this point.

❑ The location within Ireland of a cited family is not always evident from the title. In some cases an indication of location has been added (see Placename index). Otherwise, it may be useful to establish (from the abbreviation list) if the periodical in which the article appears has a specific area of interest. The majority of the periodicals cited are concerned with specific counties or areas. Articles rarely appear in such journals unless there is some local significance.

❑ The references are almost always listed according to the name form used in the article cited. You should therefore be aware of all possible variations of the family name of interest and search under each one. References useful for this purpose are:
- Edward McLysaght 'Irish families: their names, arms, and origins. Dublin: Irish Academic Press, 1985 (and others in this series):
- Robert Bell's 'Book of Ulster Surnames' Belfast 1988;
- Robert E. Matheson's 'Special Report on Surnames in Ireland together with varieties and synonyms of surnames and Christian names'. Reprinted by Genealogical Pub. Co., Baltimore (1968);
- Patrick Woulfe 'Irish Names and Surnames' Dublin: M.H. Gill & son, Ltd., 1923.

❑ The referenced articles deal with the history of families in Ireland. Further articles and books exist which deal with the history of Irish families in their country of emigration. These have not been specifically sought, although some are listed.

❑ The lists do <u>not</u> include entries in the several major references to pedigrees of Irish families. These contain a wealth of information which it is pointless to repeat here, and they should be searched separately. They include:
- Burke's Irish Family Records. Ed. Hugh Montgomery-Massingberd. London & NY: Burke's Peerage Ltd; 1976.
- A Genealogical & Heraldic History of the Landed Gentry of Ireland. Sir John B. Burke. London 1912.
- O'Hart, John. Irish Pedigrees or the Origin and Stem of the Irish Nation. McGlashan & Gill, Dublin, 1876; and New York; Murphy & McCarthy (1923). (Origins of the Gaelic families of Ireland)
- Visitation of Ireland: 1897-1918. Joseph J. Howard & Frederick A. Crisp. Genealogical Pub. Co. Baltimore 1973. (6 Volumes of pedigrees of major Gentry of Ireland)

An analysis of the families which are the subject of the cited articles and books will show that they do not accurately reflect the popularity of the family names. Unsurprisingly, the bulk of the families which are the subjects of these studies are the prominent families. The landed gentry are a particular subject for these studies. Another factor is the existence of a local journal in which to publish. Families in counties with long-established and active local history journals (e.g. Kildare, Cork & Kilkenny) are more likely to be featured than those in counties where local history publication is a more recent activity (e.g.Mayo, Longford).

Articles in periodicals are referenced according to a standard format, which provides the details in the following sequence and with parentheses '( )' as indicated:

Title of article   This may be very brief or very detailed according to the policy of the editors.

Name of Periodical This is usually abbreviated – see Abbreviations (p. 11)for explanation & further information.

Volume Number   Periodicals appear in volumes, annually or less frequently according to the policy of the publishers.

(Part No.)   Volumes are often published in separate 'parts', eg. on a quarterly basis.

(Year/s)   The year of publication, which is often a critical requirement when ordering a periodical.

Page number(s)   The series of pages occupied by the article.

For example: *The Nagles of Mount Nagle, Annakissy. Ir.Gen. 11 (2) (1954) 337–48* shows that the article on the Nagles appeared in Volume 11, part 2 of the Irish Genealogist which was published in 1954. It occupies pages 337 to 348 of this volume.

Most of the periodicals cited are specialist genealogical or local history journals and are in most major genealogical libraries with an Irish holding. The International Standard Serial Number (ISSN) is provided (where available) and will assist libraries in tracing copies. Failing this, copies of articles may be obtained through inter-library loan or photocopy schemes. In the list of Abbreviations and Sources (page 11) the website or other contact details for many of the journal publishers is provided. Back-copies of these journals can often be purchased. If no website is listed, it may still be useful to do a web search for the publishers, since new websites are being created every day. Note that many periodicals are published by voluntary local groups and the frequency and standard of publication may vary widely over time. Some periodicals also cease publication after a few issues.

Book references contain the information: Title; Author; Place of publication and Publisher; Year of Publication. Where available, an ISBN (International Standard Book Number) is given, which will make it easy for your librarian or bookseller to find a copy. This is only available for modern books. The call number for the National Library of Ireland, and/or the Mormon Library system is given for rarer books, or donated monographs.

Some of the **books** or **booklets** cited are very difficult to obtain. Many have been privately published (usually by the author) in small numbers for distribution to family members and friends. Even many of those recently published do not contain an ISBN (International Standard Book Number) or Library of Congress number or other reference which would make them easier to trace. However, major genealogical libraries have large collections of such titles. If no library copy can be found, it may be possible to trace an original copy through bookshops specialising in Irish antiquarian books. Some examples with websites are:

- ❏ **Kenny's Bookshop**, High Street, Galway, Ireland. (Website: http://www.kennys.ie/)

- ❏ **DeBurca Rare Books**, 27 Priory Drive, Blackrock, Co. Dublin, Ireland (website: http://indigo.ie/~deburca/)

- ❏ **Bantry Bookstore**, New Street, Bantry, Co. Cork, Ireland (website: http://www.bantrybk.com/)

A final useful source are the **family histories** or **papers** which are specific to a particular library. For instance, the National Library of Ireland and the LDS libraries have a large collection of family histories donated by individuals, which may not be available elsewhere. The Leader Collection in the Irish Genealogical Research Society, also contains material (varying from 'a few lines' to detailed pedigrees) on Cork families. If you are unable to visit an Irish library yourself, a researcher may be contracted to do so. Lists of researchers are available on the website of the National Library of Ireland (Website: http://www.nli.ie) and also from the Association of Professional Genealogists of Ireland (Website: http://indigo.ie/~apgi/)

Abbreviations and Sources

Abbreviation	Periodical or description of abbreviation
Anal. Hib.	Analecta Hibernica; published by the Irish Manuscripts Commission (Website: http://www.irmss.ie)
Ardagh & Clonmacnois Antiq. J.	Pub. by Ardagh & Clonmacnoise Antiquarian Society from 1926. (NLI 794105 a1)
Ardmore J.	Ardmore Journal (ISSN: 0790-312X)
Bantry Hist.& Arch Soc. J.	Bantry Historical and Archaeological Society Journal (ISSN 0791-6612)
Breifne	Published by Breifne Historical Society (Cumann Seanchas Bhreifne) Co. Cavan.
Carloviana	Published by the Old Carlow Society. (ISSN 0790-0813)
Cathair na Mart	Published by Westport Historical Society (ISSN: 0332 4117)
CLAHJ	County Louth Archaeological & Historical Journal (ISSN 0070 1327)
Clogher Record	Journal for the Diocese of Clogher (comprising Cos. Fermanagh, Monaghan and part of Tyrone) (Each edition has a separate ISBN number)
Clongownian	Pub. by Clongowes Wood College (NLI Ir 37941 c6)
Clonmel	Clonmel Archaeological & Historical Society Journal
Comp.	compiled (by)
Dal gCais	Journal on history & archaeology of Co. Clare. (ISSN 0790-7303).
Decies	Journal of Waterford Archaeological & Historical Soc. (ISSN 1393-3116)
	(Website: http://www.infohwy.com/~gfewer/decies.htm)
Donegal Ann.	Donegal Annual; pub. By Co. Donegal Historical Society (ISSN 0416-2773)
Dublin Hist. Rec.	Dublin Historical Record: Journal of the Old Dublin Society (ISSN: 0012-6861)
Duiche Neill	Journal of O'Neill Country Historical Society, Co. Tyrone (ISSN 0964 4970)
Dun Laoghaire J.	Dun Laoghaire Journal: pub. by Dun Laoghaire Borough Historical Society (ISSN:07913680))

Eigse	Eigse: A Journal of Irish Studies. Pub. by National University of Ireland.
Eire-Ir.	Eire-Ireland (ISSN 0013-2683) Pub. by Irish American Cultural Inst. (Website: http://www.irishaci.org/)
Familia	Familia: Ulster Historical Review (ISSN: 0950-8481) pub. by Ulster Historical Foundation, 12 College Sq. E., Belfast BT1 6DD.
Family Links	(ISSN: 02607816)
Family Names of Co. Cork	Book by Diarmuid O'Murchada. Dublin: Glendale Press 1985. (ISBN 090760630X). Reprint Collins Press, Cork: 1996 (ISBN 1898256136)
Friends Hist. Lib.	Friends Historical Library, Swanbrook Hse., Morehampton Rd., Dublin 4, Ireland
Gaelic Gleanings	Pub. by Magee Publications, Santa Ana, California
Galway Roots	pub by Galway Family History Society (ISSN 0791 8526)
Gateway to the Past	Journal of Ballinteer Branch of the Irish Family History Society. (ISSN: 0791-9654)
Gen.	The Genealogist (UK)
Geneal. Mag.	Genealogists Magazine. Pub. by the Society of Genealogists, London (Website: http://www.sog.org.uk)
The Glynns	Pub by the Glens of Antrim Historical Society
GO	Genealogical Office (now a part of the NLI q.v.)
GSI	Genealogical Society of Ireland (website: http://welcome.to/ genealogyIreland)
IAL	Irish Army List (Illustrations historical and genealogical of King James's Irish Army List (1689) Dublin, John D'Alton, ND. Background information on the (mainly Catholic) officers of the Army of King James' II in the campaign of 1689-1692
IGRS	Irish Genealogical Research Society, c/o The Irish Club, 82 Eaton Square, London, SW 1, UK. The Leader Collection was compiled by Michael Leader (see Ir. Gen. 10 (2) (1999) p. 173-201). The collection contains files on the history of many Cork families, some of which 'may be very detailed and some just a few lines'.
Ir.Am. Gen.	Irish-American Genealogist. Pub. by Augustan Society, Torrance, California 1974 -. (Issues 1-4 called Irish Genealogical Helper) (NLI Ir 9291 i3)
Ir. Anc.	Irish Ancestor (ISSN: 00471437)
Irish Builder	Irish Builder and Engineering Record. NLI Ir 6905 i42
Irish Family History	Journal of the Irish Family History Society (http:// homepage.tinet.ie/~ifhs). (ISSN: 0790-7060)

Ir. Gen.	Irish Genealogist - Pub. by IGRS (q.v) (ISSN 0306-8358).
Irish Heritage Links	Pub by Irish Heritage Association, Belfast (ISSN: 0957-0837)
Irish Sword	Journal of the Military History Society of Ireland. (ISSN 0021-1389)
JAPMD	Journal of the Association for the Preservation of Memorials of the Dead
J. Butler Soc.	Journal of the Butler Society: Wellbrook Press, Kilkenny (ISSN 0572 5828)
JCHAS	Journal of the Cork Historical and Archaeological Society (Website: http://homepage.tinet.ie/~chasoc/)
JCKAS	Journal of the Co. Kildare Archaeological Society (ISSN 0085-2503).
JGAHS	Journal of the Galway Archaeological & Historical Society (ISSN: 0332-415X)
J. Gen. Soc. I.	Journal of the Genealogical Society of Ireland (ISSN: 1393-936X)
JKAHS	Journal of the Kerry Archaeology & History Society (ISSN: 0085-2503)
J. Old Athlone Soc.	Journal of the Old Athlone Society (Co. Westmeath & Roscommon)
J. Old Drogheda Soc.	Journal of the Old Drogheda Society (Co. Louth) (ISSN 8602 1356)
JOWS	Journal of the Old Wexford Society
JRSAI	Journal of the Royal Society of Antiquaries of Ireland (ISSN: 0035-9106)
JW&SEIAS	Journal of the Waterford & Southeast Ireland Archaeological Society (NLI Ir 794105w1)
J. West Wicklow Hist. Soc.	Journal of the West Wicklow Historical Society (ISSN 0790 1739)
Kerry Arch. Mag.	Kerry Archaeological Magazine
King James' IAL	King James's Irish Army List: D'Alton, John. Illustrations historical and genealogical of King James's Irish Army List (1689) Dublin, John D'Alton.
LDS Lib.	(Church of)Latter Day Saints Library. The library system of the Mormon church based in Salt Lake City, Utah with local branches in many countries.
Leader Collection	see IGRS
Lough Gur Hist. Soc. J.	Lough Gur & District Historical Society Journal
Mallow Field Club J.	Mallow Field Club Journal; pub. by Mallow Archaeological & Historical Society WWW: http://www.rootsweb.com/~irlmahs/

Mf.	microfilm
Ms.	Manuscript
NAI	National Archives of Ireland (Website: www.nationalarchives.ie)
Nat. Gen. Soc. Qtly.	National Genealogical Society Quarterly (Website: http://www.ngsgenealogy.org/)
n.d.	Not dated
NLI	National Library of Ireland, Kildare St., Dublin 2 (Website http://www.nli.ie)
N. Munster Antiq. J.	North Munster Antiquarian Journal. Published by the Thomond Archaeological Society. (ISSN 0332-0820) (called N. Munster Archaeological J. until 1944)
N.p.	No publisher or place of publication stated.
Old Kilkenny Review	Published by: Kilkenny Archaeological Society: (ISSN 0332 0774)
Old Limerick J.	Journal of Old Limerick Society. (NLI Ir 05 I38)
Ossory	Transactions of the Ossory Archaeological Society (NLI 794105)
p.	page
Past	Past: published by the Ui Ceinnsealaigh Historical Society
pr.pr.	privately printed (usually indicating that the author printed a limited number for circulation to family and friends)
Proc. R.I.A	Proceedings of the Royal Irish Academy (http://www.ria.ie) (ISSN: 0035-8991)
PRONI	Public Record Office of Northern Ireland (Website: proni.nics.gov.uk/)
Pub.	published
RCB Library	Representative Church Body Library (website:www.ireland.anglican.org/library/library.html)
Ref(s).	Reference(s)
Reportorium Novum	Journal of the Dublin Diocesan Historical Society
RIA	Royal Irish Academy (Website http://www.ria.ie)
Riocht na Midhe	Records of the Meath Archaeological and Historical Society (ISSN: n/a)
Seanchas Ardmhacha	Journal of the Armagh Diocesan Historical Society (ISSN: 0488-0196)
Sliabh Aughty	J. of East Clare Heritage Society, Tomgraney, Co. Clare. (ISSN 0791-4571)
S. Mayo Family Res. J.	South Mayo Family Research Journal
Studies	Studies: An Irish Quarterly Review (ISSN: 0039-3495) (Website: http://www.jesuit.ie/studies/)

Swanzy Notebooks	Notebooks compiled by H.B. Swanzy containing information on Irish genealogies. They are held at the RCB Library, Dublin (qv)
Teathbha	Journal of the Longford Historical Society (ISSN: 0332-0839)
The Other Clare	Journal of the Shannon Archaeological Society (Co. Clare) (ISSN 0332-088X)
Tipp Hist. J.	Tipperary Historical Journal (ISSN: 0791-0665) (Website: http://www.iol.ie/~tipplibs/Journals.htm)
Ulster Gen. & Hist. Guild	Ulster Genealogical & Historical Guild. Published by Ulster Historical Foundation.
Ulster J. Arch.	Ulster Journal of Archaeology. Published by the Ulster Archaeological Society (ISSN: 0082-7355)
Ulster Local Studies	Pub. by: The Federation for Ulster Local Studies Ltd. (ISSN 0266-3473)
Wexford Gentry	The Wexford Gentry. Art Kavanagh & Rory Murphy. Irish Family Names, Wexford. Vol 1 (1994) ISBN 0952478501: Vol 2 (1996) ISBN 0952478536

Listing of Family Sources

Abercorn

Abercorn (Hamilton) Family Records (1611–1890). PRONI Ms. DOD 623.

Acheson

Family pedigrees, notes and letters for the following families: Acheson (Co.Armagh), Bell (Newry, Co. Down), Wyly (Thomastown, Co. Kildare), Black (Newry, Co. Down), Gaussen, Fleming (Monaghan), Gray, Johnston, Campbell, McGill, Moore (Carlingford), Armagh Co. Museum; LDS Mf.1279354.

Acheson families, Co. Armagh. Armagh Co. Museum. Ms, N8; LDS Mf.1279356.

Pedigree of Acheson Family of Cork: IGRS Library (Leader Collection).

Acton

Acton Papers (Stradbrook, Co. Dublin). Anal. Hib. 25: 3–13.

Adair *see* **Boyd, Lockhart**

Adams

A genealogical history of Adams of Cavan. M.R.W. Adams. London: Mitchell & Hughes 1903.

A history of the families of Adams & Peers. B.W. Adams & M.R.W. Adams. Calcutta: Traill & Co., 1891. (Adams of Cavan) LDS Lib. 929.2415 Ad17ab.

Adderley

Pedigree of Adderley Family of Cork: IGRS Library (Leader Collection).

Agnew

The Agnews in Co. Antrim. Ulster J. Arch. 7, 2nd ser. (1901) 166–71.

The East Ulster bardic family of Ó'Gnímh. Éigse 20 (1984) 106–217 (Anglicised as O'Gneiffe or Agnew).

Ahearne or **Aherne**

The Seven generations: 1757-1977. (O'Brien & Ahearne). LDS Lib. Ms. 929.2415 A1 no. 36.

Pedigree of Ahern/Aherin Family of Cork: IGRS Library (Leader Collection)

Ahern/ Ahearn/Hearn in 'Family Names of Co. Cork' (see abbrevs.) (Notes on origins & members in Co.Cork).

Aher

Pedigree of Aher Family of Cork: IGRS Library (Leader Collection).

Aitkenhead
> Pedigree of Aitkenhead Family of Cork: IGRS Library (Leader Collection).

Alcock
> Pedigree of Alcock Family of Cork: IGRS Library (Leader Collection).

Alcorn *see* **Moore**

Aldworth
> Pedigree of Aldworth Family of Cork: IGRS Library (Leader Collection).

Alen *see* **Allen**

Alexander *see* **Glasson**
> The Alexander family of Boom Hall. Robert Alexander. Londonderry, n.d.

Algoe *see* **Moore**

McAlindon *see* **Anderson**

Alison *see* **Rothwell**

Allen or Alen *see also* **Pearson**
> Alen of St. Wolstan's. Henry J. B. Clements. JCKAS 1 (5) (1892–95) 340–
> 41.
> An account of the family of Alen, of St. Wolstan's, Co. Kildare. JCKAS 4 (2)
> (1903–05) 95–110; 5(1906–08) 344–47.
> Ladytown and the Allens. JCKAS 9 (1918–21) 60–69.
> David Allens: the history of a family firm. W. E. D. Allen. London, 1957.
> Notes on Punchestown & Cradockstown. (The Allen family of Kildare) JCKAS
> 5 (1) 1906, pp. 37-46.
> Pedigree Book for Allen Family of Cork: IGRS Library (Leader Collection)
> The Pooles of Mayfield. Rosemary ffolliott. Dublin: Hodges Figgis (1958).
> (Refs to Allens of Cavan, Tipperary & Cork: 1600s to 1750s).
> The Allens of Ulster: some descendants of John Allen of Killynumber,
> Kilcronaghan, Loughinsholin, Co. Londonderry. Roy Allen. Mississauga,
> Ont: 1995. LDS Lib. 929.2415 AL53a (refs to Roy, Rutherford, Denford,
> Brayman, Clifton).

Amory
> Descendants of Hugh Amory, 1605–1805. G. E. Meredith. London, 1901.

McAnally or **McEnally** *see* **Lawless**

Ancketill *see* **Anketell**

Anderson *see also* **Mullan**
> The Andersons of Co. Kilkenny. A. L. B. Anderson. Simla, 1931.
> Pedigrees of Anderson, Burleigh, Hollingsworth, McAlindon, McBride,
> Peebles, Whaley, Woodhouse, and Smith. LDS Mf.1279327.
> Family descent of Anderson of Flush & Bawn, Sixmilecross, Co. Tyrone (1543
> to 1977). Robert H. Anderson ; revised edition by J.G.T. Anderson. Omagh:
> Tyrone Constitution, 1977.

Andrews
> Nine generations: a history of the Andrews family, millers of Comber. Ed.

John Burls from the manuscript of Sydney Andrews. Belfast, 1958. LDS Lib. 929.2415 An26a. (NLI Call No. Ir9292 a9).

Annesley

Annesley of Camolin. Wexford Gentry Vol. 1 (see abbreviations).

Anson

The Ansons at Ardmore. Ardmore J. 5(1988) 44–50.

Anstis

Pedigree of Anstis Family of Cork: IGRS Library (Leader Collection).

Anthony

The Anthony Family of Carrigcastle and Seafield. Decies 16 (1981) 15–22.

Anketell or **Ankitel**

A short history, of the . . . family of Ancketill or Anketell compiled by one of its members. Augusta Anketell. Belfast, 1901. (NLI Call No. Ir 9292 a6).

Pedigree of Ankitel Family of Cork: IGRS Library (Leader Collection).

Archbold

Capt William Archbold (of Athy, Co Kildare) in 'King James' IAL' (Notes on family members pre-1700)

Archdale

Memoirs of the Archdales with the descents of some allied families. Henry Blackwood Archdale. Enniskillen: Impartial Reporter, 1925.

Archdeacon or **Archdekin** *see also* **Cody**

Archdeacon Family in the American South (1730 1875). Old Kilkenny Review 51 (1999) 28.

The ten civic families of Kilkenny. Old Kilkenny Review, 7 (1954) p.1-19. (Refs. to early histories of Archdekin, Archer, Cowley, Langton, Lett, Knaresborough, Lawless, Raggett, Rothe & Shee).

Archer *see also* **Archdeacon**

An inquiry into the origin of the family of Archer in Kilkenny, with notices of other families of the name in Ireland. JRSAI 9 (1867) 220–32.

Pedigree of Archer Family of Cork: IGRS Library (Leader Collection).

Armstrong *see also* **Waldron**

Armstrong of Tipperary. 'Swanzy Notebooks'. RCB Library, Dublin.

Francis Armstrong of Ireland and his descendants in America. Brenda Robertson. 1995.

Pedigree of Armstrong Family of Cork: IGRS Library (Leader Collection).

Arnoldi

Arnoldi of Dublin, 27 Entries in the Family Bible. JAPMD 8 (1910–12) 71.

Arnup

Pedigree of Arnup Family of Cork: IGRS Library (Leader Collection).

Arthur *see* **McLysaght**

MacArtney *see* **MacAulay.**

Ash or **Ashe**

> The Ash manuscript and other family records. Ed. Rev. E.T. Martin. Belfast, 1890.
>
> Notes on the Cooke, Ashe and Swift Families, all of Dublin. JAPMD 9 (1912–16) 503.
>
> Ashe Families. Genealogists Mag. 6 (8) (Dec 1933).
>
> Ash family records, inc. a history of the Ash family of Londonderry, 1736. (GO Ms. 514; LDS Mf. 257821).
>
> Pedigree of Ashe Family of Cork: IGRS Library (Leader Collection).

Ashmur

> Family pedigrees: Ashmur, Atkinson, Blackham, Blair, Campbell, Carr, Caulfield, Gartlan, Gordon, Grey, Hamill, Harshaw, Henry, Hutchinson, Jennings, Johnston, Maguire, Martin, McCleneham, McCormick, Mitchell, Morell, Nesbitt, Nunn, Townley, Walker, Watson, Wright. Armagh Co. Museum Ms. F6: LDS Mf.1279353.

Aston *see* **Chamberlain**

Athy

> Captain George Athy (of Galway & Maryland) and his descendants: a guide to the first 6 generations of the Athy, Athey, Atha, Athon family in America. Lawrence F. Athy. Houston, Texas 1987.

Atkin

> Pedigree of Atkin or Atkins Family of Cork: IGRS Library (Leader Collection).

Atkinson *see also* **Ashmur**

> Pedigrees of Atkinson, Beck, Chambers, Cole, Jackson, and Pilleys or Pillows. LDS Mf. 1279354.

Auchinleck

> Brief Genealogies of Auchinleck et al in 'The History of 2 Ulster Manors'. Earl of Belmore, London/Dublin, 1903.

Auchmuty *see* **Lyons**

MacAulay or **McAuley** *see also* **McGawley**

> Gleanings in Family History from the Antrim Coast: The MacAuleys & MacArtneys. Ulster J. Arch. 8 (1860) 196–210.

McAuliffe

> McAuliffe in 'Family Names of Co. Cork' (see abbrevs.) (Notes on family origins to 1700).

Austen

> Pedigree of Austen Family of Cork: IGRS Library (Leader Collection).

Aylmer

> The Aylmer Family. JCKAS 1 (5) (1893–95) 295–307; 3 (1899–1902) 169–78; 4 (1903–05) 179–83.
>
> Donadea and the Aylmer family. JCKAS 3 (1899–1902) 169–78.

The Aylmers of Lyons, Co. Kildare. JCKAS 4 (1903–05) 179–83.

The Aylmers of Ireland. F. J. Aylmer. London, Mitchell, Hughes & Clark, 1931.

Reminiscences of Donadea Castle JCKAS 14 (1968) 362-364. (Aylmer).

Capt Gerald Aylmer (of Kildare) in 'King James' IAL' (Notes on family members pre-1700).

Aylward

The family of Aylward. Ir.Gen. 4 (1970) 157–66, (1971) 252–66, (1972) 397–416.

Babington

The Babingtons of Cavan. Breifne 5(21) (1982–83).

Babington Family. Genealogists Mag. 9 (8) (Mar 1943).

Bagenal

Vicissitudes of an Anglo-Irish family, 1530–1800. P. H. Bagenal. London, 1925.

Bagge

Genealogical account of the Bagge family of Co. Waterford. Dublin, 1860.

Bagot

The Bagots of Nurncy. JCKAS 7 (5) (1912–14) 317–24.

Bagwell

History of the Bagwell family. HarietBagwell. 1930(?) NLI Ms 32,617. (Marlfield House, Clonmel, Co. Tipperary).

Bailie

History and genealogy of the family of Bailie of the north of Ireland. George A. Bailie. Augusta, GA: 1902.

Baird

Baird, S. Dennie, & Jennie M. Baird. The Bairds: A condensed chronology of an ancient house with genealogical tracings of its American descendants. Wisconsin: Stephen A. Baird, 1909.

Baker *see also* McNamara

Baker of Co. Cavan. Pedigree in 'Swanzy Notebooks'. RCB Library, Dublin.

The Bakers of Lismacue: A family chronicle. Tipp.Hist.J. 7 (1994) p. 115-128.

Pedigree of Baker Family of Cork: IGRS Library (Leader Collection).

Balbirnie *see* Vance

Baldwin

The genealogy of Baldwins from Queen's County. William Baldwin. New York, 1918.

Pedigree of Baldwin Family of Cork: IGRS Library (Leader Collection).

Ball

Records of Anglo-Irish families of Ball. W. B. Wright. Dublin, 1887.
Pedigree of Ball Family of Cork: IGRS Library (Leader Collection)
Genealogical Memoirs of some Ball families of GB, Ireland and America. W.
Ball Wright. York, 1908.

Barbour or **Barbor** *see also* **Mullan**

Papers relating to the Bond family and Barbor family, Longford. NAI 8462–
8562: T 768–773.

Barclay

The Barclays of New York and some other Barclays. R. Burnham Moffat. R
G Cooke, New York, 1904.

Barcroft

A Quaker Wedding at Lisburn, Co. Down 1867 (Barcroft/Malcolmson). Ir.
Anc. 1392 (1981) 90–92.

Barker

The Barkers of Waterford. H. T. Morris, Decies 17 (1981) 17–28.

Barnard

The Barnards. Derry, 1897.
Pedigree of Barnard Family of Cork: IGRS Library (Leader Collection).

Barnewall, Barnwall or **Barnwell**

The family of Barnewall. Ir.Gen. 3 (1959–66) 124–35, 173–6, 198–209, 249–
56, 311–21, 384–8, 445–54; & 5(2) (1975) 181–85.
Barnewall of Rowestown Co. Meath. Ir.Gen. 4(1978)174–82.
Barnwell of Kilbrew, Co. Meath. Ir. Gen. 6 (1) (1980) 9–17.
The Barnwalls. Riocht na Midhe 1 (1957) 64–68.
The Barnewalls of Turvey. Reportorium Novum 1 (2) (1956) 336–41.

Barrett

Pedigree of Barrett Family of Cork: IGRS Library (Leader Collection).
Barrett in 'Family Names of Co. Cork' (see abbrevs.) (Notes on family origins and members up to 1700).

Barrington

The Barringtons: a family history. Amy Barrington. Dublin, 1914.
The Barringtons of Limerick. N. Munster Antiq. J. 7(3) (1956) 23–8.
The Barringtons of Limerick. Old Limerick J. 24 (1985) 5-18.
Pedigree of Barrington Family of Cork: IGRS Library (Leader Collection).
Barrington chart pedigrees (Queens, Wexford, Dublin & Wicklow) LDS Lib.
929.2415 B277b.
Barrington's private burial Ground (Cabinteely, Co. Dublin) in Memorial In-
scriptions of Dun Laoghaire – Rathdown, Co. Dublin Vol. 1. Published
by GSI (2000).
The Barringtons of Glendruid (Cabinteely, Co. Dublin). Moira Laffan. Foxrock
Local History Club. Dublin: 1990.

Barrington of Ballymacane. Wexford Gentry Vol. 1 (see abbreviations).

Barron

Distinguished Waterford Families: Barron. JW&SEIAS 17 (1914) 47–65, 128–34, 137–52; 18 (1915) 69–87, 91–104.

Pedigree of Barron Family of Cork: IGRS Library (Leader Collection).

A History of the Barron family. Robert Barron. Belfast, 1931.

Barrow

The Descendants of an Irish Orphan in Australia Ann Barrow, ancestor of Sir Ronald East, who as a 17 year old was sent to Australia from the Mallow Workhouse in 1848. Mallow Field Club J. 11 (1993).

Barry *see also* **Bellingham, Harold, Maxwell**

Etude sur l'histoire des Bary-Barry. de Barry. Vieux-Dieu-Les Anvers, 1927.

De l'origine des Barry d'Irlande. Alfred de Bary. Guebwiller, 1900.

Capt John Barry (of Cork) in 'King James' IAL' (Notes on family pre-1700).

Pedigree Book for Barry Family of Cork: IGRS Library (Leader Collection).

Barry/DeBarra in 'Family Names of Co. Cork' (see abbrevs.) (Notes on family origins and members up to 1700).

Barrymore. JCHAS 5(1899) 1–17, 77–92, 153–68, 209–24; 6 (1900) 1–11, 65–87, 129–46, 193–209. 7 (1901) 1–16, 65–80, 129–38, 193–204; 8 (1902) 1–17, 129–50.

The last earls of Barrymore. G. J. Robinson. London, 1894. (Barry family).

Barrymore. records of the Barrys of county Cork from the earliest to the present time with pedigrees. Rev. E. Barry. (Reprint from JCHAS) Cork; Guy & Co. 1902.

Barrington chart pedigrees (Queens, Ballymacane, Wexford, Dublin, Wicklow) Ms. 929.2415 B277b.

Memoirs of the Barry-Place family. A narrative of the family of Rev. John Barry, of Bandon, Wesleyan minister, and a pioneer missionary. Compiled in 1911. JCAHS, 33 (1928) 19–21.

Barter

The Irish Barters. Ir.Gen. 3 (1961) 221–7.

Pedigree Book for Barter Family of Cork: IGRS Library (Leader Collection).

Barton *see also* **Hargreaves**

Barton, Bertram Francis. Some account of the family of Barton drawn from Ms. & records. Dublin: Cahill & Co., 1902.

The family of Barton. JCKAS 4 (2) (1903–05) 111–13.

Basnett

The Basnetts during the sixteenth and seventeenth centuries. S. T. B. Percival. Chester, 1962.

Basquill

The origins of the Basquills of Co. Mayo. Cathair na Mart 17 (1997) 49-65.

Bassett

Pedigree of Bassett Family of Cork: IGRS Library (Leader Collection).

Bateman

Pedigree of Bateman Family of Cork: IGRS Library (Leader Collection).

Bathe or **De Bathe**

The Bathes of Drumcondra. Reportorium Novum 1 (2) (1956) 328–30.

Lt. Peter Bathe (of Kilkenny) in 'King James' IAL' (Notes on family pre-1700).

The De Bathes of Knightstown (Meath). Ríocht na Mídhe 2 (4) (1962) p.70.

Bayly

Bayly Papers. [Ballyarthur, Co. Wicklow]. Anal. Hib. 25, 95–122.

Beale

The Earth between them. Edgar Beale. Sydney 1975. (Re. Beale of Mountmellick).

Beamish

Pedigrees of the families of Beamish. R. P. Beamish. Cork, 1892.

Beamish. C. T. M. Beamish. London, 1950.

Pedigree of Beamish Family of Cork: IGRS Library (Leader Collection).

Beatagh or **Betagh**

Lt. Thomas Beatagh (of Meath) in 'King James' IAL' (Notes on various family members pre-1775).

Beatty or **Beattie** *see also* **Kenny**

Copies of documents re the history of the Beatty family. Philip Crossle (1919/20). NLI Ms 32,509.

Becher

The Pooles of Mayfield. Rosemary ffolliott. Dublin: Hodges Figgis (1958). (Deals with Becher of London and Munster: 16th to 18th c.).

Beck

A brief history of the family of Beck in Northern Ireland. John W. Beck. Barking, 1929.

Pedigrees of Atkinson, Beck, Chambers, Cole, Jackson, and Pilleys or Pillows. LDS Mf. 1279354.

Beirne & O'Beirne

The Family O'Beirne. Bryan Patrick Beirne. USA: Riffle & Poole 1997 (Info from MVMAG@aol.com).

Bell *see also* **Acheson, MacCormick, Guinness**

Bell of Tipperary. 'Swanzy Notebooks'. RCB Library, Dublin.

Bellew

Some Notes on the Family of Bellew of Thomastown, Co. Louth. CLAHJ 5(1923) 193–97.

John Bellew of Willistown. CLAHJ 6 (4) (1928) pp. 229-237.

The Bryan-Bellews of Jenkinstown and Bawnmore. Old Kilkenny Review,

19 (1967) p.29-38.

Col. John Lord Bellew (of Louth) in 'King James' IAL' (Notes on family members pre-1700).

Dominic Bellew (1745-1812). Seanchas Ardmhacha 6(2) (1972) 333-371. (Short account of Louth family on p. 332-3).

The Bellews of Mount Bellew: a Catholic gentry family in 18th Century Ireland. Karen J. Harvey. Dublin: Four Courts Press 1998. ISBN 1851823514.

Bellingham

History of Santry and Clogher. B. J. Adams. London, 1883.

Benn

Benn family of Belfast & Glenravel. Ulster Local Studies 5(2) (1980) 21-23; 6(1) (1980) 12-16.

Bennett

Pedigree of Bennett Family of Cork: IGRS Library (Leader Collection).

Benson *see* **Gower**

Bentley

The Bentley family of Hurdlestown, Co. Clare, The Other Clare 10 (1986) p.26-27.

Beresford

An historical account of the Beresford family. Geneal. Mag. (1898) 11–15.

The Beresford family. J. F. McCarthy. Clonmel, 1 (1954) 61–3.

Beresford Family Papers (1800–1922). PRONI DOD 519 and LDS Mf. 247312.

Berford

The Berfords of Kilruc (Meath). Riocht na Midhe 6 (4) (1978/79) 89–118.

Berkley

Berkley family records: Pedigrees, correspondence and notes of Barony of Berkley (or Berkeley). GO Ms. no. 515; LDS Mf.257821.

George Berkeley – His Connections With North Cork. Mallow Field Club J. 10 (1992).

Bermingham or **Birmingham**

Notes on the Bermingham pedigree. JGAHS 9 (1915–16) p. 195–205. (refs to FitzGerald, FitzMaurice, FitzThomas).

The Bermingham family of Athenry (Galway). JGAHS 10 (1917–18) 139–54.

Carbury and the Birminghams country. JCKAS 2 (1896–99) 85–110 (Carbury, Co. Kildare).

Manual of origin, descent, etc., of Barony of Athenry. Dublin, 1820.

John & William Bermingham (of Ballynamalough, Co Kildare) in 'King James' IAL' (Notes on family pre-1700).

The de Birminghams of Leinster, 1170-1370: a study of an Anglo-Norman family. Nora M. Hickey. LDS Lib. 929.2415 B537hn (refs to FitzGerald, de Lacy and de Burgh).

Bernard

A memoir of James Bernard, M.P., his son, the first earl of Bandon, and their descendants. 1875.

The Bernards of Kerry. J. H. Bernard. Pr.pr. Dublin, University Press, 1922. (refs to Jeffcoat, Milligan, Turton, Clifford, Hamilton, Duke and Humphreys).

Berry

Pedigree of Berry Family of Cork: IGRS Library (Leader Collection).

Besnard

Notes on the Besnard family. JCHAS 39 (1934) 92–9.

Betson

Pedigree of Betson Family of Cork: IGRS Library (Leader Collection).

Bettesworth

Pedigree of Bettesworth Family of Cork: IGRS Library (Leader Collection).

Bevan

Bevan of Co. Limerick. Ir. Anc. 6 (1) (1974) 1–5.

Pedigree of Bevan Family of Cork: IGRS Library (Leader Collection).

Bewley

The Bewleys of Cumberland and their Irish and other descendants. E. T. Bewley. Dublin, 1902.

Biggs

Pedigree of Biggs Family of Cork: IGRS Library (Leader Collection).

Bingham

Memoirs of the Binghams. R. E. McCalmont. London, 1913.

Birch

The Birch family of Birchgrove. Ir.Gen. 3 (1960) 185–7.

Bishop *see* **Gower**

Bisset

Irish chiefs and leaders. Rev. Paul Walsh. Ch. v. Dublin, 1960.

Black *see also* **Mullan, Acheson**

The Black family. Ulster J. Arch., 2nd ser., 8 (1902) 176–88.

Blackall or **Blackhall** *see also* **McNamara**

Abstracts from Blackall family records. Ir.Gen. 1 (1941) 265–75.

Pedigree of Blackhall Family of Cork: IGRS Library (Leader Collection).

Blacker

History of the family of Blacker of Carrickblacker in Ireland. L. C. M. Blacker. Dublin:Hodges & Figgis 1901.

Blacker of Woodbrook. Wexford Gentry Vol. 1 (see abbreviations).

Blackham *see also* **Ashmur**

Blackney

The Blackneys of Ballyellen (Co. Carlow). Ir.Gen. 3 (1957–58) 44–5, 116.

Blackwell *see* **Murphy**

Blackwood

Helen's tower. Harold Nicholson. London, 1937.

Clandeboye & the Dufferin & Ava family (Bibliography of books & articles about Blackwood family). Ballynahinch, Co. Down: South Eastern Education & Library Service, 1981. LDS Lib. 929.2415 A1 no. 27

The Dufferin Papers (PRONI: D/1071, D/1231, MIC/22 and T/3636) (Blackwood of Clandeboye, Co. Down).

Blair *see also* **Ashmur**

Pedigree of Blair Family of Cork: IGRS Library (Leader Collection).

Blake *see also* **Darcy, Forster, Morris, McNamara**

Blake family record 1300-1600. Martin J. Blake. London: Elliott Stock 1902–05.

Blake-Butler family records: Pedigrees and notes of Blake-Butler families of Cos Clare & Tipperary, inc. MacBrien, McCarthy, Fitzgerald, Power, O'Meagher, Ryan, Purcell, Plunkett, O'Carroll, Burke, Travers, MacGrath, Tobyn and related families. GO Ms. no. 521, LDS Mf.257821.

Blakeney

Blakeney family papers: in the possession of the Soc. of Genealogists. (refs to Beytaugh, Burke, Gunning, Netterville, Staunton) LDS Lib. 929.2415 B584b.

Blaney or **Blayney**

Blancy of Lurgan, Co. Armagh. Ir. Anc. 3 (1) (1971) 32–39.

Notes on the Families of Blaney, Co. Monaghan, and Denny of Tralee, Co. Kerry. JAPMD 7 (1907–09) 373.

The family of Blayney. Notes re Blayney family of Montgomeryshire & Ireland. E. Rowley-Morris. London, 1890.

Blatchford

Pedigree of Blatchford Family of Cork: IGRS Library (Leader Collection).

Blennerhassett

The Blennerhassets of Kerry: earlier English stock. JKAHS (Old Series) 5(1919) 34–9.

Pedigree of Blennerhassett Family of Cork: IGRS Library (Leader Collection).

Selections from old Kerry records, historical & genealogical. Mary A. Hickson. London: Watson & Hazell, 1872: LDS Mf. 941.96 H2hi. (genealogy of Blennerhasset (1580-1736) & allied families of Conway, Cross, Brown, Gun).

The Blennerhassetts of Kesh. Clogher Record 16 (3) (1999) 112-126.

Blood

Notes on the Blood family of Corofin (Co. Clare). The Other Clare 16 (1992) p. 49-52.

Bloxham or **Bloxsom**
  The Bloxham/Bloxsom story (Co. Clare) Sliabh Aughty 2 (1990) p. 20-22.
Blunden
  Blundens of Kilkenny. Old Kilkenny Review 3 (5) (1988) p. 456-467.
Boate
  Pedigree of Boate Family of Cork: IGRS Library (Leader Collection).
Boland
  Some memories. John P. Boland. Dublin, 1928.
Bolster
  Pedigree of Bolster Family of Cork: IGRS Library (Leader Collection).
Bolton
  Bolton families in Ireland. C. K. Bolton. Boston, Goodspeed's Bookshop 1937.
    LDS Lib. 929.2415 B639b.
  The Boltons of Co. Waterford. Ir. Gen. 7 (2) 186–200; 7 (3) 405–420; 7 (4)
    615–641.
Bond *see also* **Tweedy**
  Papers relating to the Bond family and Barbor family, Longford. NAI 8462–
    8562: T 768–773.
Bor
  The family of Bor of Holland and Ireland. Reprint from Miscellanea
    Genealogica, Dec. 1911.
Borough
  The Borough family of Querrin (Co. Clare). The Other Clare 9 (1985) p. 41;
    corrigendum Vol. 10 p.55.
Boswell
  James Boswell's Irish Cousins. Genealogists Mag. 16 (3) (Sep 1969).
Bourchier
  The Bourchier Tablet in the Cathedral Church of St. Canice, Kilkenny, with
    Some Account of That Family. JRSAI 34 (1904) 365–79; 35(1905) 21–
    33.
Bourke *see also* **Burke**
  Descendants of Grainne O'Malley by her second husband (Richard Bourke).
    Ir.Gen. 1 (1940) 211–21.
  Notes on the history of the Burgh family. Elizabeth Jane Hussey de Burgh.
    Dublin, 1890.
  The Bourkes of Clanwilliam. JRSAI 19 (1889) 192–203.
  The de Burgos or Bourkes of Illeagh. N. Munster Antiq. J. 1 (2) (1937) 67–
    77.
Bourne or **Bournes**
  Pedigree of Bourne Family of Cork: IGRS Library (Leader Collection).
  The Bourne(s)Families of Ireland. Strange, Mary A. USA: Stramer Corpora-
    tion, 1970.

Bowden

Pedigree of Bowden Family of Cork: IGRS Library (Leader Collection).

Bowen

Ballyadams in the Queen's County, and the Bowen Family. JCKAS 7 (1912–14) 3–32.

Bowen's Court. Elizabeth Bowen. London, 1942.

Pedigree of Bowen Family of Cork: IGRS Library (Leader Collection).

Bowen Papers (Bowenscourt). Anal. Hib. 15, 1–34.

Bowes *see* **Wandesforde**

Boxwell *see also* **Kelly (Ainsworth misc)**

The Boxwells, a planter family. JOWS 13 (1990-1) p.82-91.

Boxwell of Butlerstown. Wexford Gentry Vol. 1 (see abbreviations).

Boyd *see also* **Stewart**

History of the Boyd family in Ireland since 1680. W. P. Boyd, Rochester N.Y. 1912.

Abstracts of Some Boyd Wills. Ir. Anc. 9 (1) (1977) 53–55.

Boyds & Lockharts of Donegal. Comp. by James W, Devitt. LDS Lib. 929.2415 B692d (refs to Adair, Busby, Dean, Devitt, Given, Long, McBride, Morrow, Nesbitt).

Boyd-Montgomery-McBride Families. Genealogists Mag. 16 (3) (Sep 1969).

Boyd of Kiltra. Wexford Gentry Vol. 1 (see abbreviations).

Boylan

The Boylan Family of Carbury Area. JCKAS 14 (3) 1968, p. 346-361.

Boylan of Dungimmon, Kilbride, Co. Cavan. Rosemary Ffolliott for A. J. Boylan. LDS Lib.Ms.929.2415 A1 no. 6.

Boyle or **O'Boyle** *see also* **Jephson**

Memoirs of the illustrious family of the Boyles. Eustace Budgell. Dublin, 1755.

Genealogical memoranda relating to the family of Boyle of Limavady. E. M. F-G. Boyle. Londonderry, 1903.

The Orrery papers. Ed. by The Countess of Cork & Orrery. London: Duckworth & Co.1903. LDS Lib. 929.2415 Or7o.

Calendar of the Orrery papers, 1620 to 1689. E. MacLysaght. Dublin, 1941.

Thoughts on the Boyle name. Daniel C. Boyle. LDS Lib. 929.2415 A1 no. 66.

Boyse

Boyse of Bannow. Wexford Gentry Vol. 1 (see abbreviations).

Brabazon

Genealogical history of the family of Brabazon. H. Sharp. Paris, 1825. (LDS Lib. 929.2415 B72g.

Bracken

The Brackens. Bill Coffey. Victoria: Author-published: 1990 (ISBN: 0646002279).

Braddell
> Braddell of Bullingate (Wexford). Wexford Gentry Vol. 2 (see abbreviations).

Bradfield
> Pedigree of Bradfield Family of Cork: IGRS Library (Leader Collection).

Bradshaw
> The Bradshaws of Bangor & Mile-Cross, in the Co. of Down. Ulster J. Arch. 8 (1902) 4–6, 55–57.
> The Dubliner who negotiated peace between Britain and Nepal: Lt. Col. Paris Bradshaw of the East India Co. Ir.Gen. 10 (3) (2000) 259-304.

Brady
> Pedigree of Brady Family of Cork: IGRS Library (Leader Collection).

Braly
> A history of the Bralys. David Braly. Princeville, Oregon 1975.

Bray
> Pedigree of Bray Family of Cork: IGRS Library (Leader Collection).

Brayman *see* **Allen – Allens of Ulster**

Bredin
> Bredin of Drumcagh, Co. Fermanagh. Pedigree in 'Swanzy Notebooks'. RCB Library, Dublin.

Breen
> The Breens of Co. Carlow. Irish Roots (1) (1993) 24–25.
> The Breens of the Donner Party. Carloviana 39 (1991/2) 4-9.
> Breen of Coolbawn. Wexford Gentry Vol. 1 (see abbreviations).

Brennan or **O'Brennan**
> A History of the O'Brennans of Idough, Co. Kilkenny. T.A. Brennan. New York, 1975. (LDS Lib. 929.273 B75bt.
> Pedigree of Brennan Family of Cork: IGRS Library (Leader Collection).
> The O'Brennans and the ancient territory of Hy-Duach. Nicholas Murphy. Ossory, 1 (1874–79) 393–407.

Brereton
> A memoir of the Brereton family. Fortunatus Dwannis. London, 1848.
> The Breretons of Co. Carlow and Co. Kildare. Ir. Anc. 3 (1971) 10–26, 124.

Brett *see also* **Darbyshire**
> Long shadows cast before: nine lives in Ulster, 1625-197. C.E.B. Brett. (Brett family) Edinburgh ; London: John Bartholomew & Son 1978. (LDS Lib. 929.2415 B756b.

Brettridge
> Pedigree of Brettridge Family of Cork: IGRS Library (Leader Collection).

McBride *see also* **Boyd (x 2)**
> Pedigrees of … McBride, Peebles, Whaley, Woodhouse, and Smith. LDS Mf. 1279327.

McBrien *see* **Blake**

O'Brien or **Brien** *see also* **Bryant, McLysaght, Osborne, Watson**

Carrigogunnell Castle & the O'Briens of Pubblebrian in Co. Limerick. JRSAI 37(1907) 374–92. 38(1908) 141–59.

The O'Briens in Munster after Clontarf. N. Munster. Antiq. J. 2 (1941) 141–52.

The sept of Mac-I-Brien Ara. JCHAS 3 (1897) 10–21.

Pedigree of O'Brien Family of Cork: IGRS Library (Leader Collection).

Historical Memoir of the O'Briens, With Notes, Appendix and a Genealogical Table of their Several Branches. John O'Donoghue. Dublin: Hodges, Smith & Co., 1860.

History of the O'Briens from Brian Boroimhe A.D. 1000 to 1945. Hon. Donough O'Brien. London: Batsford 1949.

The O'Briens. W. A. Lindsay. London, 1876.

Genealogical notes on the O'Briens of Kilcor, Co. Cork. 1887.

The Inchiquin manuscripts. ed. J. F. Ainsworth. Dublin, 1960.

Noel and the genealogy of the O'Briens: being a history of the town of Noel, Nova Scotia, its inhabitants and descendants. R. G. O'Brien. New Bedford, Mass. [1925].

The O'Brien family. Ir.Gen. 1 (1939) 164–70.

The family register of the O'Briens of Newcastle, Ballyporeen, Co. Tipperary. Ir.Gen. 2 (1953) 308–10.

The Cratloe O'Briens. Ir. Gen. 6 (1980) 48–53.

The O'Briens of Glencolumbkille. Ir.Gen. 7 (1) (1986) 51–53. (Co. Donegal).

An O'Brien family in France. Ir. Gen. 8 (2) (1991) 207–209.

William O'Brien and The Kingston Estate. Mallow Field Club J. 12 (1994).

The Briens of Brawney. Riocht na Midhe 7 (4) (1980/81) 80–98.

O'Brien of Thomond;The O'Briens in Irish History: 1500–1865. O'Brien, Ivar. Phillimore, 1986.

The O'Briens of Dromore Castle (Co. Clare). The Other Clare 11 (1987) p.58-59.

O'Brien and Leddin Families. Irish Family History 4 (1988) 80-82.

The case of the prince of Thomond. Nat. Gen. Soc. Qtly. 50 (4) 1962.

The Seven generations: 1757-1977. (O'Brien & Ahearne). LDS Lib. Ms. 929.2415 A1 no. 36.

Origin & distribution of surname O'Brien. Fort Collins, Colo:A.J. Morris, c1984. (LDS Lib. 929.2415 A1 no. 41.

History of the O'Briens from Brian Boromhe A.D. 1000 to A.D. 1945. London: B. T. Batsford, 1949. (LDS Lib. 929.2415 Ob6h.

These my friends & Forebears: The O'Briens of Dromoland. Grania R. O'Brien. Ballinakella Press: 1991 (ISBN: 0946538034).

Genealogy of O'Brien family of Ennistymon House, by Michael O'Reilly. GO Ms. no. 559, LDS Mf.257821.

Brinkley
> Pedigree of Brinkley Family of Cork: IGRS Library (Leader Collection).

Brinsley *see* **Sheridan**

Briody
> The origins of Clann Bhruaideadha (Briody). Éigse 31 (1999) 121.

Britton
> Pedigree of Britton Family of Cork: IGRS Library (Leader Collection).

Brocas
> The Brocas family, notable Dublin artists. University Review, 2 (6)(1959) 17–25.
>
> The Brocas family, notable Dublin artists. Dublin Hist. Rec. 17(1) 25-36.

Broderick
> Pedigree of Broderick Family of Cork: IGRS Library (Leader Collection).

(Mac) Brody
> Material for the history of Clann Bhruaideadha. Eigse, 4(1) Part 1, (1943) 48–66.

Brohen
> Pedigree of Brohen Family of Cork: IGRS Library (Leader Collection).

Bronte *see* **Brunty**

Brooke *see also* **Monck**
> Brooke, Victor. A memoir of his life and extracts from his letters. Oscar Leslie Stephen. London: John Murray, 1894.
>
> The Brimming River: Raymond F. Brooke. Dublin: Allen Figgis & Co.:1961. (Brooke) (LDS Lib.929.2415 B79b.
>
> Brooke Family. Genealogists Mag. 14 (3) (Sep 1962).

Brooks or **Brookes**
> Census Returns relating to Brooks (1841) NAI Mf. 5248 (1).
>
> Pedigree of Brooks Family of Cork: IGRS Library (Leader Collection).
>
> 300 years of the Brookes & other Ascendancy families at Lough Eske. Donegal Ann. 45 (1993) p.94-103. (also Wray & Young families).

Brotherton
> Pedigree of Brotherton Family of Cork: IGRS Library (Leader Collection).

Browne or **Brown** *see also* **Mullan, Darcy, Blennerhasset**
> The Kenmare manuscripts ed. E. MacLysaght. Dublin, 1942.
>
> Pedigree of the Brownes of Castle MacGarrett. JGAHS 5 (1907/8) 48–59, 165–77, 227–38.
>
> Notes on Brown of Mayglass (including pedigree). JAPMD 9: 403.
>
> Pedigree Book for Browne Family of Cork: IGRS Library (Leader Collection).
>
> The Pooles of Mayfield. Rosemary ffolliott. Dublin: Hodges Figgis (1958). (Browne of Riverstown, Cork: 17-18th c.).
>
> Col. Francis W.N. Wogan-Browne. Clongownian 11(2) (1927) pp. 103-4.

(Browne of Co Clongowes, Co. Kildare).

The Brownes of Clongowes. Clongownian 4 (1) (1905) pp. 44-50. (Browne of Clongowes, Co. Kildare).

The Brady Browne family of Newgrove, Tulla, Co. Clare. The Other Clare 8 (1984) p. 5-6.

The Emigration of the Brownes from Clonoulty to Australia—Part I (1853–1857). Tipp.Hist.J. 8 (1995) p.117-132.

Westport House & the Brownes. Marquess of Sligo. Ashbourne: Mooreland Pub., 1981. (LDS Lib. 929.2415 B816b).

Col Valentine Brown, Lord Kenmare (of Kerry) in 'King James' IAL' (Notes on family members pre-1757).

Brownlow *see* **Chamberlain, Swift**

Brownrigg *see* **Spedding.**

Brucher

Brucher family of Ulster Province: Armagh Co. Museum Ms. N8: LDS Mf.1279356.

Brunty or **Prunty**

The road to Haworth: the Brontës' Irish ancestry. John Cannon. London: Weidenfeld & Nicolson, 1980 (LDS Lib. 929.2415 B789c. (Brunty or Prunty).

The Bronte's Irish Ancestry. Edward Chitham. McMillan 1986. (ISBN: 0333386639).

Bryan *see also* **Bellew**

Bryan's of Jenkinstown. Old Kilkenny Review 2 (3) 1981.

The Claim of Pierce Bryan of Jenkinstown 1717. Old Kilkenny Review 3 (1) (1984) p. 44-46.

Bryant

Genealogical Information on the Bryant, O'Brien and Fitzgerald families. G & J Catherell. Pr.pr.: Morris, Mn. 1981. (NLI Call No. Ir 9292 b 54).

Buchanan

The Buchanan book. A. W. P. Buchanan. Montreal, 1911.

Later leaves of the Buchanan book A. W. P. Buchanan. Montreal, 1929.

Buckley

Buckley/O'Buachalla in 'Family Names of Co. Cork' (see abbrevs.) (Notes on family origins & members).

Bulby or **McBulby**

The Bulbys or the McBulbys of the Co. Kildare. JCKAS 2(6) (1898) pp 388-9.

Bullen

Pedigree of Bullen Family of Cork: IGRS Library (Leader Collection).

Bullock

Bullock or Bullick of Northern Ireland. compiled. J. W. Beck. London, 1931.

Bunce *see* **Teape**
Bunworth
> Pedigree of Bunworth Family of Cork: IGRS Library (Leader Collection).

Burdon
> Burdon Family History. David G. Burdon. pr.pr.: Buttevant 1982 (Only 10 copies: NLI Call No. LO).

De Burgh/o *see* **Burke** or **Bourke**
Burke, De Burgh or **De Burgo** *see also* **Bourke:** *also* **Blake, Darcy, Forster**
> The family of Gall Burke, of Gallstown, in the Co. of Kilkenny. JRSAI 6 (1860) 97–120.
> The Rt. Hon. Edmund Burke (1729–97). A basis for a pedigree. JCHAS 60 (1955) 69–74.
> Some notes on the Burkes. M. R. JGAHS 1 (1900–01) 196–7.
> The De Burgo clans of Galway. JGAHS 1 (1900–01) 123–31; 3 (1903–04) 46–58; 4 (1905–06) 55–62.
> Portumna and the Burkes. JGAHS 6 (1909) 107–09.
> The Burkes of Marble Hill. JGAHS 8 (1913–14) 1–11.
> Seanchus na mBurcach & Historia et Genealogia Familae De Burgo. JGAHS 13(1926–27) 37–137; 14 (1928–29) 30–51, 142–66.
> The wives of Ulick, first Earl of Clanricarde. JGAHS 21 (1945) p. 174-183 (Burke Family)
> The de Burghs of Oldtown. JCKAS 4 (1903–05) 467–72.
> Notes on the history of the De Burgh family. E. J. Hussey de Burgh. Dublin, 1890.
> Burke: people and places. Eamonn Bourke. Ballinakella Press, 1984
> History of the Burke/Bourke clan. Maureen O'Brien. Kansas City, Mo.: Clan Pubs: 1991. (ISBN 0962907405)
> St Clerans : the tale of a manor house. William Henry,Galway :Merv Griffin, 1999. (Burke family)

Burleigh
> Pedigrees of Anderson, Burleigh et al. LDS Mf. 1279327.

Burnell *see also* **McNamara**
> The Burnells and the Penal Laws. Ir.Gen. 4 (1969) 74–80.

Burnett
> Pedigree of Burnett Family of Cork: IGRS Library (Leader Collection).

Burnside
> Burnside of Corcreevy, some family descents. Smyth Burnside. Dublin, pr. pr., 1880.

Burrows or **Burrowes** *see also* **Borough**
> Burrows of Stradone. Pedigree in 'Swanzy Notebooks'. RCB Library, Dublin.
> Burrowes of Fernsborough. Pedigree in 'Swanzy Notebooks'. RCB Library,

Dublin.
Burton
The Burton family. Carloviana 1(2) (1953) 10–12.
The Burtons of Pollacton. Carloviana 2 (21) (1972) 44-45.
Bury
Burys in and out of Dublin. J. Gen. Soc. I.2(1) (2001) 53-56.
Busby *see* **Boyd, Lockhart**
Bush *see* **Ireton**
Busteed
Pedigree of Busteed Family of Cork: IGRS Library (Leader Collection).
Butler *see also* **Blake, Gerrard, McNamara, O'Shaughnessy**
Journal of the Butler Society. All issues have information of relevance to Butler family history.
Calendar of Ormond deeds, 1172–1603 ed. Edmund Curtis. Vols. I–VI. Dublin, 1932–43.
Some account of the family of Butler, but more particularly of the late Duke of Ormonde. London: J. Morphew 1716.
Genealogical memoranda of the Butler family. W. Butler. Sibsagor, Assam, 1845.
A genealogical history of the noble house of Butler in England and Ireland. London, 1771.
The testamentary records of the Butler families in Ireland. Rev. Wallace Clare. Peterborough, 1932.
The Butlers of Co. Clare. N. Munster Antiq. J. 6 (1952) 108–29; 7 (1953) 153–67; 7 (2) (1955) 19–45.
The Butlers; and Cloghrennan and the Butlers. Old Kilkenny Review, 15, 18, 19 (1964–66).
Butler family history. Lord Dunboyne. Kilkenny. 1969.
The Butlers of Lower Grange, Viscounts Galmoy. Old Kilkenny Review, 16 (1964) p.16-22
The Butlers of Cregg. JGAHS 28 (1959) 23–41.
Original docs relating to Butler lordship of Achill, Burrishoole & Aughrim (1236–1640). JGAHS 15 (1931–33) 121–8.
The Butlers of Poulakerry and Kilcash. JW&SEIAS 15 (1912) 24–9.
The Butlers of Kilcash. Old Kilkenny Review, 21 (1969)83
The descendants of James, ninth earl of Ormond.. JRSAI 59 (1929) 29–44.
An Irish legend of the origins of the barons of Cahir. JRSAI 55 (1925) 6–14.
The Butlers of Dangan and Spidogue. JRSAI 30 (1900) 330–3.
The Butlers of Duiske Abbey. JRSAI 10 (1868–69) 62–75.
The Butler archbishops of Cashel. N. Munster Antiq. J., 7, (2) (1955) 1–11.
Butler, The Barony of Dunboyne. Ir. Gen. 2 (1945) 66; (1946) 107; (1947) 130; (1948) 162.

The origin of the Butlers of Ireland. Ir.Gen. 1 (1937-39) 58, 147–57.

Thomas Le Botiller, prior of Kilmainham 1402–1419 (& some descendants). Ir.Gen. 1 (1942) 362–72.

The Butlers of Ballyslatteen: two Famine notebooks. Tipp.Hist.J. 10 (1997) p.166-177.

The barony of Dunboyne. Ir.Gen. 2 (1945–48) 66–81, 107–21, 130–6, 162–4.

Poems of the Butlers of Ormond, Cahir and Dunboyne (A.D. 1400–1650) ed. James Carney. Dublin. 1945.

The Butlers. Old Kilkenny Review, 19 (1967) p.5-13

Cloghrennan and the Butlers. Old Kilkenny Review, 18 (1966) p. 25-34

Butler family records: Pedigrees etc. of the Butler family of Co. Clare. GO Ms. no. 522, LDS Mf. 257821

Genealogy of the Butlers of Ireland. T. Blake Butler. Ms. LDS Lib. 929.2415 B976b

Testamentary records of Butler families & abstracts from Diocesan wills to 1800. New London, N. H.: The Butler Society n.d. (refs to Bourke, Burke, Fitzgerald, Power)

Butt

Pedigree of Butt Family of Cork: IGRS Library (Leader Collection).

Byrne or **O'Byrne**

The Byrnes of Co. Louth. CLAHJ 2 (1908–11) 45–49.

Byrnes and Wickhams of Wexford. Irish Family History 9 (1993) 55–58.

Capt. Sir Gregory Byrne (of Tymogue, Laois) in 'King James' IAL' (Notes on family pre-1757).

Leabhar Branach. The Book of the O'Byrnes ed. Sean Mac Airt. Dublin: Dublin Institute for Advanced Studies, 1944. (Text mainly in Irish: pre-17th century genealogies and poems). (LDS Lib. 929.2415 Ob9m).

The O'Byrnes and their descendants. John Edge. Dublin, 1879.

Historical Reminiscences of O'Byrnes, O'Tooles, O'Kavanaghs and Other Irish Chieftains. G. O'Byrne. London: M'Gowan, 1843.

History of the Clan O'Byrne and Other Leinster Septs. P.L. O'Toole. Dublin: M.H. Gill and Son, 1890. (LDS Lib. 929.2415 Ob9o).

The O'Byrnes country in Co. Wicklow in the 16th century. JRSAI 63 (2) (1933) 224-242; 66 (1) (1936) 41-66.

The O'Byrnes of Baile na Coille. JRSAI 68(2) (1938) 272-280.

MacCabe

The Fomorians and Lochlanns. Pedigrees of MacCabe of Ireland and MacLeod of Scotland. Ulster J. Arch., 1st ser., 9 (1861–62) 94–105.

A United Irish Family: The McCabes of Belfast. Familia 2 (10) (1994).

The McCabes of Belfast. Familia 13 (1997) pp. 1–24.

O'Cahane

Capts. Francis & Roger O'Cahane (of Derry) in 'King James' IAL' (Notes on family members pre-1700).

Cairns or **Cairnes**

History of the family of Cairnes or Cairns. H.C.Lawlor. London, 1906. NLI Call No. Ir 9292 c1.

Notes on the Family of Cairnes, Co. Tyrone. JAPMD 12 (1926–31) 297.

Cairnes of Stameen (Co. Louth). J.Old Drogheda Soc. 7 (1990).

Caldwell

The Caldwells of Coleraine, Co. Londonderry & Baxters Harbour, King's Co., Nova Scotia, Canada. Irish Heritage Links 3 (6) 19-22.

The Caldwells of Quebec. Familia 2 (10) 1994.

McCall

Copies of 1841 Census Returns for McCall Family. NAI Mf. 5248 (10).

Clonmore and the McCalls. Carloviana 1 (15) (1966) 28-30

O'Callaghan or **Callaghan**

The chieftains of Pobul-I-Callaghan, Co. Cork. JCHAS 3 (1897) 201–20.

To Hell or to Clare-Donogh O'Callaghan, Chief of his name, a transplanter, The Other Clare 9 (1985) p.68-75.

Pedigree of O'Callaghan Family of Cork: IGRS Library (Leader Collection).

The O Callaghans and the rebellion of 1641. JCHAS 95 (254) (1990) p.30-40.

Lt.Col. Donogh O'Callaghan (of Clonmeen, Cork) in 'King James' IAL' (Notes on family members pre-1710).

The India Callaghans. Irish Family History 11 (1995) 32-33.

O'Callaghhan in 'Family Names of Co. Cork' (see abbrevs.) (Notes on family origins and members up to 1700).

Dromaneen Castle: an O'Callaghan Stronghold. Mallow Field Club J. 17 (1999).

Callan

Dr Callan family Papers. Seanchas Ardmhacha 5(1) (1969) 133-139 (Some info on Callan of Dromiskin & Dowdstown, Co. Louth 1660-1850).

Callender *see* **Sheridan**

Camac

Memoirs of the Camacs of Co. Down & account of their predecessors. Frank O. Fisher. Norwich, 1897 (50 copies).

Campbell *see also* **Acheson, Ashmur, Devlin, Moore**

The genealogy of Robert Campbell of Co. Tyrone. F. Campbell. New York, 1909.

Campbell of Co. Monaghan. Pedigree in 'Swanzy Notebooks'. RCB Library, Dublin.

Campion

The late Rev. Edward I. Campion PP. Carloviana 2 (23) (1974) 12-14. (Campion of Bracknagh, Co. Offaly).

Candler

Candler family, Coca Cola; the Callan Connection. Old Kilkenny Review, (1991) 885.

McCann or **McCana**

The Descendants of Robert McCann of Cloghoge, Co. Armagh. Ir. Anc. 5(1) 1–6.

Origin of the McCanns: with a history of the sept. Anthony Mathews. Drogheda: A. Mathews, 1978. (LDS Lib. 929.2415 M126m (Ref to Hamilton).

McCana or McCann of Clanbrassil: an ancestral and family history. John D. Macan. Ashgrove, Queensland 1997. (ISBN 0646316907).

Canning

Would that their ghosts be heard: A Canning family history 1866-1990. Margaret Love. Bacchus March 1990. (ISBN 0646024736) NLI Ir 9292 p28(1).

O'Cannon

A history of the O'Cannons of Tirchonaill. Donegal Ann. 12 (2) (1978) 276–315.

Cantillon

Cantillon de Ballyheigue. Ir. Eccl. Record, Sept. 1921, 275–85.

Richard Cantillon of Ballyheigue (Co Kerry). Studies, 21 (81) (1932) 105–22. (Also spelt Conron).

Cantwell

A Cantwell miscellany. Brian J. Cantwell. Greystones, 1960.

Caraher

Caraher of Cardistown family papers. CLAHJ 16 (3)(1967) 169–90.

MacCarragher/Caraher civil registration list: indexes of marriages & deaths, 1845-1900. Caraher Family Hist. Soc., 6 (1987). (LDS Lib. 929.2415 A1 no. 61.

Journal of the Caraher Family History Society. Perthshire UK (ISSN 02608391) NLI Ir 9292c40.

Irish Carahers in Australia who made their mark. Irish Family History 5 (1989) 104-106.

The Carraghers of Corrytanty. Clogher Record 13 (2) (1989) 131.

O'Carragher Clan Association Clogher Record 15 (1) (1994) 128.

Carbery

Pedigree of Carbery Family of Cork: IGRS Library (Leader Collection).

Carden

Some Particulars re Family and Descendants of John Carden of Templemore. J. Carden. 1912.

Cardiff

Catherine Cardiff Emigrated from Glenmore Ireland to Australia 1869. Irish Family History 15 (1999).

Cardigan

Pedigree of Cardigan Family of Cork: IGRS Library (Leader Collection).

Carew

The Shapland Carew papers ed. A. K. Longfield. Dublin, Stationery Office, 1946. (LDS Lib. 929.2415 C187L).

The Carews of Cork (Part 2). JCHAS 99 (1994) p. 66-82.

Carew of Castleborough (Wexford). Wexford Gentry Vol. 2 (see abbreviations).

Carey

Pedigree of Carey Family of Cork: IGRS Library (Leader Collection).

Carlile *see also* **Hargreaves**

Anne Jane Carlile and her descendants. R.H. Crofton. Sussex:King Bros. & Potts, 1930. (LDS Lib 929.2415 C194c. (refs to Crofton, Geoghegan, Harden, Hayes, Jamieson).

Pedigree of Carlisle Family of Cork: IGRS Library (Leader Collection).

Carlin

Theories on the name Carlin. William P. Carlin. Switzerland:William P. Carlin, 1993 (LDS Lib. 929.2415 C194cw).

Carr *see* **Ashmur**

Carragher *see* **Caraher**

O'Carroll or **Carroll** *see also* **Blake, Dungan, Ireton**

Pedigree of the O'Carroll family. E. O'Carroll. Dublin: 1883.

True version of the pedigree of Carroll of Carrollton, Maryland. JRSAI 16 (1883) 187–94.

Capt James Carroll (of Tipperary) in 'King James' IAL' (Notes on family members pre-1756).

Drogheda (Co. Louth) families of Carroll, Clinton, McGovern & Skelly. J.Old Drogheda Soc. 11 (1998).

Virginia Carrolls and Their Neighbors: 1618-1800s. Elizabeth Carroll Foster. Heritage Books, USA. 1999.

Descendants of James Carrell and Sarah Dungan. Ezra P. Carrell. Hatboro, Pennsylvania. 1928.

A long way from Tipperary (Carroll). June O'Carroll Robertson. Images Pub., UK 1994. (LDS Lib. 929.2415 C239c.

Princes of Ireland, Planters of Maryland. A Carroll Saga 1500-1782. Ronald Hoffman. Univ. N. Carolina Press 2000 (ISBN 0 8078 2556 5).

Valley of the milk: a history of the Carroll family of Luggawannia, Headford, Co. Galway. Michael H. Carroll. Headford,Galway: 2000. ISBN 0953650006.

McCarron

The McCarrons of Monaghan. Clogher Record 7 (2) (1970) 354.

Carson

Carson of Shanhoe, Co. Monaghan. T. W. Carson. Dublin, Davidson & McCormack 1909. (NLI Call No. Ir 9292 c3).

Short history of Carson family of Monanton, Co. Monaghan. James Carson. Belfast, 1879. (LDS Lib. 929.2415 C236r.

MacCarthy *see also* **Blake, Walsh**

The Pedigree and Succession of the House of MacCarthy Mor. JRSAI 51 (1921) 32–48.

The Clann Carthaigh. JKAHS (Old Series) 1 (1908–12) 160–79, 195–208, 233–51, 320–38, 385–402, 447–66; 2 (1912–14) 3–24, 53–74, 105–22, 181–202; 3 (1914–16) 55–72, 123–39, 206–26, 271–92; 4 (1917) 207–14.

The MacFinnin MacCarthys of Ardtully. JCHAS 2 (1896) 210–14.

The MacCarthys of Drishane. JCHAS 23 (1917) 114–15.

Some McCarthys of Blarney and Ballea. JCHAS 59 (1954) 1–10, 82–88; 60 (1955) 1–5, 75–79.

A historical pedigree of the MacCarthys. D. MacCarthy. Exeter, 1880.

Pedigree of McCarthy Family of Cork: IGRS Library (Leader Collection).

The MacCarthys of Munster. Samuel T. McCarthy. Dundalk: Dundalgan Press, 1922. (LDS Lib. 929.2415 M127m.

Gleanings from Irish history. W. F. Butler. London, 1925.

McCarthy in 'Family Names of Co. Cork' (see abbrevs.) (Notes on family origins and members up to 1700).

History of the name MacCarthy. J.D. Williams. Cork: Mercier Press, 1978.

McCarthy People and Places. Alicia St Leger. Ballinakella Press 1991 (ISBN: 0946538263).

Historical pedigree of the Sliocht Feidhlimidh; the McCarthys of Gleannacroim . . . Exeter 1877.

Macartney

Macartney of Lissanoure 1737-1806. Ulster Gen. & Hist. Guild 6 (1983).

Carttar *see* **Ferrar**

Casey *see also* **Murphy**

Pedigree of Casey Family of Cork: IGRS Library (Leader Collection).

Cashman

Pedigree of Cashman Family of Cork: IGRS Library (Leader Collection).

Cassell or **Castle**

Did Richard Castle have family connections in Ireland? Ir. Anc. 11(2) (1979) 119-120.

Cassidy

Clogherici: muintir Caiside. Clogher Record 1 (1956) 4, 137–60.

Castle *see* **Cassell**

Caters

> Caters of Irish Quarter, Carrickfergus. Ir. Anc. 10(1) (1978) 31–33.

MacCathmhaoil or **McCaul** *see also* **Devlin**

> The MacCathmhaoils of Clogher. Clogher Record 2 (1) (1957) 25-49.

McCaughan

> The McCaughans of Scotland & Ireland. John A. McCaughan. Ir.Am. Gen. 7 (25-28) (1982) 450-471.

Caulfield *see also* **MacCathmhaoil, Ashmur**

> A short biographical notice of the Clan Cathmhaoil or Caulfield family. Bernard Connor. Dublin, 1808.
>
> Caulfield family of Ulster Province: Armagh Co. Museum Ms. N8: LDS Mf.1279356.

Macausland or **McCausland** *see also* **McClintock**

> Macausland Family Papers (Strabane, Co Tyrone;1250–1942). PRONI DOD 669; LDS Mf. 248300.

Cavenagh *see* **Kavanagh**

MacCawell *see* **Caulfield**

Chadwick

> Pedigree of Chadwick Family of Cork: IGRS Library (Leader Collection).
>
> The Chadwicks of Guelph and Toronto. Toronto, pr. pr., 1914.

Chamberlain(e) *see also* **Sheridan**

> The Chamberlains of Nizelrath. T. G. F. Paterson. CLAHJ 10 (1944) 324–6.
>
> The Chamberlains of Nizelrath. Notes on allied families of Clinton, Aston, O'Doherty, Brownlow. CLAHJ 11 (3) (1947-8) p.175-185.

Chambers

> Pedigrees of Atkinson, Beck, Chambers, Cole, Jackson, and Pilleys or Pillows. LDS Mf. 1279354.
>
> Chambers family of Ulster Province: Armagh Co. Museum Ms. N8: LDS Mf.1279356.

Charleton

> The family of Charlton of Clonmacnoise. Ir.Gen. 4 (1969) 117–121.

Charley *see* **Darbyshire**

Chartres

> Pedigree of Chartres Family of Cork: IGRS Library (Leader Collection).

Chatterton

> Pedigree of Chatterton Family of Cork: IGRS Library (Leader Collection).

Cheetham *see* **Ireton**

Chenevix

> The family of Chenevix. R. A. Austen-Leigh. Proc. of Huguenot Soc. of Ireland, 17 (1945) 4.

Cherry *see* **Cleland**
>Pedigree of Cherry Family of Cork: IGRS Library (Leader Collection).

Chetwood
>Chetwoods of Woodbrook in the Queen's Co. JCKAS 9 (1918–21) 205–26.

Chichester
>The history of the family of Chichester. Alexander P. B. Chichester. Pr.pr.
>London, 1871. (Chichester family, Marquesses of Donegal).

Chinnery
>George Chinnery, 1774–1852, with account of his family and genealogy.
>JCHAS 37 (1932)11–21; 38 (1933) 1–15.
>Pedigree of Chinnery Family of Cork: IGRS Library (Leader Collection).
>Chinnery of Co. Cork. Ir. Anc. 7 (2) (1975) 67–69.

Chivers
>Pedigree of Chivers Family of Cork: IGRS Library (Leader Collection).

Christian
>Pedigree of Christian Family of Cork: IGRS Library (Leader Collection).

Claffey
>Pedigree of Claffey Family of Cork: IGRS Library (Leader Collection).

Clancarty *see also* **Monck**

Clancy
>Clancy – MacFhleannchaidh, a brief family history. Maria Clancy, 1979.
>The Clancy & Huss families of Ireland, Luxembourg & America. Marie E.
>Clancy. pr.pr.: Jackson Heights, NY 1980. (NLI Call No. Ir 9292 p.20).

Clare *see* **Guinness**

Clark or **Clarke**
>The history and genealogy of the Clark family and its connections. C. L.
>Clark. Detroit, 1898.
>Pedigree of Clarke Family of Cork: IGRS Library (Leader Collection).
>History of Patrick & Catherine (Wade) Clarke & their ancestors & descend-
>ants. William P. Clarke. Toledo,Ohio: 1946.

McClatchey
>Notes on the surname McClatchey in Ireland. Ulster Gen. & Hist. Guild. 9
>(1986) 87-88.

Clayton
>Some account of the Clayton family of Thelwall, Co. Chester, afterwards of
>St. Dominick's Abbey, Doneraile, and Mallow, Co. Cork. J. P. Rylands,
>Liverpool, 1880.
>Pedigree of Clayton Family of Cork: IGRS Library (Leader Collection).
>Clayton family, Co. Cork. JCHAS 5(1889) 194–7.

Cleland *see also* **Rose**
>The Clelands of Co. Down; extracts from Presbyterian records: with Cherry,
>Mulligan, Vance notes. D. Stewart. LDS Lib. 929.2415 C589sd.

McClement *see* **Orr**
Clements
> Pedigree of Clements Family of Cork: IGRS Library (Leader Collection).

McClenehan *see* **Ashmur**
Clenlow
> Clenlow of Co. Down. Pedigree in 'Swanzy Notebooks'. RCB Library, Dublin.

O'Clery
> The Ó Cleirigh family of Tir Conaill. Rev. Paul Walsh. Dublin: Three Candles 1938.
>
> The Muintir Cleirigh of Tirawley. JRSAI 75 (1945) 70–5.

Cliffe
> Cliffe of Bellevue. Wexford Gentry Vol. 1 (see abbreviations).

Clifford *see* **Bernard, Moore**
Clifton *see* **Allen – Allen of Ulster**
McClintock
> McClintock family papers: genealogical notes on McClintock et al. P. V. E. McClintock. Lancaster, 1986. (ISBN/ISSN: 095118170X) (Refs to McCausland, Hime, Robertson, Dobbs, Powell).

Clinton *see also* **Chamberlain.**
> The Clinton Family in Co. Louth. CLAHJ 3 (1912) 1–15.
>
> Clinton Records. CLAHJ 12 (1950) 109–16.
>
> Some notes on Drogheda (Co.Louth) families of Carroll, Clinton, McGovern & Skelly. J.Old Drogheda Soc. 11 (1998).
>
> Clinton family of Ulster Province: Armagh Co. Museum Ms. N8: LDS Mf.1279356.

Clune
> The Clunes: from the Dalcassians to modern times. Conor F. Clune. Cork: Quinville Press (199?). (LDS Lib. 929.2415 C628cc.

McClure
> Our Haddon, McClure, Curry and allied families. Eliza H. Brevort & Doris B. Wheeler. Burkert-Walton Co. 1952.
>
> An Account of Research on the McClure Family. Familia 2 (10) 1994.

Coakley
> Pedigree of Coakley Family of Cork: IGRS Library (Leader Collection).

Coane
> Pedigree of Coane Family of Cork: IGRS Library (Leader Collection).

Coats *see also* **Waldron**
> Pedigree of Coates Family of Cork: IGRS Library (Leader Collection).

Cockburn or **Coburn** *see* **Stinson, Nesbitt**
Codys or **MacCodys** *see also* **Archdekin**
> The Archdekins or MacCodys. Old Kilkenny Review 4 (2) (1990) p. 745-759.

Codd

Castletown Carne and its owners. JRSAI 41 (1911) 246–58. 42 (1912) 34–45.

Genealogies of Esmond, Codd, Jacob, and Redmond. GO Mf. 279.

Coffey

Genealogical and historical records of the Sept Cobhthaigh, now Coffey. H. A. Coffey. Dublin, 1863.

Cogan or **DeCogan**

Pedigree of Cogan Family of Cork: IGRS Library (Leader Collection).

The de Cogan family. JRSAI 84 (1959) 41–56.

Cogan, De Cogan or Goggin in 'Family Names of Co. Cork' (see abbrevs.) (Notes on origins & members in Co. Cork).

Coghill *see also* **Cramer, Somerville, Swift**

Pedigree of Coghill Family of Cork: IGRS Library (Leader Collection).

Coghlan, MacCoghlan, Coughlan or Cohalan.

The MacCoghlans of Delvin Eathra. Ir. Gen. 4 (1970) 534–546; 5(1971) 21–32.

Coghlan, Coughlan or Cohalan in 'Family Names of Co. Cork' (see abbrevs.) (Notes on family origins etc to 1700).

Colburn

Pedigree of Colburn Family of Cork: IGRS Library (Leader Collection).

Colclough

Colclough Papers. [Tintern Abbey, Co. Wexford]. Anal. Hib. 20, 3–16.

Pedigree of Colclough Family of Cork: IGRS Library (Leader Collection).

The Colclough Family. JOWS 10 (1984-5) p. 44-54.

Colclough of Tintern. Wexford Gentry Vol. 1 (see abbreviations).

Cole *see also* **Monck**

Memoirs of Sir (Galbraith) Lowry Cole. Maud Lowry Cole. London: Macmillan & Co., 1934.

Cole of Co. Cork. Gen., 3 (1879) 289–91.

The Cole family of West Carbery. R. L. Cole. Belfast: Bell & Logan, 1943. (LDS Lib. 929.2415 C674c.

Genealogy of the family of Cole, Co. Devon, with branches in Ireland. James E. Cole. 1867.

Pedigrees of Atkinson, Beck, Chambers, Cole, Jackson, and Pilleys or Pillows. LDS Mf.1279354.

Belleisle and its owners. Clogher Record 16 (2) (1998) 7-44. (Cole family).

Coleman or **Colman**

Coleman or Colman in 'Family Names of Co. Cork' (see abbrevs.) (Notes on origins & members in Co. Cork).

Colgan and McColgan

The McColgans of Inishowen. JRSAI 12 (1871) 1; 23 (1893) 243-250; 32 (1902) 291-329.

Colhoun

A Donegal-Virginia connection. Donegal Ann. 47 (1995) p. 113-115. (Patton & Colhoun families).

Colkin

Colkin of Cavan. Pedigree in 'Swanzy Notebooks'. RCB Library, Dublin.

Colles or **Collis**

Records of the Colles family. R. W. Colles. Dublin, 1892.

Pedigree of Collis Family of Cork: IGRS Library (Leader Collection).

Colley

Two Colley inscriptions in Castle Carbury churchyard: notes on the family founder. JCKAS 8(5) (1917) p. 368-387.

The last days of the Colleys on Carbury Hill. JCKAS Vol. 17 (1989-91) p. 96-98.

Collins

Collins in 'Family Names of Co. Cork' (see abbrevs.) (Notes on origins & members in Co.Cork).

Colpoys

Colpoys of Ballycarr (Co. Clare). JRSAI 27 (1898) 71–72.

Colquhoun or **Calhoun**

Colquhoun/Calhoun and their ancestral homelands. Ellen R. Johnson. Heritage Books, USA 1993.

Colville *see also* **Wandesforde**

The Colville family in Ulster. Ulster J. Arch. 5 (1899) 139–45, 202–10.

The Colville family. Ulster J. Arch. 6 (1900) 12–16.

McComb *see* **McCuskey**

Comerford

The Comerford family. Old Kilkenny Review, 24 (1972) p.29-32.

John Comerford of Ballybur (1598-1667) tracing his later life. Old Kilkenny Review 46 (1994) p.23-36.

Comyn

The origin of the Comyns. Ancestor 10 (1905) 104–19; 11 (1905) 129–35.

Notes on the Comyn pedigree. N. Munster. Antiq. J. 3 (1913) 22–37.

The early Irish Comyns. JRSAI 86 (1956) 170–86.

Concannon

The story of the Concannons. M. Concannon O'Brien. Dublin: Clan Publications, 199?. (LDS Lib. 929.2415 C744o.

McCone

The Territory of Ballymacone and its association with the McCones. Seanchas Ardmhacha 1(1) (1954) 132-150. (Early history of the McCone family).

Condon

Pedigree of Condon Family of Cork: IGRS Library (Leader Collection).

Condon, DeCondon, DeCanton in 'Family Names of Co. Cork' (see abbrevs.)

(Notes on origins & members in Co.Cork).

The Condons of Clonleigh. JCHAS 2 (1896) 477–85, 509–15.

Condons Aboos: the history of an ancient family. Robt J Condon. Florida: Condon Press 1995. (NLI Ir 9292 c 49).

MacConmara

The Pedigrees of MacConmara of Co. Clare with Some Family Reminiscences. 1908.

McConnell *see also* Orr

Pedigree of McConnell Family of Cork: IGRS Library (Leader Collection).

Conn

The Scottish & Irish Background of Rev. Hugh Conn of the Colonial Clergy of Maryland. Familia 2 (10) 1994.

Connell or O'Connell *see also* Stinson

O'Connell family tracts. Basil M. O'Connell. Dublin: Browne & Nolan 1947, 1948, 1951. (LDS Lib. 929.2415 Oc5o (Extracts of biographies of prominent O'Connells).

Pedigree of O'Connell Family of Cork: IGRS Library (Leader Collection).

O'Connell in 'Family Names of Co. Cork' (see abbrevs.) (Notes on origins & members in Co.Cork).

Conner

Conner Papers. (Manch, Co. Cork.) Anal. Hib. 15: 153–59.

Connery

The Connerys: the making of a Waterford legend. Brendan Kiely. Dublin: Geography Pubs. 1994 (ISBN: 0906602246).

Connolly or Conolly

Clogherici: the Connollys of Fermanagh and Co. Monaghan. Clogher Record 2 (1957) 172–6.

The Connollys of Castletown: a family history. QBIGS (1968) p 1-46.

Notes on some families of the Clones (Co. Monaghan) area: the Connolly family of Clones Estate. Clogher Record 13(3) (1990) p.115-124.

Pedigree of Conolly Family of Cork: IGRS Library (Leader Collection).

The Dickson and Connolly families of Ballyshannon. Donegal Ann. 4 (1959) 111–17.

Speaker Conolly and his connections. Privately pr., 1907.

O'Connor or O'Conor *see also* Goodbody, Henchy

The O'Conors of Connaught: An historical Memoir. C. O'Conor Don. Dublin: Hodges & Figgis, 1891.

Memoirs of Charles O'Connor of Belenagare, with historical account of the family O'Conor. C. O'Conor. Dublin, 1796.

Memoir of the O'Connors of Ballintubber, Co. Roscommon. R. O'Connor. Dublin, 1859.

Lineal descent of the O'Connors of Co. Roscommon. Roderic O'Connor. Dublin. 1862.

Historical and genealogical memoir of the O'Connors, kings of Connaught. Roderic O'Connor. Dublin, 1861.

The O'Conor family: families of Daniel and Matthias O'Connor of Corsallagh House, Achonry, Co. Sligo, Ireland, A.D. 1750. Watson B. O'Connor. Brooklyn, 1914.

Pedigree of O'Connor Family of Cork: IGRS Library (Leader Collection).

The Royal O'Connors of Connaught. P. O'Connor. Old House Press, Mayo: 1997.

The O'Connor Papers: Their Significance to Genealogists. Eire-Ireland 11(2) (1976) 104–18.

The O'Connor Henchys of Stonebrook. JCKAS 2 (1896–99) 407–12.

O'Connor: people and places. Hugh W. L. Weir. Clare: Ballinakella Press, 1994 (ISBN 0946538174) (LDS Lib. 929.2415 Oc5w).

O'Connors of Swinford, Co. Mayo: A family history. Patrick O'Connor. Swinford Old House Press 1998. (ISBN 0952992825) NLI Ir 9292 o76.

Memoir of a Controversy Respecting the Name Borne by the O'Connors of Ballintobber, The title of Don and the Legal Representatives of the Family. Roderic O'Conor Esq. Dublin, 1857.

O'Conor; Roderic O'Conor, 1860-1940. Paula Murphy. 1992.

The duel between two of the O'Connors of Offaly … 1583. JRSAI 40 (1910) 1-5.

Conron *see also* **Cantillon**

The Conron family of Co. Cork. H. D. Gallwey. Ir.Gen. 3 (9) (1964) 341–50. (Refs to Copinger, Gallwey & O'Shea).

Conway or **McConway** *see also* **Blennerhasset**

The Conways of Kerry. S. J. M. JKAHS (Old Series) 5(1920) 71–91.

Three Kerry families: O'Mahony, Conway and Spotswood. S. T. MacCarthy. Folkestone [1923].

Lt. Edward McConway (of Kerry) in 'King James' IAL' (Notes on family members pre-1784).

Conwil

The Village Schoolmaster: John Conwil (1802-1880). Carloviana 37 (1989-90) 3-7. (Rathornan, Co. Carlow).

Conyers *see* **Wandesforde**

Conyngham

William Burton Conyngham, 1733–1796. Riocht na Midhe 8 (1987) 113–129.

An old Ulster house & the people who lived in it. Mina Lenox-Conyngham. Dundalk: W. Tempest, 1946. (LDS Lib. 929.2415 C769L (Conyngham & Lenox-Conyngham families).

Cook or **Cooke**

Notes on the Cooke, Ashe and Swift Families, All of Dublin. JAPMD 9 (1912–16) 503.

Notes on Cooke of Tomduff. JAPMD 1 (1888–91) 519.

Lt. Matthew Cooke (of Painstown, Carlow) in 'King James' IAL' (Brief notes on family members pre-1691).

Cooper *see also* **O'Hara.**

Pedigree Book for Cooper Family of Cork: IGRS Library (Leader Collection)

Butterhill and Beyond: an illustrated history of the Cooper family of Byfleet, Killenure Castle, Co. Tipperary and Abbeville House, Co. Dublin. R. Austin Cooper. Pr.pr. Reading 1991 (100 copies) (ISBN 0951773607).

Coote

Historical and genealogical records of the Coote family. Rev. A. de Vlieger. Lausanne:Bridel 1900.

Cope

The Cope family of Loughgall (including Swift connections). Armagh Co. Museum Ms. M9; LDS Mf.1279356.

Copinger or **Coppinger**

History of Copingers or Coppingers of Co. Cork. W.A. Copinger. London: Sotheran, 1884. (LDS Lib. 929.2415 C791c).

Capt Henry Copinger (of Cork) in 'King James' IAL' (Notes on family pre-1700).

Copley

Pedigree of Copley Family of Cork: IGRS Library (Leader Collection).

Corballis or **Corbally**

Corballis/Corbally families of Co. Dublin. Irish Family History 8 (1992) 84–93.

The Corbally family of Co. Dublin. Dublin Hist. Rec. 46 (1) (1993) p.66.

The Corballis-Corbally families of Co. Dublin. Dublin Hist. Rec. 45 (2) (1992) p.91-100.

Corban

Pedigree of Corban Family of Cork: IGRS Library (Leader Collection).

Corbet

Pedigree of Corbet Family of Cork: IGRS Library (Leader Collection).

Corker

The Pooles of Mayfield. Rosemary ffolliott. Dublin: Hodges Figgis (1958). (Deals with Corker of Manchester, Dublin and Cork: 17th to early 19th c.).

MacCormick or **McCormack** *see also* **Ashmur**

Scotch-Irish in Ireland and in America, as shown in sketches of the pioneer Scotch-Irish families McCormick, Stevenson, McKenzie & Bell. Andrew P. McCormick. New Orleans, 1897.

Pedigree of McCormick Family of Cork: IGRS Library (Leader Collection).

Surname report on the bearers of the great Irish name of MacCormack. Kansas City, Mo.: Irish Genealogical Foundation, 1981. (LDS Lib. 929.2415 A1 no. 15.

Corry

The History of the Corry Family of Castlecoole. Lowry-Corry, Somerset R. London: Longmans, Green & Co., 1891. (LDS Lib. 929.2415 C817b & NLI Call No. Ir 9292 c8) (also refs to Lowry family).

Brief Genealogies of the Families Corry, Crawford, Auchinleck, Dane, Rampain, and Leslie, in 'The History of 2 Ulster Manors'. Earl of Belmore, London/Dublin, 1903.

The Corrys of County Monaghan. J.C.Bond. Nepean,Ont.: J.C. Bond, 1995. (LDS Lib. 929.2415 C817bj.

Cosby

The Autobiography of Pole Cosby, of Stradbally, Queen's County (1703–1737). JCKAS 5 (1906–08).

Cosgrove

Pedigree of Cosgrove Family of Cork: IGRS Library (Leader Collection).

Cossett

Cossett of Co. Down. Pedigree in 'Swanzy Notebooks'. RCB Library, Dublin.

Costello *see also* **Nolan**

Pedigree of Costello Family of Cork: IGRS Library (Leader Collection).

Cotter

Notes on the Cotter Family of Rockforest, Co. Cork. JCHAS 14 (1908) 1–12.

Pedigree of Cotter Family of Cork: IGRS Library (Leader Collection).

The Cotter Family of Rockforest, Co. Cork. JCHAS 43 (1938) 21–31.

Cotter, McCoitir in 'Family Names of Co. Cork' (see abbrevs.) (Notes on origins & members in Co. Cork).

Coughlan

Capt. Terence Coughlan (of Offaly) in 'King James' IAL' (Notes on family pre-1700).

Coulson

Coulson of Belmont. Pedigree in 'Swanzy Notebooks'. RCB Library, Dublin.

Courthope

The Pooles of Mayfield. Rosemary ffolliott. Dublin: Hodges Figgis (1958). (Deals with Courthopes of Kent, England & Cork: 1500 to 1700 approx.).

Cowan *see* **Switzer**

Cowley *see also* **Archdeacon**

Some notice of the family of Cowley in Kilkenny. JRSAI 2 (1852) 102–14.

Cramer

A Genealogical Note on the Family of Cramer or Coghill. JCHAS 16 (1910) 66–81, 143.

Crawford

The Crawfords of Donegal and how they came there. R. Crawford. Dublin, 1886.

Brief Genealogies of the Families Corry, Crawford, Auchinleck, Dane, Rampain, and Leslie, in 'The History of 2 Ulster Manors'. Earl of Belmore, London/Dublin, 1903.

McCrea *see* **Gower**

Creagh *see also* **McNamara**

Pedigree of Creagh Family of Cork: IGRS Library (Leader Collection).

Ulster Creaghs. JRSAI 3 (1854) 240.

Creany *see* **Stinson**

Crichton

Genealogy of the Earls of Erne (Crichton). J. H. Steele. Edinburgh, 1910.

The pedigree of the Earl of Erne. John H. Steele. R. & R. Clark, Edinburgh, 1891. (LDS Lib. 929.2415 A1 no. 1.

Crocket

Pedigree of Crocket Family of Cork: IGRS Library (Leader Collection).

Crofton *see also* **Carlile & Hargreaves**

Pedigree of Crofton Family of Cork: IGRS Library (Leader Collection).

Crofton memoirs: account of John Crofton of Ballymurray, Co. Roscommon, his ancestors and descendants and others bearing his name. H. T. Crofton. York: Yorkshire Printing Co., 1911. (LDS Lib. 929.2415 C874c.

The Story of Mote (Family History of Lord Crofton) Francis Crofton. pr.pr. 1895.

Crofts

Pedigree of Crofts Family of Cork: IGRS Library (Leader Collection).

Croker

The family of Croker. Herald & Genealogist 8 (1874) 377–91.

Pedigree of Croker Family of Cork: IGRS Library (Leader Collection).

Crone

Crone of Co. Cork. Ir. Anc. 1 (1969) 77–88.

Cronin

Pedigree of Cronin Family of Cork: IGRS Library (Leader Collection).

Cronin in 'Family Names of Co. Cork' (see abbrevs.) (Notes on origins & members in Co.Cork).

Crooke

Pedigree Book for Crooke Family of Cork: IGRS Library (Leader Collection).

Crookshank

Entries from the Family Bible of Alexander and Esther Crookshank. Ir. Anc. 9 (2) (1977) 1–2.

Crosby

Harrigans and Crosbys: A genealogical study. J. Gen. Soc. I. 1(1) 8-12.

Bing Crosby's Irish Roots: The Harrigan family of Co. Cork, New Brunswick, Minnesota & Washington. Ir.Am. Gen. 29-32 (1984) 487-489.

Cross *see also* **Blennerhasset**

Pedigree of Cross Family of Cork: IGRS Library (Leader Collection).

Crossle or **Crossley**

Descent and alliances of Croslegh, or Crossle etc of Scaitliffe. C. Croslegh. London: De La More Press 1904.

Crowley or **O'Crowley**

A Defeated Clan, (The O'Crowleys). JCHAS 36 (1931) 24–28.

O'Crowley Pedigree from the Carew Mss. and Other Sources. JCHAS 35(1930) 89.

The O'Crowleys of Coill t-Sealbhaigh. JCHAS 56 (1951) 91–94; 57 (1952) 1–6, 105–09; 58 (1953) 7–11.

(O) Crowley in 'Family Names of Co. Cork' (see abbrevs.) (Notes on origins & members in Co.Cork).

Cruise

Capt. Francis Cruise (of Dublin) in 'King James' IAL' (Notes on family members pre-1700).

Crushell *see* **Donnelly**

Crymble *see* **Payton**

Cudahy

Cudahys: an Irish-American success story. Old Kilkenny Review, (1996) 133.

Cudmore

Pedigree of Cudmore Family of Cork: IGRS Library (Leader Collection).

Cuffe

Maurice Cuffe of Ennis (Co. Clare) and his family. The Other Clare 18 (1994) p.28-31.

Pedigree of Cuffe Family of Cork: IGRS Library (Leader Collection).

O'Cuinneagan

O'Cuinneagan family. JRSAI 13(1873) 392- ; 60 (1931) 79.

Cullen

Cullen; Biographical Material. Reportorium Novum 1 (1) (1955) 213–27.

Pedigree of Cullen Family of Cork: IGRS Library (Leader Collection).

The Early Cullen Family. Reportorium Novum 2 (1) (1958) 185–202.

Cullinane and Cullinan

The Cullinan & Cullinane family genealogy. Michael W. Cullinan. Ms. LDS Lib. 929.2415 C898c.

McCullagh

Pedigree of McCullagh Family of Cork: IGRS Library (Leader Collection).

Cummins

Pedigree of Cummins Family of Cork: IGRS Library (Leader Collection).

Cunningham *see* **Payton**

Cunningham, Hagan, McKiearnan family history. Harriette W. Rochford. Alpha, Illinois 1984 (NLI Call No. 9292 r21).

Cuppaidge

Pedigree of Cuppaidge Family of Cork: IGRS Library (Leader Collection).

Curneen or **O'Curneen**

The learned family of O Cuirnin. in: 'Irish Men of Learning'. Rev. Paul Walsh; Three Candles, Dublin (1947) (16th century & earlier references).

Curran *see also* **Hoade**

Pedigree of Curran Family of Cork: IGRS Library (Leader Collection).

John Philpot Curran and his family. D. F. Moore. Dublin Hist. Rec. 15 (1959) 50–61.

Curtin

The Curtins of Ballygarrett. Mallow Field Club J. 15 (1997).

Cusack *see also* **Warren**

Cusack Family of Meath and Dublin. Ir. Gen. 5(3) (1976) 298–313; 5(4) (1977) 464–70; 5(5) (1978) 591–600; 5(6) 1979: 673–84; 6 (2) (1981) 130–53; 6 (3) (1982) 285–98.

The Cusacks of Killeen, Co. Meath. Riocht na Midhe 7 (4) (1980/81) 3–35.

The Cusacks of Portraine and Rathaldron. Riocht na Midhe 4 (4) (1970) 58–61.

Capt. Nicholas Cusack (& Family of Meath) in 'King James' IAL' (Family line pre-1753).

McCuskey

A tree of 4 ancient stocks: a four-fold family history. Wm. H. McCuskey. pr.pr. 1916. (McCuskey, McComb, Harvey, Hughey).

Cust

Ways to wealth: the Cust family of 18th century Armagh. L.A. Clarkson & E.M. Crawford. Belfast: Ulster Soc. for Irish Hist. Studies, Queen's Univ. 1985. (LDS Lib. 929.2415 C965c.

Macutchen or **McCutchen** *see also* **Rothwell**

Pedigree of McCutchen Family of Cork: IGRS Library (Leader Collection).

Cutting *see* **MacNair**

Dacey

Pedigree of Dacey Family of Cork: IGRS Library (Leader Collection).

Dalton

Capt. Miles Dalton (of Dundonnell, Westmeath) in 'King James' IAL' (Notes on family pre-1793).

Daly and O'Daly *see also* **Ireton**

Families of Daly in Galway with Tabular Pedigrees. JGAHS 13 (1926–27) 140.

Pedigree of Daly Family of Cork: IGRS Library (Leader Collection).

Papers (e.g., deeds, leases, & pedigrees) relating to Daly et al. Longford/ Westmeath Library (Upton Papers) & LDS mf. 101011.

The O'Dalys of Muintuavara: a story of a bardic family. Dominick Daly. Dublin, 1821.

History of the Dalys. E. E. O'Daly. New York, 1937.

Dunsandle Papers. Anal. Hib. 15, 392–405.

Capt Charles Daly (of Dunsandle, Galway) in 'King James' IAL' (Notes on family members pre-1761).

Daly or O'Daly in 'Family Names of Co. Cork' (see abbrevs.) (Notes on origins & members to 1850).

History of the O'Dalys: the story of the ancient Irish sept, the race of Dalach of Corca Adaimh. New Haven, Conn.: Tuttle, Morehouse & Taylor Co., 1937. (LDS Lib. 929.2415 Od1o).

Four O'Daly manuscripts. *Eigse* 26 (1992) 43-79.

Daly family of Ladysbridge, Castlemartyr, Co. Cork. Ir.Am. Gen. 5 (1975) 59-60.

Danckert

Pedigree of Danckert Family of Cork: IGRS Library (Leader Collection).

Dane

Brief Genealogies of … Dane et al in 'The History of 2 Ulster Manors'. Earl of Belmore, London/Dublin, 1903.

Daniel(s) or **O'Daniel**

Snatches of O'Daniel, Hamilton & allied ancestry & history in Maryland & Kentucky. Victor F. O'Daniel. Somerset, Ohio, 1933.

Pedigree of Daniels Family of Cork: IGRS Library (Leader Collection).

Dannett *see* **Jephson**

D'Aran

The D'Aran family of New South Wales. Irish Family History 4 (1988) 89-92 (ref to Troy).

Darbyshire

The Darbyshire genealogy: inc. the families of Denny, Traill, Brett, Hannon, Kingan and Charley. John Harris Rea. Ms. LDS Lib. 929.2415 D242r.

D'Arcy or **Darcy** *see also* **McNamara**

An historical sketch of the family of D'Arcy from the Norman conquest to the year 1853. John C. Lyons: pub. 1882. Longford/Westmeath Library; LDS Lib. 929.2415 A1 no. 34.

Pedigree of D'Arcy family (complete of English & Irish branches) London: Elliott Stock 1901.

Count Patrick D'Arcy and pedigrees of the D'Arcy family. JGAHS 10(1918)
58–66, 158–9.

Pedigree of Darcy Family of Cork: IGRS Library (Leader Collection).

The D'Arcys from 1323 to today. Irish Link 9 (June 1986) 4-7; & 10 (Sept
1986) 10-12.

Darcy of Platten. Ir. Gen. 6 (4) (1983) 403–22.

Lt. Edmund D'Arcy: in 'King James' IAL' (Notes on family members pre-
1700).

The genealogy of the Darcys of Clonuane in Co. Clare, & Kiltolla in
Co.Galway. Darcy Burke. Dublin: J. Hill, 1796. (ref to Blake, Browne,
Burke, Fitzgerald, French, Lynch) (LDS Lib. 929.2415 A1 no. 43).

Dardis

The family of Dardis. Riocht na Midhe 6 (1976) 58–80.

Dare *see* **Hall**

Darley *see* **Guinness**

Darrah

Pedigree of Darrah Family of Cork: IGRS Library (Leader Collection).

Daunt

Account of the family of Daunt. John Daunt. Newcastle-on-Tyne, 1881.

Pedigree of Daunt Family of Cork: IGRS Library (Leader Collection).

Davies *see also* **Davys**

The descendants of V. Rev. Rowland Davies, Dean of Cork. H. E. Jones.
Ir.Gen. 3 (1966) 424–38.

The Pooles of Mayfield. R. ffolliott. Dublin: Hodges Figgis (1958). (Re: Davies
of Ludlow, England & Cork: 1550-1790).

Pedigree Book for Davies Family of Cork: IGRS Library (Leader Collection)

MacDavitt *see* **Mullally**

O'Davoren

The O'Davorens of Cahermacnaughten, Burren, Co. Clare. N. Munster Antiq.
J. 2 (2) (1912–13) 63–93; 2 (3) 149–64; 2(4) 194-211.

Davys

O'Cianain, S. F. The Davys Family Records. Records kept by members of the
Davys family, formerly of Cloonbonny, near Lanesborough, and of
Martinstown, near Roscommon, from 1693 to 1832. Printed from the origi-
nals in the possession of the family. Longford: Longford Printing Co.,
1931.

Dawson *see also* **O'Mullally**

The Dawsons of Ardee. CLAHJ 8 (1) (1933) p.22-34.

Pedigree of Dawson Family of Cork: IGRS Library (Leader Collection).

Dawson of Co. Monaghan. Pedigree in 'Swanzy Notebooks'. RCB Library,
Dublin.

Dawson St. & the Dawson family. Dublin Hist. Rec. 17 (2) (1962) 62-73.

O'Dea

O'Dea - Ua Deaghaidh: the story of a rebel clan. Whitegate: Ballinakella Press, 1992. (LDS Lib. 929.2415 Od2u.

Deacon *see* **Rothwell**

Dean or **Deane** *see also* **Boyd**

Pedigree of Deane Family of Cork: IGRS Library (Leader Collection).

De Burgh

Notes of the history of the De Burgh family. compiled by Elizabeth Jane Hussey De Burgh. Dublin: C.W. Gibbs, 1890 (LDS Lib. 929.2415 D354d.

Deady

Pedigree of Deady Family of Cork: IGRS Library (Leader Collection).

DeCourcy *see also* **Meade**

Lt. Col. Almeric DeCourcy (Kinsale, Co Cork) in 'King James' IAL' (Notes on family members pre-1719).

Deey *see* **Spedding.**

Degennes *see* **Lyons**

De Lacy *see also* **Lacy.**

Notes on the family of De Lacy in Ireland. JRSAI 49 (1919) 113–31.

Delafield

Delafield, the family history. John Ross Delafield. Pr.pr. (NY) 1945. (LDS Lib. 929.2415 D371d.

O'Dell

The O'Dells of Carriglea. Ardmore J. 3 (1986) 44–59.

Delamain

The Delamain family in Ireland. Dublin Hist. Rec. 49 (2) (1996) p.156-160.

Delamere

Memoir of the family of Delamere, Delamar, De La Mer, etc.: of Donore, Streate, & Ballynefid, Co. Westmeath. Dublin: R.D. Webb, 1857 (GO Ms. no. 518; LDS Mf. 257821).

Delany

Pedigree of Delany Family of Cork: IGRS Library (Leader Collection).

The Delanys and their links with Clogher and Derryvullan. Clogher Record 7 (2) (1970) 221.

Delanys of Delville. Dublin Hist. Rec. 9(4) (1948) 105-116.

De la Touche *see* **Latouche**

Dempsey or **O'Dempsey**

An account of the O'Dempseys, chiefs of clan Maliere. T. Matthews. Dublin:Hodges & Figgis 1903.

The O'Dempseys of Clanmaliere. Lord Walter Fitzgerald. JCKAS 4 (1903–05) 396–431.

Lt. Colonel Laurence Dempsey (of Laois/Offaly) in 'King James' IAL' (Notes on family members pre-1746).

Denham *see also* **Jephson**
> Denham of Dublin. C. H. Denham. Dublin, 1936.

Dennehy
> The family register of John Dennehy of Fermoy. W. G. Clare. Ir.Gen. 1 (1937) 23–5.

Dennison
> Pedigree of Dennison Family of Cork: IGRS Library (Leader Collection).

Denny *see also* **Darbyshire**
> The Denny family. J. King. History of Co. Kerry, 242–60. Dublin, 1910.
> Dennys of Cork. H. L. L. Denny, JCHAS 28(1922)45–46.
> Notes on the families of … Denny of Tralee. JAPMD 7 (1907–09) 373.

Denroche
> Large Pedigree Book for Denroche Family. IGRS Library (Leader Collection).

De Rinzy
> De Rinzy and Dundas of Clobemon (Wexford). Wexford Gentry Vol. 2 (see abbreviations).

McDermot *see also* **Ireton, Gower**
> Mac Dermot of Moylurg: the story of a Connaught family. Dermot MacDermot. Leitrim: Drumlin Publications, 1996 (ISBN: 1873437161). (LDS Lib. 929.2415 M143m.
> Pedigree of McDermott Family of Cork: IGRS Library (Leader Collection).
> Capt. Hugh McDermott (of Moylurg) in 'King James' IAL' (Notes on family members pre-1700).

De Ridelesford
> The De Ridelsfords. E. St. John Brooks. JRSAI 81 (1951) 115–38; 82 (1952) 45–61.

Desmond
> Desmond or O'Deasuna in 'Family Names of Co. Cork' (see abbrevs.) (Notes on origins & members in Co.Cork).

D'Esterre *see also* **Guinness**
> Pedigree of Captain D'Esterre, who was fatally wounded by Daniel O'Connell in a duel in 1815. JCHAS 34 (1929) 47.
> D'Esterre of Rosmanagher. Ir. Gen. 6 (1979) 720–727.

Devaney *see* **Donnelly**
O'Develin
> The O'Devlins of Tyrone: the story of an Irish sept. J. C. Develin. Rutland, Vermont: 1938. (LDS Lib. 929.2415 Od2d.

Devenish
> Sylvester Devenish (Athlone & Roscommon) in 'King James' IAL' (Notes on family members pre-1700).

De Verdon

The De Verdons of Louth. JRSAI 25 (1895) 317–28: 29 (1899) 417-419.

Two De Verdon seals. CLAHJ 11 (3) (1947-8) p.292-296.

The De Verdons and the Draycotts. CLAHJ 5(3) (1923) p. 166-172.

Devereux

Account of the Anglo-Norman Family of Devereux of Balmagir, Co. Wexford. G.O.Redmond. Irish Builder: Dublin 1891. NLI Ir 9292 d1.

Devereux of the Leap. Ir. Gen. 4 (5) (1972) 450–60.

Devereux of Ballymagir and Adamstown. JOWS 3 (1970) p. 43 50.

Devereux and Skrine of Ballyrankin (Wexford) Wexford Gentry Vol. 2 (see abbreviations).

Devenish

Records of the Devenish families. Robert T. Devenish and Charles H. MacLaughlin. Chicago, 1948.

Devitt *see* **Boyd, Moore**

Devlin or **O'Devlin** *see also* **O'Hagan**

O'Neill's 'own country' and its families. Seanchas Ardmhacha 6(1) (1971) 3-23. (Origins & early history of families associated with the O'Neills of Tyrone: O'Devlin, O'Quinn, O'Hagan, O'Donnelly, McCathmail [or McCaul, Campbell] and Murphy).

Devoy *see also* **Flynn**

Outline history of the Devoy family of Courtwood, Ballybrittas, Co. Leix. Ballinderry, Co. Westmeath 1999(?) (NLI Ir 9292 d37) (also refs to Walsh family).

Dexters

The Dexters of Dublin and Annfield, Co. Kildare. Ir. Anc. 2 (1) (1970) 31–42.

Dickson

Dickson genealogy. C. T. M'Cready. Dublin, 1868.

The Dickson and Connolly families of Ballyshannon. Donegal Ann., 4 (1959) 111–17.

Digby

Digby family records: collection of pedigree charts etc for Digby (or Digbie) & related families (1590-1750) GO Ms 169; LDS Mf 257822.

Dignam

Chronicle of the Dignam family. Toronto, pr. pr., 1962.

Dill

Worthies of the Dill family. J. R. Dill. Belfast, 1888 (2nd ed. Belfast: 1892). (LDS Lib. 929.2415 D58d.

The Dills of Fanad. Donegal Ann. 34

The Pattons and Dills of Springfield. Donegal Ann. 11 (1) (1974).

Dillon

Cnoc Diolun: a genealogical survey of the Dillon family in Ireland. Gerald Dillon. Ir.Gen. 2 (1955) 361–7.

The Dillons of Carlow. W. E. C. Davisson-Houston. Ir.Gen. 3 (1962) 7, 245–8.

Dillon Papers. [Clonbrock, Co. Galway]. Anal. Hib. 20, 17–55.

Col. Henry Dillon (of Westmeath) in 'King James' IAL' (Notes on family members pre-1794).

Disney

Disneys of Stabannon: a review of an Anglo-Irish family from the time of Cromwell. Hugh Disney.

Oxford: 1995 (ISBN 0952590808). (LDS Lib. 929.2415 D632di.

Dix

Dix Family of Dublin, Entries from Family Bible. JAPMD 11 (1921–25) 490.

Dixon

Dixon of Kilkea Castle. JCKAS 9 (5) (1918–21) 392–4.

Dixon of Castlebridge, Co. Wexford. Ir.Gen. 6 (5) 1984 p 640.

Dobbs *see also* **McClintock**

Pedigree of Dobbs Family of Cork: IGRS Library (Leader Collection).

Dobbyn or **Dobbin**

Pedigree of Dobbin Family of Cork: IGRS Library (Leader Collection).

Ancient and Illustrious Waterford Families: The Dobbyns and Waddings. JW&SEIAS 4 (1955) 247–50.

Dodwell

Notes on the Dodwells of Manor Dodwell, Co. Roscommon. Ir.Gen. 1 (1941) 315–17.

O'Doherty, Dogherty or **O'Dochartaigh** *see also* **Chamberlain, Switzer**

O'Doherty Info Pack: History & Genealogy. Derry Youth & Community Workshop,1985. (LDS Lib.929.2415 A1 no.48).

Pedigree of Dogherty Family of Cork: IGRS Library (Leader Collection).

Origin and history of the O'Dohertys. Anthony Mathews. Pr.pr.Drogheda, Ireland, 1978. (LDS Lib. 929.2415 A1 no. 22).

O'Dochartaigh Clan History (O'Dochartaigh Family Research Association) Donegal 1984.

Lt. Con O'Doherty (of Inishowen, Co. Donegal) in 'King James' IAL' (Notes on family members pre-1700).

Mac Daibhéid: descendant of Pug-Nosed Ó Dochartaigh. Donegal Ann. 44 (1992) p.110-113.

O'Doherty family of Inishowen. JRSAI 7(1862) 387; 8 (1864) 155-162; 43(1912) 43-119; 45 (1915).

O'Doherty family of Inishowen. CLAHJ 11(3).

Rosa O'Dogherty; a Gaelic woman. Seanchas Ardmhacha 10(1) (1980-81) 42-62. (Family notes from 1588-1660).

Dolan

Dolan of Pulbawn (Co. Mayo). S. Mayo Family Res. J. 7 (1994) 62-65.

Domville *see* **Bellingham.**

McDonagh

Pedigrees of McDonagh Clan of Corann & Tirerill & Other Families of Co. Sligo. McDonagh Mss. No. 1, Sligo Co. Library.

The McDonagh Family of Co. Sligo. McDonagh Mss. No. 5 and 23, Sligo Co. Library.

The Lords of Ella: the MacDonoghs of Duhallow. JCHAS 3 (1894) 157–62.

MacDonald

The MacDonalds of Mayo. JGAHS 17 (1936–37) 65–82.

Manuscript History of the McDonalds. PRONI D 358/1–4.

A fragment of an Irish manuscript history of the MacDonalds of Antrim. Rev. Archibald MacDonald. Bruceton Mills, W. Va.: Unicorn Inc., 1988. (LDS Lib. 929.2415 A1 no. 3).

The Antrim McDonalds (Family history of the McDonnell family, Earls of Antrim) 205-1977 AD. Angela Antrim. LDS 929 2415 M146a.

Donaldson

Alexander Ban Donaldson, our ancestor, 1691-1776: historical & genealogical account of the Ban Donaldson family of Co. Armagh, & descendants worldwide. Ron Donaldson. Kansas City, Mo. 1989. (LDS Lib. 929.2415 D714d).

Donelan or **Donnellan**

Capt. McLaughlin Donelan (of Clanbrasil, Co Galway) in 'King James' IAL' (Notes on family members pre-1742).

Dongan *see also* **Dungan**

The Dongan family in the County of Kildare at the commencement of the 17th century. JCKAS 4 (1) (1903) 67-70.

Colonel Lord Dongan (of Castletown, Co. Kildare) in 'King James' IAL' (Notes on family members pre-1700).

Ancestry of Governor Dongan. Frederick Van Wyck. Boston: A. A. Beauchamp, 1935. (LDS Lib. 929.2415 D717v).

John Dongan of Dublin, an Elizabethan gentleman. JRSAI 118 (1988) 101-117.

Donnan

Living in Dunsilly: History of Donnan family of Antrim. Leo G. Donnan. Antrim & Dist. Hist. Soc. 1990. (ISBN 0951528017).

MacDonnell

An historical account of the Macdonnells of Antrim: including notices of some other septs, Irish and Scottish. George Hill. Belfast: Archer & sons, 1873. Facsimile ed. Published by Glens of Antrim Historical Soc., 1976.

The Macdonnells of Tinnakill Castle. JCKAS 4 (1903–05) 205–15.

Chiefs of the Antrim MacDonnells Prior to Sorley Boy. Ulster J. Arch. 7, 1st ser. (1859) 247–59.

Notices of the Clan Iar Vor, Clan-Donnell Scots, especially of the branch settled in Ireland. Ulster J. Arch., 1st ser., 9

The MacDonnells of Antrim and on the continent. Micheline Walsh (O'Donnell lecture). Dublin, 1960.

Irish chiefs and leaders. Rev. Paul Walsh. Chs. 3, iv, vi. Dublin, 1960.

The Wild Geese of the Antrim McDonnells. Hector McDonnell. Irish Academic Press. Dublin, 1996. (ISBN 0 7165 2609 3) (McDonnells in Netherlands, France, Italy and Morocco: 1615-1820).

Col. Alexander McDonnell (of Antrim) in 'King James' IAL' (Notes on family members pre-1700).

The Irish legend of the M'Donnell & the Norman De Burgos. Archibald M'Sparran. Limavady: North-West Books, 1986 (ISBN: 0907528082). (LDS Lib. 929.2415 M146m).

The McDonnells of Tyrone & Armagh. Seanchas Ardmhacha 10(1) (1980-81) 193-219. (Early history to 1670's).

O'Donnell

The life of Aodh Ruadh O'Domhnaill, with introduction and notes by Rev. Paul Walsh. 5parts. Dublin, 1948–57.

John O'Donnell of Baltimore: his forbears and descendants. E. T. Cook. London, 1934.

Pedigree of O'Donnell Family of Cork: IGRS Library (Leader Collection).

Capt. Manus O'Donnell (of Donegal) in 'King James' IAL' (Notes on family members pre-1770).

O'Donnells of Tirconaill. Donegal Ann. 1 (4) (1950) 263-281 (Early history).

O'Donnells of Tirconaill. JRSAI 18 (1887) 342. (Early history).

O'Donnells of Killeen and the Cathach. N. Mayo Hist. & Arch. Soc. 2 (1) 13-19.

Donnellan

Family of Donnellan. Irish Builder, March 15 1887, p. 85.

Donnelly or O'Donnelly *see* Devlin, O'Hagan

Family History of the Donnellys and Crushells of Belmont, Co. Galway. James J. Donnelly. Pr.pr. Nepal, 1998. (NLI Ir 921 d 12; LDS 941.74/B4 D2d). (Refs to Dowd, Mahoney, Singleton, Russell).

MacDonogh *see* McDonagh

Donoghue or O'Donoghue

Origin and history of the O'Donoghues. Anthony Mathews. Drogheda: 1973. (LDS Lib. 929.2415 A1 no. 37).

Donovan

Col. Daniel O'Donovan (of Cork) in 'King James' IAL' (Notes on family members pre-1829).

Pedigree of Donovan Family of Cork: IGRS Library (Leader Collection).

(O')Donovan in 'Family Names of Co. Cork' (see abbrevs.) (Notes on origins & members in Co.Cork).

Donovan of Ballymore. Wexford Gentry Vol. 1 (see abbreviations).

Dooney

The Dooney Family of Co. Kildare and New Zealand. P.D. McCann. Dublin 1977.

Dopping *see* **Swift**

Dore

A history of the Dore family. Mary Cochrane. Pakenham, Victoria, Australia, 1982.

Dormer

The Dormer Family of New Ross. JRSAI 19 (1889) 133–35.

O'Dowd, O'Dowda or **O'Dubhda** *see also* **Donnelly**

Genealogies, Tribes and customs of Hy Fiachra, commonly called O'Dowda's country. John O'Donovan. Dublin: Irish Archaeological Soc. 1844. NLI Ir 9412 o2.

The O'Dubhda family history. Conor MacHale. Enniscrone: G. MacHale 1990. (NLI Call No. Ir 941 p108(5): LDS Lib.929.2415 A1 no. 79).

Colonel Baron James O'Dowda, Bonniconlon (1765-1798). N. Mayo Hist. & Arch. Soc. 2 (2) 1988/9) 11-20.

Dowdall

Dowdall deeds ed. C. McNeill and A. J. Otway-Ruthven. Dublin, 1960.

Dowdalls of Athlumney. Riocht na Midhe 3 (3) (1965) 205–10.

Dowdall family(of Louth) in 'King James' IAL' (Notes on family pre-1700).

Dowden

Pedigree of Dowden Family of Cork: IGRS Library (Leader Collection).

Dowe

Pedigree of Dowe Family of Cork: IGRS Library (Leader Collection).

O'Dowling

Women of the Ui Dunlainge of Leinster. Ir.Gen. 1 (1940) 196–206.

Dowman

The lineage of Dowman. Ir.Gen. 3 (1966) 460–7.

Pedigree of Dowman Family of Cork: IGRS Library (Leader Collection).

Downey

A History of the Protestant Downeys of Cos. Sligo, Leitrim, Fermanagh and Donegal (also of the Hawksby family of Leitrim and Sligo). L. Downey. New York, 1931. (LDS Lib. 929.2415 D758d).

Pedigree of Downey Family of Cork: IGRS Library (Leader Collection).

Downing or **Dineen**

Pedigree of Downing Family of Cork: IGRS Library (Leader Collection).

Downing or Dineen in 'Family Names of Co. Cork' (see abbrevs.) (Notes on origins & members in Co.Cork).

Dowse

Lawrence Dowse of Legbourne, England, his ancestors, descendants and connections in England, Massachusetts and Ireland. W. B. H. Dowse. Boston, pr. pr., 1926.

Doyle *see also* **Ireton**

Doyle Wells of Gorey. Irish Builder. 1888.

Pedigree of Doyle Family of Cork: IGRS Library (Leader Collection).

Doyne

Doyne of Wells (Wexford). Wexford Gentry Vol. 2 (see abbreviations).

Drake

The Drake family. JCHAS 38 (1933) 20–30.

Draycot

The De Verdons and the Draycots. CLAHJ 5 (1923) 166–72.

Draycott

The Draycott Family. CLAHJ 5 (1924) 270–75.

Draycott of Mornington. Riocht na Midhe 6 (3) (1977).

The De Verdons and the Draycotts. CLAHJ 5(3) (1923) p. 166-172.

Dreaver *see* **Jephson**

Drew

The Drews of Mocollop Castle. JCHAS 24 (1918) 4–6.

The Drews of Dromlohan: a preliminary history of Drew family from Kilcornan, Co. Limerick. Carol Baxter. St. Ives, NSW: 1996. (NLI Ir 9292 b73; LDS Lib. 929.2415 D82b).

O'Driscoll

Miscellany of the Celtic Society. John O'Donovan. Appendix p. 86–139. Celtic Society: Dublin, 1849.

The O'Driscolls and Other Septs of Corca Laidh. JCHAS 16 (1910) 24–31.

Lt.Col. Cornelius O'Driscoll (of Donelaong, Co. Cork) in 'King James' IAL' (Notes on family members pre-1700).

(O')Driscoll in 'Family Names of Co. Cork' (see abbrevs.) (Notes on origins & members in Co.Cork).

O'Dubhda *see* **O'Dowd**

Duck

Oh yes! we're British: a family history. (Duck & Duke family) Patricia Maddocks. Ipswick, Suffolk: Wolsey Press 1989. (LDS Lib. 929.2415 D885m.

Duckett

The Ducketts & Duckett's Grove. Carloviana 2 (23) (1974) 10-11.

Duffield

Pedigree of Duffield Family of Cork: IGRS Library (Leader Collection).

Duffy or **O'Duffy**

From Meath to Balmain; The story of a convict couple & their family (W.L.

& Bridget Duffy). Patricia Stemp. New South Wales, Australia, 1989.

Duggan

Duggan in 'Family Names of Co. Cork' (see abbrevs.) (Notes on origins & members in Co.Cork).

A Duggan family from Galway. Irish Family History. 15 (1999).

250 years of Highfield: a short history of the Duggan family. John Duggan. Carbury Highfield Pubs. 1997. (ISBN 0953120201).

From the cottage at Duggan's Cross: A Duggan family History (With account of the allied Heffernan family). Robert E. Nichols. Pr. pr. Homewood, Illinois 1998. (NLI Ir 9292 n11).

Duigenan or **O'Duigenan**

The learned family of O'Duigenan. in 'Irish Men of Learning' Paul Walsh; Three Candles, Dublin (1947) (17th century & earlier references).

Duke *see* **Bernard, Duck**

Dulhunty   .

The Dulhunty papers. Beryl Dulhunty. Sydney, 1959.

Dullea

Pedigree of Dullea Family of Cork: IGRS Library (Leader Collection).

Dundas *see* **De Rinzy**

Dungan *see also* **Dongan**

Descendants of James Carrell and Sarah Dungan. Ezra P. Carrell. Hathoro, Pennsylvania. 1928.

Pedigree of Dungan Family of Cork: IGRS Library (Leader Collection).

Dunleavy or **Dunlevy**

The Annals of the Dunleavy family. G. D. Kelley. Chaucer Press: Columbus, Ohio 1901.

A Genealogical history of the Dunleavy family. Pr.pr. Columbus Ohio 1901. (NLI Call No. Ir 9292 d5).

Dunlop *see* **Stewart**

Dunne

Dunne Papers (Brittas, Co. Wexford). Anal. Hib. 30: 123–47.

Papers (e.g., deeds, leases, & pedigrees) relating to .. Dunne of Brittas... Longford/Westmeath Library (Upton Papers), and LDS Mf. 101011.

Dunne: people and places. Joe Dunne. Whitegate, Co. Clare: Ballinkella Press 1996. (LDS Lib. 929.2415 D922dj.

Dunville

The Dunville family of Redburn House. Moffett, P., Holywood 1757–1940.

Durack

Kings in grass castles. Mary Durack. London, 1959.

O'Dwyer

The O'Dwyers of Kilnamanagh: the history of an Irish sept. M. O'Dwyer. London: John Murray, 1933. (LDS Lib. 929.2415 Od9o.

Records of the four Tipperary Septs. Martin Callanan. JAG Publishing, Galway 1938. (ISBN 0952660806).

The family of Michael Dwyer. J. West Wicklow Hist.Soc. 1 (1983/4) 30-36.

Eagar

The Eagar family in Co. Kerry. F. J. Eagar. Dublin, 1860.

Pedigree of Eagar Family of Cork: IGRS Library (Leader Collection).

Genealogical history of the Eagar family. F. J. Eagar. Pr.pr.: Dublin, 1861 (NLI Call No. Ir 9292 e1).

Earberry

Pedigree of Earberry Family of Cork: IGRS Library (Leader Collection).

Early

A history of the family of Early in America: The ancestors and descendants of Jeremiah Early who came from Donegal. Samuel S. Early, New York, 1896.

Eason

Pedigree of Eason Family of Cork: IGRS Library (Leader Collection).

Eastwood

Family of Eastwood. Irish Builder March 15 1888, p. 77-78.

Eaton

Pedigree of Eaton Family of Cork: IGRS Library (Leader Collection).

Echlin

Genealogical memoirs of the Echlin family. J. R. Echlin. Edinburgh, 1881.

Edgeworth

The Black Book of Edgeworthstown and other Edgeworth memories, 1585–1817 ed. H. J. Butler and H. E. Butler. London: Faber & Gwyer, 1927. (LDS Lib. 929.2415 Ed37b).

The Edgeworths: Part 2. Irish Family History 7 (1991) 51-55.

Edwards

Edwards of Newtown, Co. Kilkenny. JCHAS 34 (1929) 100–05.

Eedy

Pedigree of Eedy Family of Cork: IGRS Library (Leader Collection).

Egan or **MacEgan**

Two Irish Brehon scripts: with notes on the MacEgan family. JGAHS 6 (1909–10) 1–9.

The MacEgan family. Ir.Gen. 1 (1939) 174–6.

Pedigree of Egan Family of Cork: IGRS Library (Leader Collection).

Copies of census returns of the Egan family, Co. Longford, 1851. NAI M 5249 (65).

Annals of the Clan Egan: an account of the MacEgan bardic family of brehon lawyers (Annalá Clainne Aodhagáin). Conor MacHale. Sligo:1990. (LDS Lib. 929.2415 A1 no. 80).

The history of Clan Egan: the birds of the forest of wisdom. JJ & MJ Egan. Ann Arbor: University Microfilms, 1990. (ISBN 0835704920). (LDS Lib. 929.2415 Eg13c).

Elgee

Elgee: the maternal lineage of Oscar Wilde. Ir. Anc. 4 (2) (1972) 94–103.

Ellerd

Pedigree of Ellerd Family of Cork: IGRS Library (Leader Collection).

McElligott or **McEllicott**

Col. Roger McEllicott (of Kerry) in 'King James' IAL' (Notes on family members pre-1797).

Ellis

Notices of the Ellises of England, Scotland and Ireland. W. S. Ellis. London, 1857, Supplements 1866–81.

Pedigree of Ellis Family of Cork: IGRS Library (Leader Collection).

Ellison

'Search of My Family (Concerning the Ellison family.)'. Ellison, J., & Henry Havelock. Pr. pr. Dublin University Press, 1971. (LDS Lib. 929.2415 EL59e).

Elrington

The Elringtons in Ireland. Ir.Gen. 1 (1941) 263–4.

Elwood

The Elwood Family. Ir.Gen. 6 (4) (1983) 477–86.

Ely

Rathfarnham Castle: Adam Loftus and the Ely family. Estminster, n.d.

Ely of Loftus hall (Wexford) Wexford Gentry Vol. 2 (see abbreviations).

Emison

The Emison families. James Wade Emison Jr., 3 vols. Vincennes, Indiana, 1947, 1954, 1962.

Emmet

The Emmet family….. Thomas A. Emmet. Pr.pr. (Only 130 copies): New York 1898. (NLI Call No. Ir 9292 e4).

McEnally *see* **McAnally**

MacEneaney

Mac Eanaigh, Son of the Dean. Con McEneaney, p. pr. 1974.

The MacEneaneys. Clogher Record 4 (1&2) (1960/61) 6-7.

England *see* **McNamara**

Erley

The Manor of Erley or Erlestown, Co. Kilkenny. JRSAI 36 (1906) 154–65.

Eskildson

The Eskildson family of Denmark, Ireland and U.S.A. L. D. Melnick. Chicago. 1968.

Esmond or **Esmonde**

  Genealogies of Esmond, Codd, Jacob, and Redmond. GO Mf. 279.

  Capts. Walter & Robert Esmonde (of Wexford) in 'King James' IAL' (Notes
     on family members pre-1734).

  Esmonde of Ballynastragh. Wexford Gentry Vol. 1 (see abbreviations).

Etchingham

  The Etchinghams of Dunbrody. JOWS 1 (1968).

Eustace *see also* **FitzEustace**

  The Eustaces of Co. Kildare. JCKAS 1 (2) (1891–95) 115–30.

  Baltinglass Abbey, its possessions & their post-reformation proprietors.
     JCKAS 5(6) (1908) 378-414. (includes a Eustace pedigree).

  Kilcullen New Abbey and the FitzEustaces. JCKAS 12 (1935–45) 217–21.

  The Eustace Family and Their Lands in Co. Kildare. JCKAS 13 (6)270–87;
     13 (7)307–41; 13 (8)364–413.

  The House of Eustace. Reportorium Novum 2 (2) (1960) 245–56.

  Col. Sir Maurice Eustace (of Castlemartin, Co. Kildare) in 'King James' IAL'
     (Notes on family members pre-1720).

Evans

  Pedigree of Evans Family of Cork: IGRS Library (Leader Collection).

  The last 6 generations of the family of Evans, now represented by Nicholas
     Evans of Lough Park, Castlepollard, Co. Westmeath. W. Sloane Evans.
     1864.

Evanson

  Pedigree of Evanson Family of Cork: IGRS Library (Leader Collection).

Evatt

  Pedigree of Evatt Family of Cork: IGRS Library (Leader Collection).

  Three Ulster Evatts. Ulster J. Arch. Ser 2. 15 (1909) 182-3.

Everard

  The Family of Everard (of Fethard, Co Tipperary). Ir.Gen. 7 (3)328–348; 7
     (4)505–542; 8 (2)175–206; 8 (4)575–601; 9 (1)43–72.

  Capt. John Everard (of Tipperary) in 'King James' IAL' (Notes on family
     members pre-1750).

Everitt

  Pedigree of Everitt Family of Cork: IGRS Library (Leader Collection).

Evers

  Lt. Gerald Evers (of Meath) in 'King James' IAL' (Notes on family members
     pre-1700).

McEvoy *see* **Netterville**

Eyre

  A short account of the Eyre family of Eyre Court, and Eyre of Eyreville, in
     Co. Galway. Allen S. Hartigan. Reading, n.d. (LDS Lib. 929.2415 Ey62h).

  Hayes-McCoy, Marguerite. The Eyre Documents in University College, Galway. JGAHS 20(1942-43)57–74; 21(1945) 71–95; 23 (1948–49) 147–53.

Signpost to Eyrecourt: portrait of the Eyre family triumphant in the cause of liberty,.. Derbyshire, Wiltshire, Galway, c. 1415-1856. Ida Gantz. Bath: Kingsmead, 1975. ISBN 0901571709.

Fagan

Fagans of Feltrim. Reportorium Novum 2 (1) (1958) 103–06.

Capt. Richard Fagan (of Dublin) & others in 'King James' IAL' (Notes on family pre-1700).

Family of Fagan. Irish Builder, March 15 1887, p. 85; March 15 1888, 78-79.

Fahy *see also* **McNamara**

The Fahys of the pond: Roger & Nora Whelan Fahy (Rine-Burren, Co.Clare). Kathleen Fay Field. LDS Lib. 929.2415 F146f.

Fair *see also* **Phaire**

The Fair family of Levally, Ballinrobe, Co Mayo. S. Mayo Family Res. J. 9 (1996) 43-50.

Falkiner

The Falkiners of Abbotstown, Co. Dublin. JCKAS 8 (1915–17) 331–63.

A pedigree with personal sketches of the Falkiners of Mount Falcon. F. B. Falkiner. Dublin, 1894.

Fannins

Medical and Musical - the Fannins of Dublin. Dublin Hist. Rec. 49 (1) (1996) p.32-58.

Fawcett

Fawcett of Co. Fermanagh. Pedigree in 'Swanzy Notebooks'. RCB Library, Dublin.

McFee

Manuscript with account of McFees in Rushen, Donegal (1761-1992). Comp. by David Morgan. LDS Lib. 929.2415 A1 no. 100.

Fennessy

Fennessy of the Co. Tipperary. Richard J. Fennessy. Baltimore: Genealogical Pub. Co. (1999).

Fiangus to Fennessy: Proceedings of the Fennessy Family History Meeting at Clonmel 1998. Plymouth, Coastal Research 1999. (ISBN 0953065618).

Fenwick

Pedigree of Fenwick Family of Cork: IGRS Library (Leader Collection).

Ferguson

The Fergusons of Belfast: A short account of the ancestry of Duchess of York. Familia 2 (2) 1986 pp. 15-22.

Ferrall *see also* **Farrell, Kelly (Ainsworth misc)**

Capt. Connell Ferrall (of Tirlickin, Longford) in 'King James' IAL' (Notes on family pre-1700).

Ferrar

The Limerick Huntingdon Ferrars. by 'One of Them'[Michael Lloyd Ferrar]. Plymouth: Underhill 1903 - Frankfort Press (50 copies only). (LDS Lib. 929.2415 F412h) (refs to Hughes, Venable, Lloyd, Minchin, Carttar, Hardy).

Fetherston

Papers (e.g., deeds, leases, and pedigrees) relating to Fetherston. RIA: (Upton Papers), and LDS Mf. 101011.

Fetherton

The Fetherton Family of Ardagh. Teathbha 2 (1) (1980) 17–32.

ffolliott *see also* **Folliott**

The Pooles of Mayfield. R. ffolliott. Dublin: Hodges Figgis (1958). (ffolliott of Worcestershire & Ireland: 15-17th c.).

ffolliott of Co. Meath. Ir. Anc. 1 (1) 27–33.

Fiddes

Fiddes of Co. Fermanagh. Pedigree in 'Swanzy Notebooks'. RCB Library, Dublin.

Finnerty

Finnerty: O'Fionnacta ui siol Muireadach: or descendents of Muireadach, king of Connacht. Richard M. Finnerty. Ms. LDS Lib. 929.2415 F497f.

Finucane

Finucane of Co. Clare. Ir. Anc. 1 (1) (1969) 1–11; 1 (2) 144.

MacFirbis or **Forbes** *see also* **O'Mullally**

The learned family of MacFirbisigh. in 'Irish Men of Learning' Rev. Paul Walsh. Three Candles, Dublin (1947) (16th century & earlier references).

The celebrated antiquary Dubhaltach Mac Firbhisigh (c1600-1671): his lineage, life and learning. N. O'Muraile. Maynooth: An Sagart 1996. (ISBN: 1870684532).

Fish

The Family of Fish of Castlefish, Co. Kildare. Ir. Anc. 14 (1) 1982.

Fisher

Pedigree of Fisher Family of Cork: IGRS Library (Leader Collection).

Fitton

Pedigree of Fitton Family of Cork: IGRS Library (Leader Collection).

Fitzell

Pedigree of Fitzell Family of Cork: IGRS Library (Leader Collection).

FitzEustace *see also* **Eustace**

FitzEustace of Baltinglass. JW&SEIAS 5(1899)190–95.

Kilcullen New Abbey and the FitzEustaces. JCKAS 12 (1935–45) 217–21.

Fitzgerald *see also* **Blake, Bryant, Darcy, McNamara.**

Geraldines, Earls of Desmond. C. P. Meehan. Dublin, 1852.

Sketch of the History & descent of the Geraldines of Queen's Co. from 1550-

1893. Mountmellick 1913.

Pedigree of Fitzgerald Family of Cork: IGRS Library (Leader Collection).

The Earls of Kildare and their ancestors from 1057-1773. Marquis of Kildare. Dublin 1858.

The Fitzgeralds of Lackagh. JCKAS 1 (1892–95) 245–64.

The Fitzgeralds and the MacKenzies. JCKAS 2 (1896–99) 269.

The Fitzgeralds of Ballyshannon (Co. Kildare), and Their Successors Thereat. JCKAS 3 (1899–1902) 425–52.

The history of Morett Castle, and the Fitzgeralds. JCKAS 4 (1903–05) 285–96.

Extracts from Athy Parish Register. JCKAS 6 (2) 1909 pp 181-2. (Family of Robt Fitzgerald, Grangemellon d. 1697).

Unpublished Geraldine documents. JRSAI 10 (1869) 365–416; 12 (1871) 591–616; 14 (1876–77) 14–52, 157–66, 246-64, 300–35.

The Geraldines of Desmond. From Michael O'Clery's Book of pedigrees. ed. Canon Hayman. JRSAI 15 (1880–81) 215–35, 411–40; 17 (1885) 66–92.

The Geraldines of the Co. Kilkenny. JRSAI 22 (1892) 358–76; 23 (1893) 179–86, 408–20; 32 (1902) 128–31.

The Fitzgeralds of Rostellane in the Co. Cork. JRSAI 25 (1895) 163–70.

The Desmonds' castle at Newcastle Oconyll, Co. Limerick. Thomas J. Westropp. JRSAI 34 (1909) 42–58, 350–68.

The Fitzgeralds of Glenane, Co. Cork. JRSAI 42 (1912) 164–9.

The Fitzgeralds, Barons of Offaly. JRSAI 44 (1914)99–113.

The origin of the Fitzgeralds. Ancestor 7 (1903) 67–70.

The last Baron of Cluain. JW&SEIAS 4 (1898) 36-46 (Edward Fitzgerald, Kilkenny)

The Fitzgeralds of Farnane, Co. Waterford. JW&SEIAS 13 (1910) 112-121, 168-175; 14 (1911) 27–39, 72–81; 15(1912) 168–76.

The story of the Slught Edmund (1485 to 1819). An episode in Kerry history. JKAHS (New Ser.) 3 (1915) 186 205.

The Geraldines. Brian Fitzgerald. London and New York, 1951.

The Red Book of the Earls of Kildare ed. G. Mac Niocaill. Dublin, 1964.

The descendants of the Earls of Desmond. John O'Donovan. Ulster J. Arch., 1st ser., 6 (1858) 91–7.

Descents of the Earls of Kildare, and their wives. The Marquis of Kildare. Dublin. 1869.

Memoirs of an Irish family, Fitzgerald of Decies. M. MacKenzie. Dublin, 1905.

Initium, incrementum et exitus familiae Geraldinorum Desmoniae. Dominic O'Daly. 1655.

The descendants of Oliver FitzGerald of Belagh. Ir.Gen. 4 (1968–70) 2–9, 93–109, 194–200.

Dromana: the memoirs of an Irish family (Fitzgerald). Thérèse M. Macken-
zie. Dublin: Sealy, Bryers & Walker,1906. (LDS Lib. 929.2415 F576m.
Fitzgerald in 'Family Names of Co. Cork' (see abbrevs.) (Notes on origins &
members in Co. Cork).
Col. Sir John Fitzgerald (of Rathcoole & Lucan, Co. Dublin) in 'King James'
IAL' (Notes on family pre-1773).

FitzGibbon

Earl of Clare: mainspring of the union (FitzGibbon). Elliot Fitzgibbon. London: Research Pub. Co. 1960 (LDS Lib. 929.2415 F577f).

FitzMaurice

The Fitzmaurices, Lords of Kerry. JCHAS 26 (1920) 10–18.
The Fitzmaurices of Duagh, Co. Kerry. Ir.Gen. 3 (1956–57) 25–35, 64–6.
Glanerought and the Petty-Fitzmaurices. The Marquis of Lansdowne. Lon-
don: Oxford Univ. Press, 1937. (LDS Lib. 929.2415 L291L.
The Fitzmaurices of Kerry. JKAHS (New Series) 3 (1970) 23–42.
Fitzmaurice, Barons of Kerry & Lixnaw. Genealogists Mag. 1 (1) (Apr 1925).
The family of Fitzmaurice. Carloviana 1 (16) (1967) 23-25.
Ardfert friary and the Fitzmaurices of Kerry. JRSAI 27 (1897) 232-242.

FitzPatrick

Fitzpatricks of Ossory. Old Kilkenny Review 2 (3) (1981) p. 254-268.
Capt Bryan Fitzpatrick (Lord Upper Ossory) in 'King James' IAL' (Notes on
family members pre-1732).

Fitzrery

The Fitz Rerys, Welsh Lords of Cloghran, Co. Dublin. CLAHJ 5(1921) 13–
17.

Fitzsimon

The Story of a Picture (The Fitzsimons Family on Foynes Island). Mallow
Field Club J. 14 (1996).

Fitzwilliam *see also* **Watson**

Catholic families of the Pale (Fitzwilliam of Merrion….). Reportorium Novum
2(1) (1958) 88–108.

O'Flaherty

The flight of the O'Flahertys, lords of Moy Soela, to Iar Connaught. J. Fahy.
JRSAI 27 (1897) 19–27.
Descendants of Grainne O'Malley by her first husband (Teige O'Flahertie).
Ir.Gen. 1 (1940) 218–19.
Iar Connaught. Roderic O'Flaherty. Dublin, 1846.
The origin of the surname O'Flaherty. Anthony Mathews. Dublin, 1968.
Lt. Col. Morrogh O'Flaherty (of Culvin, Co. Westmeath) in 'King James'
IAL' (Notes on family members pre-1768).

Flanagan *see* **McNamara**

The Woulfe Flanagan family of Roscommon and Dublin. Irish Family History 11 (1995) 110-118.

Flannery

Flannery: Irish Origins & world-wide progress. Flannery Clan: Dublin 2000.

Flatesbury

The Family of Flatesbury of Ballynascullogue and Johnstown, Co. Kildare. JCKAS 4 (2) (1903) 86–94.

Fleetwood

The Fleetwoods of the Co. Cork. JRSAI 38 (1908) 103–25.

An Irish branch of the Fleetwood family. Gen. 24 (1908) 217–41; 25 (1908) 21–2.

Fleming *see also* **Acheson**

Historical and genealogical memoir of the family of Fleming of Slane. Sir W. Betham. 1829.

The Pooles of Mayfield. Rosemary ffolliott. Dublin: Hodges Figgis (1958). (Deals with Flemings of Glasgow and New Court, Cork: 1700 to 1950s).

Fleming and Conyngham of Slane. Riocht na Midhe 7 (2) (1982/83) 69–75.

A family on the Shannon: the Flemings of Richmond Harbour, Co. Longford. Shirley McGlynn. LDS Lib. 929.2415 F629ms.

Col. Christopher Fleming, Lord Slane (of Meath) in 'King James' IAL' (Notes on family members pre-1772).

Fleming of Ballylagan, Co. Meath: A branch of the Barons of Slane. Ir. Am. Gen. 2 (1974) 18-20.

O'Flynn or **Flynn**

The O'Flynns of Ardagh. JCHAS 11 (1905) 99–101.

(O') Flynn in 'Family Names of Co. Cork' (see abbrevs.) (Notes on origins & members in Co.Cork).

History of the O'Flynns. Chas. P. Flynn. Patterson, NY: Irish Heritage Research: 1994. (LDS Lib. 929.2415 A1 no. 83.

Outline history of the Flynn family of Coolroe, Ballybrittas in Co. Leix and a sketch of their descendants since 1800. (Also the Devoy family of Courtwood). Mullingar, Co. Westmeath 1995. NLI Ir 9292 t15.

Flood *see also* **Ireton**

Flood family triad: A family history in England, Ireland and America from AD 1550 to 1850. Chas. R Patterson. Pr.pr.: Charlottesville, VA. 1982.

Follin

Follin family. Gabriel Edmondston. Washington, 1911. (NLI Call No. Ir 9292 f4).

Folliott *see also* **ffolliott**

The Folliotts of Londonderry and Chester. Sir Edmund Bewley. 1902.

The Folliotts, Wardstown Castle and the Colleen Bawn. Donegal Ann. 43 (1991) p. 61-75.

Foott

Pedigree of Foott Family of Cork: IGRS Library (Leader Collection).

Forbes *see also* **MacFirbis, O'Mullally**

Memoirs of the Earls of Granard. John Forbes. London: Longmans, Green & Reader: 1868. (LDS Lib. 929.2415 F741f).

Forrestall

The Forrestals in Australia. Irish Family History 11 (1995) 4-8.

Fortescue

The Fortescues of County Louth. CLAHJ 24 (1) (1997) p. 5-20.

Forster *see also* **McNamara**

The story of my family. (History of the Forster family of the former Clooneene estate (now Ashfield), near Gort, Galway). Francis J. P. Forster. Burlingame, Calif.: Forbach, 1978. (LDS Lib. 929.2415 F733f . (Refs to: Forster/Foster, Blake, de Burgo/Burke, Ffrench, Hogan, Shannon, Whelan.)

Forsythe *see* **Mullan**

Foster *see also* **Forster**

The Foster family and the Parliamentary Borough of Dunleer (1683-1800). CLAHJ 17 (3) (1971) p. 156-163.

Fowkes

Pedigree of Fowkes Family of Cork: IGRS Library (Leader Collection).

Fox or **Foxe**

Some notes on the Fox family of Kilcoursey in King's Co. M. E. Stone. pr.pr. Chicago, 1890.

Pedigree of Fox Family of Cork: IGRS Library (Leader Collection).

The Foxes of Muintir Thaidgean. Riocht na Midhe 4 (4) (1970) 6–23.

Franklin

Pedigree of Franklin Family of Cork: IGRS Library (Leader Collection).

Frayne

Frayne of Co. Wexford. Ir.Gen. 4(3) (1970) 213–20.

Frazer or **Fraser** *see also* **Lyons**

Notes & papers connected with Persifor Frazer in Glasslough, Ireland & his son John Frazer of Philadelphia 1735-1765. P. Frazer. pr.pr. 1906.

Freeman

Pedigree of Freeman Family of Cork: IGRS Library (Leader Collection).

Freke

Pedigree of Freke Family of Cork: IGRS Library (Leader Collection).

French *see also* **Darcy, Forster, Lynch, Nixon.**

Field Marshal Sir John French. JGAHS 8 (4) (1913-14) 247-251.

French families of Dures, Cloghballymore & Drumharsna, with tabular pedigree. JGAHS 10 (1917–18) 125–38.

Notes: Frenches of Drumharsna. JGAHS 11 (1) (1919) 77-78.

The French family pedigree-a correction. JGAHS 23 (1949) p.161

The origin of the families of French of Connaught, with tabular pedigree of

John French of Grand-Terre in 1763. JGAHS 11 (1920–21) 142–9.

Pedigree of French Family of Cork: IGRS Library (Leader Collection).

Some Account of the Family of French of Belturbet. Ulster J. Arch. 2nd ser. 8 (1902) 155–60.

The families of French and their descendants. H. B. Swanzy, Dublin; 1908.

Memoir of the French family (Da la Freyne, De Freyne, Frenshe, ffrench). John D'Alton. Dublin, 1847.

The Families of French of Belturbet and Nixon of Fermanagh and their descendants. H.B. Swanzy. Dublin: Alex. Thom, 1908. (LDS Lib. 929.2415 F887s.

Capts Matthew & Christopher French (of Galway) in 'King James' IAL' (Notes on family members pre-1700).

Friel

Friel history from Ireland. GO Ms. (6 Pages); (LDS Lib. 929.2415 A1 no. 3

Frith

The Friths of Fermanagh. Ir.Gen. 1 (1941) 218–20.

Fry

Annals of the late Major Oliver Fry, with notes on his descendants. Wm. Fry. London, 1909.

Pedigree of Fry Family of Cork: IGRS Library (Leader Collection).

Fuller

The family of Fuller: some royal, noble, and gentle descents of the Kerry branch. compiled by James F. Fuller Dublin: John Wilson. Dublin: 1880. (LDS Lib. 929.2415 F958f.

Pedigree of Fuller Family of Cork: IGRS Library (Leader Collection).

Pedigree of the Family of Fuller of Cork, Kerry, and Halstead. J.F.Fuller. 1909.

The Fuller Family. In 'History of Co. Kerry'. J. King. Dublin, 1910: 208–11, 346–52.

Fullerton *see* **Stewart**

Fulthorpe *see* **Wandesforde**

Fulton

Memoirs of the Fultons of Lisburn. Sir Theodore C. Hope. London: Richard Clay, 1903. (LDS Lib. 929.2415 F959h.

Furlong

Lt Joseph Furlong (of Wexford) in 'King James' IAL' (Notes on family pre-1827).

Pedigree of Furlong Family of Cork: IGRS Library (Leader Collection).

The Furlongs of Co. Wexford. JOWS 6 (1976-7) p. 73.

Gage

Gage Family Papers (1610–1837). PRONI; LDS Mf. 248301.

Galbraith

The Galbraiths of Cappard. Ir. Gen. 4 (1968) 25–8.

O'Gallagher

In 'Irish chiefs and leaders'. Rev. Paul Walsh. Ch. x. Dublin, 1960.

Muintir Gallchobhair. Donegal Ann. 10 (3) (1973) 295-315. (In Gaelic/Irish language).

The O'Gallager Septs of Tirconaill to 1600-1630. Irish Book Lover 27 (5).

Galwey *see also* **Meade**

The Galweys of Lota. C. J. Bennett. Dublin, 1909.

Pedigree of Galwey Family of Cork: IGRS Library (Leader Collection).

The Genealogy of Galwey of Lota. JCHAS 30 (1925) 59–74.

The Galweys of Munster. JCHAS 71-74 (1966–69).

Gamble *see also* **Gower**

Pedigree of Gamble Family of Cork: IGRS Library (Leader Collection).

Ganley

The Family Bible of John Ganley, William St., Limerick. Ir. Anc. 9 (2) (1979) 84–85.

O'Gara

Col. Oliver O'Gara (of Sligo) in 'King James' IAL' (Notes on family members pre-1734).

Garde

Pedigree of Garde Family of Cork: IGRS Library (Leader Collection).

The Garde family. JCHAS 5(1899) 200–2.

Gardiner

Pedigree of Gardiner Family of Cork: IGRS Library (Leader Collection).

Gartlan or **Gartland** *see also* **Ashmur**

The Gartlands of Augher, Co. Tyrone. Clogher Record 12 (3) (1987) 397-398.

Garvey or **McGarvey(vie)**

An enquiry re the Garvey family. JGAHS 15 (3 & 4) (1931-33) 162-163.

Kilkenny to Murrisk: a Garvey family history. Rosemary Garvey. Pr. Pr. Mayo. 1992 (ISBN 0952061902).

McGarvie Family History 1884-1994. McGarvie Family History Editorial Committee, Melbourne 1995. (ISBN 0959013946) (NLI Ir 9292 m75).

Gates *see* **Warren**

Gaughran or **Gauran** *see* **McGovern**

Gault *see* **Kenny**

Gaussen *see* **Acheson**

McGawley *see also* **McAuley**

Capt. Patrick McGawley (of Tulliwood, Co. Westmeath) in 'King James' IAL' (Notes on family members pre-1709).

Gayer

Memoirs of the Gayer family in Ireland. A. E. Gayer. Westminster, 1870.

MacGee *see* **Magee.**

Gelston

Pedigree of Gelston Family of Cork: IGRS Library (Leader Collection).

Geoghegan or **MacGeoghegan** *see also* **Carlile, McNamara(Geigan) Mageoghan**

The MacGeoghegans. Rev. Paul Walsh. Mullingar, 1938.

Major Conly Geoghegan (of Westmeath) in 'King James' IAL' (Notes on family members pre-1745).

Geraghty

Copies of census returns of the Geraghty family, Co. Longford, 1841. NAI 5248 (21).

The Geraghty of Murrisk na Boll. Ed. R. O. P. Geraghty. Calif. Pr.pr. 199. (LDS Lib. 929.2415 G31g.

Gernon

Lt. George Gernon (of Dunany, Co Louth) in 'King James' IAL' (Notes on family members pre-1700).

Gerrard

Gerrards and Geraldines. JCHAS 34 (1929) 30–5, 71–5.

Gerrard family records: Inc. pedigrees, ...notes etc for Gerrard, Inglefield & related families. (GO Ms. 654; LDS Mf. 257819).

McGettigan

Early history of McGettigan scpt. Donegal Ann. 42 (1990) 63-68.

Gettys

The Gettys of Ireland, 1631-1865: abstracts & notes. Robert C. Gettys. LDS Lib. 929.2415 G335g.

Gibbs

Pedigree of Gibbs Family of Cork: IGRS Library (Leader Collection).

McGill *see* **Acheson**

Gillespie

Distribution of Gillespie households in Ireland according to Tithe applotments (1823-1838) & Griffith's valuation (1848-1864). W. Robert Gillespie. LDS Lib. 929.2415 A1 no. 25.

Gillman or **Gilman**

Searches into the history of Gillman or Gilman family in Ireland. A. W. Gillman. London: E.Stock 1895. (NLI Call No. Ir 9292 g3).

Pedigree of Gillman Family of Cork: IGRS Library (Leader Collection).

The Gillman family and some myths. Gen. 14 (1898) 152–62.

MacGillycuddy or **McGillicuddy**

The McGillycuddy papers. W. Maziere Brady. Longman's: London 1867. (NLI Call No. Ir 9292 m3).

The Macgillycuddy family. JKAHS (Old Series) 3 (1915) 176–85.

Short history of the clan McGillycuddy. R.B.MacGillycuddy. Dublin: MacGillycuddy Press, 1991. (LDS Lib. 929.2415 A1 no. 74).

Given *see* **Boyd**

Gleeson or **Glasson**

Pedigree of Gleeson Family of Cork: IGRS Library (Leader Collection)

A Record of the Descendants of John Alexander, of.. Scotland, and his wife, Margaret Glasson, who emigrated from Co. Armagh to Pennsylvania, A.D. 1736. (Pub. 1878) reprint by Heritage Books, USA 1999.

Godkin

Pedigree of Godkin Family of Cork: IGRS Library (Leader Collection).

Godson

Pedigree of Godson Family of Cork: IGRS Library (Leader Collection).

Goff *see also* **Gough**

Six Generations of Friends in Ireland 1655-1890. Jane M. Richardson. London 1895. (Goffs of Co Wexford).

Goff of Horetown (Wexford) Wexford Gentry Vol. 2 (see abbreviations).

Going

Going of Munster. Ir. Anc. 9 (1) (1977) 21–43.

Gollick

Pedigree Book for Gollick Family of Cork: IGRS Library (Leader Collection).

Good

Pedigree of Good Family of Cork: IGRS Library (Leader Collection).

Goodall

Goodall of Wexford. Ir.Gen. 3(12) (1967) 487–500.

An Irishman in India: Abraham Goodall FRCS (1801-1892). Ir.Gen. 10(2) 1999, 133-143.

Goodbody

The Goodbody family of Ireland. Michael Goodbody. Essex: Barton House 1979. (LDS Lib. 929.273 G611g) (refs to Grattan, Haughton, Hudson, O'Connor, Pim).

Pedigree of Goodbody Family of Cork: IGRS Library (Leader Collection).

The Goodbodys of Clara. Margaret Stewart. Dublin 1965.

Goold

Cornet Robert Goold (of Cork city) in 'King James' IAL' (Notes on family pre-1800).

Gordon *see also* **Ashmur**

Gordons of Salterhill and their Irish descendants. J. M. Bulloch. Keith. 1910.

Gore

Pedigree of Gore Family of Cork: IGRS Library (Leader Collection).

Gorges

The story of a family through eleven centuries. Raymond Gorges. Boston, 1944. (Gorges family).

O'Gormley

Ceneal Moain and the O'Gormleys in E. Donegal & W. Tyrone. Familia 2 (6) (1990).

Gosnell or **Gosnold**

Pedigree of Gosnell/Gosnold Family of Cork: IGRS Library (Leader Collection).

Gough

The story of an Irish Property. Robt. S. Rait. Pr.pr.: Oxford Univ. Press 1908. (NLI Call No. Ir 94124 r1) (refs. To O'Shaughness, Gough & Prendergast).

MacGovern

An Irish sept: Being a history of the McGovern or MacGauran clan. J. B. & J. H. McGovern. Manchester, 1886.

Genealogy and historical notes of the MacGauran or McGovern clan. J. H. McGovern. Liverpool, 1890.

The book of Magauran ed. Lambert McKenna. Dublin 1947.

Some notes on Drogheda (Co. Louth) families of Carroll, Clinton, McGovern & Skelly. J.Old Drogheda Soc. 11 (1998).

O'Gowan

A memoir of the name of O'Gowan, or Smith. 'An O'Gowan'. Tyrone, 1837.

Gower

The descendants of Roger Gower. Sir David Gamble. Pr.pr. St. Helens, England 1897. (LDS Lib. 929.2415 G747g). (Refs to Benson, Bishop, Gamble, McCrea, McDermott, O'Neill, Sheridan, Young).

Grace

A survey of Tullaroan, etc., being a genealogical history of the family of Grace. Dublin, 1819.

Origin of the Grace Family of Courtstown, Co. Kilkenny, & their title to the Tullaroan estate. JRSAI 30 (1900) 319–24; 32 (1902) 64–67.

Memoirs of the family of Grace. Sheffield Grace. London, 1823.

The Graces. Old Kilkenny Review 19 (1967) 26-28.

Col. John Grace (of Courtown) in 'King James' IAL' (Notes on family members pre-1700).

O'Grady

O'Grady of Cappercullen (Co. Limerick). N. Munster Antiq. J. 7 (4) (1957) 20–22.

O'Grady Papers. [Kilballyowen, Co. Limerick]. Anal. Hib. 15: 35–62.

Graham *see* **Waldron**

Granard

Pedigree of Granard Family of Cork: IGRS Library (Leader Collection).

Grant

The Grant Families of Co. Tipperary. JCHAS 77 (226) (1972) 65–75.

Pedigree of Grant Family of Cork: IGRS Library (Leader Collection).
Grants of Ulster and the Pale. CLAHJ 20 (1972) 230–234.

McGrath *see* **Blake**

Grattan *see also* **Goodbody**

Grattan family links with Canada. Breifne 2 (1965) 376–412.

Graves

Some notes on the Graves family. H. G. MacDonnell. pr. pr. Dublin 1889.

Gray or **Grey** *see also* **Acheson, Ashmur**

The Gray family of Co. Leitrim. Fr. Mark Breen, 1980.
The Gray Family of Claremorris (Mayo). Ir. Gen. 7 (4) 551–562.
Pedigree of Gray Family of Cork: IGRS Library (Leader Collection).
Gray of Cork City and Lehana. Ir. Anc. 7 (1) (1975) 11.
Gray of Co. Cork. Pedigree in 'Swanzy Notebooks'. RCB Library, Dublin.
A divided family in 1798: the Grays of Whitefort and Jamestown (Wexford).
     JOWS 15 (1994/5) 52-66.

Greatrakes

Pedigree of Greatrakes Family of Cork: IGRS Library (Leader Collection).
Selections from General Acct. Book of Valentine Greatrakes 1663-79.
     JW&SEIAS 11(1908) 211-224 (with pedigree).

Green or **Greene**

Pedigree of the family of Greene. J. Greene. Dublin, 1899 (Kilkenny, Tipp.,
     Limerick, Waterford, Kildare, Meath).
The Greenes of Kilmacow. Old Kilkenny Review, 12 (1960) p.38-42.
Pedigree of Green Family of Cork: IGRS Library (Leader Collection).
The family of Green of Youghal, Co. Cork: an attempt to trace descendants of
     Simon Green. H.B. Swanzy & T.D. Green. Dublin: Alex. Thom, 1902.
     (LDS Lib. 929.2415 G82s).
The Greenes & Kilranelagh House. J. West Wicklow Hist. Soc. 2 (1985/86)
     48-51.

Greer *see* **Nesbitt**

Gregg

Large Pedigree Book for Gregg Family. IGRS Library (Leader Collection).

Gregory

A Guide to Coole Park. Colin Smythe, London, 1979.
Pedigree of Gregory Family of Cork: IGRS Library (Leader Collection).
The house of Gregory. V. R. T. Gregory. Dublin: Browne & Nolan 1943.
     (LDS Lib. 929.2415 G862g).

Grier

Grier of Gurteen. Pedigree in 'Swanzy Notebooks'. RCB Library, Dublin.

Grierson

King's printers: Notes on the family of Grierson of Dublin. Ir.Gen. 2 (1953)
     303–37.

The Griersons of Co. Meath. Ir.Gen. 2 (1953) 303–37; & 3 (1959)136–43.

Griffin

Limerick and Gerald Griffin. N. Munster Antiq. J. 2 (1) (1940) 4–13.

Griffith

The Griffiths of Laurelhill, Co. Monaghan & associated families. Clogher Record 14 (3) (1993) p. 111-124.

The Griffith Family. Irish Family History 13 (1997).

Grubb

The Grubbs of Tipperary: Studies in Heredity & Character. Geoffrey Watkins Grubb. Cork: Mercier Press 1972.

Gubbins

The Gubbins Family of Kilfrush. Lough Gur Hist. Soc. J. 9 (1996).

McGuckin

The McGuckins of Desertmartin, Co. Londonderry. Familia 2 (8) 1992.

McGuckin burial inscriptions at Ballinderry, Co. Derry. Ir.Am.Gen. 17-20 (1980) 305-307.

Guinness or **McGuinness** *see also* **Magennis.**

The Guinness family. Henry S., & Brian, Guinness. 2 vols. London: Lund Humphries, 1953. (LDS Lib. 929.2415 G947g) (refs to Bell, Clare, Darley, d'Esterre, Hill (Hills), Kennedy, Mackenzie, Phipps, Thompson).

The Guinness saga. Dublin Hist. Rec. 16 (1960) 50–7.

Origin of surname McGuinness, with a short history. Anthony Mathews. Dublin:1968. (LDS Lib. 929.2415 A1 no. 49).

The Silver Salver: the story of the Guinness family. Frederic Mullally. London; NY: Granada, 1981. (ISBN 0246112719). (LDS Lib. 929.2415 G948m).

MacGuire

The Maguires and Irish learning. in 'Irish Men of Learning' Rev. Paul Walsh. Dublin, 1947.

Irish chiefs and leaders. Rev. Paul Walsh. Dublin, 1960

A Maguire family in France. Clogher Record 5(la) (1964) 222–6.

Patrick and Rose Anne McGuire and their descendants. Betty Patterson, Madison, Wisconsin, pr. pr. 1980.

Conor Mac Guire (of Fermanagh) in 'King James' IAL' (Notes on family members pre-1700).

Gun or **Gunn** *see* **Blennerhasset**

Gunning *see* **Blakeney**

Hackett

Mullinahone, 1789–1917: Hackett land holdings. Tipp.Hist.J. 5 (1992) p. 140-147.

Hadsor

The Hadsors and some other Louth Exiles in France and Spain. CLAHJ 18 (4) (1976) 263-272.

Lt. Bartholomew Hadsor (of Louth?) in 'King James' IAL' (Notes on family members pre-1700).

O'Hagan

Gleanings from Ulster History. Seamus O'Ceallaigh. Cork: Univ Press: 1951. Republished Belfast: Ballinascreen Hist.Soc.:1994 (ISBN: 09951175998) (Re: O'Neill, O'Hagan, O'Quinn, O'Donnelly, O'Devlin).

O'Hagerty or **O'Hegerty**

Two letters to Benjamin Franklin from Peter Charles Daniel Count O'Hagerty: with documents concerning him and his family in the National Archives of France. John C. Hagerty. Typescript: LDS Lib. 929.2415 Oh2h.

Haines

Pedigree of Haines Family of Cork: IGRS Library (Leader Collection).

Halahan

Pedigree of Halahan Family of Cork: IGRS Library (Leader Collection).

Hall

Jottings re Narrow Water & Hall family. Ed. F.C. Crossle. Armagh Co. Museum Ms. P8 (LDS Mf.1279356).

Pedigree of Hall Family of Cork: IGRS Library (Leader Collection) Pedigree of Hamilton.

Hall family of Ulster Province: Armagh Co. Museum Ms. N8: LDS Mf.1279356.

Hall-Dare of Newtownbarry. Wexford Gentry Vol. 1 (see abbreviations).

Halliday

Pedigree of Quaker family of Halliday (Armagh, Westmeath, Dublin et al). Thos. H. Webb. Ms. at Friends Hist. Lib.

Hallinan

The Hallinan Family of Quartertown. Mallow Field Club J. 9 (1991) 70-81.

O'Halloran *see also* **Ireton**

The O'Halloran family. In J. King 'History of Co. Kerry' p. 212–13. Dublin, 1910.

Thady O'Halloran of Ballycuneen, Co. Clare (1727-1798). N. Munster Antiq. J. 5(4) (1948) 102–06; 7 (3) (1956) 12–17 (gives diary of births/marriages, etc. from 1758–1912 & pedigree).

A brief history of the families of John O'Halloran & Fanny Lacey of Inishbofin, Co. Galway. Mary Lyden. LDS Lib. 929.2415 A1 no. 73. (refs to Lyden, Lacey, King).

O'Halloran, Halloran and variants. Laurence Halloran. Sydney: L. Halloran, 1987. (LDS Lib. 929.2415 Oh1h) (Collection of history, genealogy, .. including Hallorans in Australia).

The O'Hallorans in South Australia. Old Limerick J. 23 (1998) 30-34.

Haly *see* **Healy**

Hamill *see* **Ashmur, Hargreaves**

Hamilton *see also* **Bernard, McCann, Gerrard, Lowry, Swift**

Monea Castle, Co. Fermanagh, & the Hamiltons. Ulster J. Arch. 1 (1895) 195–208, 256–77.

The Hamiltons. E. W. Hamilton. Dublin, pr. pr. 1889.

Pedigree of Hamilton family of Fermanagh & Tyrone. J. F. Fuller. London, 1889.

Hamilton Manuscripts. ed. T. K. Lowry. Belfast. 1848.

Hamilton memoirs. E. Hamilton. Dundalk, 1920.

Snatches of O'Daniel, Hamilton, and allied ancestry and history in Maryland and Kentucky. Victor F. O'Daniel. Somerset, Ohio, 1933.

Hamilton: a short family & personal history. R. W. Hamilton. Pr.pr. Hollywood, Co. Down 1995. (NLI Ir 9292 h180)

The Hamilton manuscripts: containing some account of the settlement of the territories of the Upper Clandboye, Great Ardes, and Dufferin. J. Hamilton. Archer & Sons, 1867.

Copies of census returns for the following years: Hamilton - 1821,'31,'41 & '51; NAI Mf. 5246 (9,12).

Vestry records of the Church of St. John, Parish of Aghalow with an account of the family of Hamilton of Caledon 1691–1807. Ed. John J.Marshall. Dungannon, 1935 (NLI Ir 27411 a2).

Abercorn Papers; Hamilton family (1250–1942). PRONI DOD 669; LDS Mf. 248300.

Hamilton family: in 'King James' IAL' (Notes on 3 family members pre-1700).

Additional notes on the Hamiltons. Clogher Record 14 (2) (1992) 132.

Sketches of Waldron & Hamilton history (1135-1927). Jane W. Patterson. Stafford: W. H. Smith. 1927. (LDS Lib 929.2415 W147p) (Refs to Armstrong, Coats, Graham, Potterton).

Hammet

Pedigree of Hammet Family of Cork: IGRS Library (Leader Collection).

Hanbidge

The memories of William Hanbidge and chronicles of the Hanbidge family. Mary Hanbidge. St. Albans, 1939.

Hanley, O'Hanley or **O'Hanly**

O'Hanly and the Townland of Kilmacough. Ir. Gen. 3 (3) (1963) 101–08.

Hanlon or **O'Hanlon** *see* **Moore**

Redmond Count O'Hanlon's pedigree. CLAHJ 2 (1908–11) 61.

Capt. Colin Hanlon (of Armagh) in 'King James' IAL' (Notes on family members pre-1700).

O'Hanlon family records: Notes re the family O'Hanlon anciently of Orior,
Co. Armagh. (Inc. listing of pedigrees from and Irish poems.) GO Ms. no.
517, LDS Mf.257821.

The O'Hanlons, O'Neills and the Anglonormans in 13th c. Armagh. Seanchas
Ardmhacha 9(1) (1978) 70-94.

Hannon *see* **Darbyshire**

Hanrahan

Hanrahan family History. Patrick L. Hanrahan. Pr.pr. Portland Oregon 1983.
(NLI Ir 9292 h10).

O'Hara *see also* **Stewart**

The Book of O'Hara. Ed. Lambert McKenna. Dublin Institute for Advanced
Studies, 1980. (Collection...of Bardic poems dealing with the O'Hara's:
1597-1612) (LDS Lib. 929.2415 Oh1b).

Capt Daniel O'Hara (of Antrim) in 'King James' IAL' (Notes on family pre-
1793).

Capt. Cormuck O'Hara (of Cooloney, Co. Sligo) in 'King James' IAL' (Notes
on family members pre-1700).

Harden *see* **Carlile**

Hardy *see* **Ferrar**

Hare

Pedigree of Hare Family of Cork: IGRS Library (Leader Collection).

Hargreaves

The children of Edmonstown Park: memoirs of an Irish family. Denis H.
Crofton. England: Volturna Press, 1980. (LDS Lib. 929.2415 H325c) (Refs
to Barton, Carlile, Crofton, Hamill, Hargreaves, Savile, Smith).

Harman or **Harmon**

Pedigree of Harman Family of Cork: IGRS Library (Leader Collection).
The Harmons of Cork. Ir.Gen. 3 (1967) 524–8.

Harney

Harneys in Ireland – 1850's: from Griffith's valuations. Linda H. MacDonald
1989. (LDS Lib.929.2415 A1 no. 65).

Harold

Capt. Nicholas Harold (of Dublin) in 'King James' IAL' (Notes on family
pre-1700).

Harold-Barry Papers. [Ballyvonare, Co. Cork]. Anal. Hib. 15, 129–33.

Harper or **Harpur**

Roots of the Harper Family, Co Monaghan. Irish Heritage Links 3 (7) (1989)
35-41.

Large Pedigree Book for Harpur Family. IGRS Library (Leader Collection).

Harrigan *see* **Crosby**

Harrington

Harrington in 'Family Names of Co. Cork' (see abbrevs.) (Notes on origins &
members in Co.Cork).

Harris
Pedigree of Harris Family of Cork: IGRS Library (Leader Collection).
Harrison
Pedigree of Harrison Family of Cork: IGRS Library (Leader Collection).
Hart, O'Hart & Harte
Family history of Hart of Donegal. H. T. Hart.London: Hughes & Clark 1907. (NLI: Ir 9292 h2: LDS 929.2415 H251h).
Harte of Co. Limerick. Pedigree in 'Swanzy Notebooks'. RCB Library, Dublin.
Pedigree of Hart Family of Cork: IGRS Library (Leader Collection).
The last princes of Tara, or a brief sketch of the O'Hart ancient royal family. J. O'Hart. Dublin, 1873.
Hartland
The Hartland Nursery Family of Mallow & Cork. Mallow Field Club J. 3 (1985).
Hartpole
Notes on the district of Ivory, Coolbanagher Castle, and the Hartpoles. JCKAS 4 (1903–05) 297–311.
Harvey
The Harvey families of Inishowen, Co. Donegal. G. H. Harvey. Folkestone, 1927.
Harvey Family of Co. Wexford, Sixteen Births 1798–1801. JAPMD 9 (1912–16) 572.
The Harvey-Waddy Connection. JOWS 8 (1980–81).
Harvey of Kyle. Wexford Gentry Vol. 1 (see abbreviations).
Harvey of Bargy. Wexford Gentry Vol. 2 (see abbreviations).
Hassard
Some account of the family of Hassard with a list of descendants in England and Ireland. Henry B. Swanzy. Dublin: Alex. Thom & Co., 1903. (NLI Call No. Ir 9292 h4).
The genealogy and history of the Hassards. H. Short Hassard. York. 1858.
Hatch
The family of Hatch of Ardee. CLAHJ 16 (1968) 205–23; 17 (1969) 19–21.
Hatchell
Hatchell of Co. Wexford. Ir. Gen. 4 (5) (1972) 461–76.
Hatfield
Papers (e.g., deeds, leases, and pedigrees) relating to; Hatfield of Killimor ..et al. Longford/Westmeath Library; RIA:Upton Papers), and LDS Mf. 101011.
Haughton *see also* **Goodbody**
Memoirs of the family of Haughton in Ireland. T. W. Haughton Pr. pr. 1929.
The Rev. Samuel Haughton. Carloviana 2(28) (1980) 12-14; 2(29) (1981) 10-12.

Hawkes

Pedigree Book for Hawkes Family of Cork: IGRS Library (Leader Collection).

Hawkins

Pedigree of Hawkins Family of Cork: IGRS Library (Leader Collection).

Hawksby *see* **Downey**

Hawkshaw

Pedigree of Hawkshaw Family of Cork: IGRS Library (Leader Collection).

Hay *see* **Moore**

Hayden

A brief history of the Haydens of Caherlesk (Co. Kilkenny). Old Kilkenny Review 49 (1997) p. 33-47.

The Haydens of Caherlesk in North America. Old Kilkenny Review 50 (1998) p. 24-42.

The Haydens in Tipperary: A 700 year journey. Tipp.Hist.J. 7 (1994) p. 142-154.

Hayes *see also* **Carlile**

Pedigree of Hayes Family of Cork: IGRS Library (Leader Collection).

From the Minehouse: A Hayes family History 1819-1994. Patrick C. Hayes. Wachope Australia 1995. (ISBN 0646244728).

Hayman *see* **Holmes**

Hazelton

Pedigree of Hazelton Family of Cork: IGRS Library (Leader Collection).

O'Hea *see also* **Hayes**

The O'Heas of South-west Cork. JCHAS 51 (1951) 97–107.

O'Hea or Hayes in 'Family Names of Co. Cork' (see abbrevs.) (Notes on origins & members in Co.Cork).

Healy

The Healys of Donoughmore. JCHAS 48 (1943) 124–32.

(O')Healy, Healy, Hely in 'Family Names of Co. Cork' (see abbrevs.) (Notes on origins & members in Co.Cork).

The Healy story: heritage of an Irish name (or Oidreacht Mhuintir Ui Ealaithe). Donal Healy. Macroom: Milini Pubs. 1996. (LDS Lib. 929.2415 H349h).

Heard

Pedigree of Heard Family of Cork: IGRS Library (Leader Collection).

Hearn *see* **Ahearn**

Heffernan *see also* **Duggan**

The Heffernans and their times. Patrick Heffernan. London 1940.

O'Hegarty *see also* **O'Hagerty**

History of the noble O'Hegerty family: ancient lords of Magherabeg & Clainsullagh, in Co. Donegal. John C. Hagerty. Charleston, 1959. (LDS Lib. 929.2415 Oh2hj).

(O')Hegarty in 'Family Names of Co. Cork' (see abbrevs.) (Notes on origins
    & members in Co.Cork).
The O'Hegarty's of Ulster & kindred families. Donegal Ann. 1(2) (1948) 86-
    92. (Early pedigree).

Helsham
The Helshams of Kilkenny. Old Kilkenny Review 2 (4) (1982) 319–27.

Henchy
The O'Connor Henchys of Stonebrook (Kildare). JCKAS 2 (1896–99) 407–
    12.

Henderson *see also* **Mullan**
Pedigree of Henderson Family of Cork: IGRS Library (Leader Collection).

Hendley
Pedigree of Hendley Family of Cork: IGRS Library (Leader Collection).

Hendy
The Hendy family of Harristown, near Nurney (Co Kildare). JCKAS 14 (2)
    (1966) 167.

Hennessey
Pedigree of Hennessey Family of Cork: IGRS Library (Leader Collection).
(O')Hennessy in 'Family Names of Co. Cork' (see abbrevs.) (Notes on ori-
    gins & members in Co.Cork)

Henry *see also* **Ashmur, Nesbitt**
The Henry family in Kildare. JCKAS 3 (1902) 386–8.
Pedigree of Henry Family of Cork: IGRS Library (Leader Collection).
Henry of Co. Down. Pedigree in 'Swanzy Notebooks'. RCB Library, Dublin.

Heppental
Pedigree of Heppental Family of Cork: IGRS Library (Leader Collection).

Herbert *see also* **Kelly (Ainsworth misc)**
Herbert correspondence ed.. W. J. Smith. Cardiff and Dublin, 1963.
Herbert Papers. [Cahirnane, Co. Kerry]. Anal. Hib. 15, 93–107.

Herlihy
(O')Herlihy in 'Family Names of Co. Cork' (see abbrevs.) (Notes on origins
    & members in Co.Cork).

Heron
Pedigree of Heron Family of Cork: IGRS Library (Leader Collection).
The Heron family of Dublin, Ireland and Melbourne. Irish Link. Sept 1985; p.
    26-27.

Herrick
The Herricks of Co. Cork. Ir.Gen. 3 (1963) 291–8.
Pedigree of Herrick Family of Cork: IGRS Library (Leader Collection).

Hewetson *see also* **Hewson**
The Hewetsons of Co. Kildare. JRSAI 39 (1909) 146–63.
Hewetson of the Co. Kilkenny. JRSAI 39 (1909) 369–92.

Hewetson of Ballyshannon, Donegal. JRSAI 40 (1910) 238–43.

Memoirs of the house of Hewetson or Hewson in Ireland. H. B. Swanzy.
London 1901; & Dublin, 1903.

Hewson *see also* **Hewetson**

Hewsons of Finuge, Kerry, of royal descent. John Hewson. 1907.

The Hewson family of Ballyshannon and Donegal. JRSAI 39 (1909) 40.

O'Heyne

Tribes and customs of Hy Fiachra. John O'Donovan. Dublin: Irish Archaeological Soc. 1844. Appendix D, 398–406.

O'Hickey, Hickey or Hickie *see also* **McNamara**

The O'Hickeys. N. Munster Antiq. J. 8(1) (1958) 38–41.

Pedigree of Hickey Family of Cork: IGRS Library (Leader Collection).

Hickie of Kilelton. Shannonside Annual 1 (1957) 65–9.

Hickson

Pedigree of Hickson Family of Cork: IGRS Library (Leader Collection).

Higgins or **O'Higgins** *see also* **Stinson**

Ambrose O'Higgins: an enquiry into his origins and ancestry. Ir. Anc. 2 (2)
(1970) 81–9.

Higginson

Descendants of Rev. Thomas Higginson (b. Ballinderry, Co. Antrim, 1700).
Thomas B. Higginson. London: Research Publishing Co. 1958.

Hill *see also* **Guinness, Stewart**

The house of Downshire from 1600 to 1868. H. MacCall. Belfast: 1880.

Hillas

Hillas of Co. Sligo. Ir. Anc. 4 (1972) 26–29.

Hilliard

Pedigree of Hilliard Family of Cork: IGRS Library (Leader Collection).

Hime *see* **McClintock**

Hoade

The Hoade family book: a genealogy of the Hoade & Curran families of Co.
Galway. Eugene Hoade. Ms. LDS Lib. 929.2415 H65h.

Hoare

Account of the early history and genealogy, with pedigrees from 1330, of the
families of Hore and Hoare with all their branches. Edward Hoare. London,
1883.

Pedigree of Hoare Family of Cork: IGRS Library (Leader Collection).

History of the Hoare family of Factory Hill, Co. Cork. Edward Hoare. n.d.

Hobson

Pedigree of Hobson Family of Cork: IGRS Library (Leader Collection).

Hodges *see* **Morgan**

Hodnett

Belvelly Castle. JCHAS 21 (1915) 105–10. (Hodnett family).

Hogan *see also* **Forster**
> The quest for galloping Hogan. Matthew J. Culligan-Hogan. NY: Crown Pubs.
> 1979. (LDS Lib. 929.2415 H678c).

Holdom *see* **Mullan**

Hollingsworth
> The Hollingsworth Register Vols 1 & 2. Inglewood, Calif., 1965 & 1966.
> Pedigrees of … Hollingsworth et al. LDS Mf. 1279327.

Hollywood
> The Hollywoods of Artane. Reportorium Novum 1 (2) 1956: 341–44.

Holmes
> The Pooles of Mayfield. R. ffolliott. Dublin: Hodges Figgis (1958). (Re Holmes
> family of Dublin & Hayman links).
> Pedigree of Holmes Family of Cork: IGRS Library (Leader Collection).

Homan
> Pedigree of Homan Family of Cork: IGRS Library (Leader Collection).
> Deeds, leases, & pedigrees relating to…Homan. RIA (Upton Papers): LDS
> Mf. 101011.

Hone
> Nathaniel and all the Hones. Dublin Hist. Rec. 23 (1969/70) 72-85.

Honner
> Pedigree of Honner Family of Cork: IGRS Library (Leader Collection).

Hopper
> The Hopper Family. Ir.Anc. 14 (2) (1982) 13–19, 59–73.

Hore
> Hore of Harperstown and Polehore (Wexford). Wexford Gentry Vol. 2 (see
> abbreviations).

Hornibrook
> Large Pedigree Book for Hornibrook Family. IGRS Library (Leader Collec-
> tion).

Hort
> The Horts of Hortland. JCKAS 7 (1912–14) 207–16.

Hosford
> Large Pedigree Book for Hosford Family. IGRS Library (Leader Collection).

Houghton
> Houghton of Kilmannock. Irish Builder. 1888.

Hovenden
> Lineage of the family of Hovenden (Irish branch). By 'A member of the family'.
> pr.pr. London, 1892.

Howard
> Pedigree of Howard Family of Cork: IGRS Library (Leader Collection).

Hudson *see also* **Goodbody**
> Pedigree of Hudson Family of Cork: IGRS Library (Leader Collection).

Hughes *see also* **Ireton, Ferrar**

 Hughes of Ballytrent and Ely House (Wexford). Wexford Gentry Vol. 2 (see abbreviations).

Huleatt

 John Huleatt of Tuamgraney (Co. Clare) and the vicissitudes of his family, The Other Clare 11 (1987) p.42-43.

Hull

 Pedigree of Hull Family of Cork: IGRS Library (Leader Collection).

Humphreys *see also* **Bernard**

 Humphreys of Knockfad, Co. Cavan. Ir. Anc. 13 (2) (1981) 88–89.

 Pedigree of Humphreys Family of Cork: IGRS Library (Leader Collection).

Huntingdon *see* **Ferrar**

Hurley, O'Hurley or **O'Hurly**

 The family of O'Hurley. P. Hurley. Cork, 1906.

 Some account of the family of O'Hurly. JCHAS 11 (1905) 105–23, 177–83; 12 (1906) 26–33, 76–88.

 Lt. John Hurly (of Galway) in 'King James' IAL' (Notes on family members pre-1700).

 Hurley or O'Muirthile in 'Family Names of Co. Cork' (see abbrevs.) (Notes on origins & members in Co.Cork).

 Hurley Families in America (in 2 Vols). William N Hurley, Jr. Heritage Books, USA 1999.

Huss *see* **Clancy**

Hutchinson *see also* **Ashmur**

 Hutchinson & Maxwell will extracts (Abstracts from Registry of Deeds, Dublin). Armagh Co. Museum. Ms. P8: LDS.

 Mf.1279356.

Hussey or **O'Hussey**

 O'Hussey. Clogher Record, 2 (1957) 1–19.

 Pedigree of Hussey Family of Cork: IGRS Library (Leader Collection).

 Capt. Thomas Hussey in 'King James' IAL' (Notes on family members pre-1700).

Hyde

 Entries from the Family Bible of James Hyde of Longford. Ir. Anc. 2(1)(1970) 23.

Hynes

 A study of the surname Hynes as found in Athlone and surrounding area. Edward A. Hynes, 1981.

Ince

 Pedigree of Ince Family of Cork: IGRS Library (Leader Collection).

Inglefield *see* **Gerrard**

Ingram
>   Pedigree of Ingram Family of Cork: IGRS Library (Leader Collection).

Ireton
>   The Iretons of Ireland, 1600-1900. Helen Gillespie & LaRoux K. Gillespie.
>   Kansas City, Mo.: Family Hist. & Genealogy Center, 1989. (LDS Lib.
>   929.2415 Ir2g) (Refs to: Bush, Carroll, Cheetham, Daly, Doyle, Flood,
>   Hughes, Kinsella, Madill, McDermont, Mosman, O'Halloran, Purcell,
>   Sheehan, Thornton).
>   Pedigree of Ireton Family of Cork: IGRS Library (Leader Collection).

Irvine, Irving *see also* **MacNair**
>   The book of the Irvines. J. B. Irving. Aberdeen, 1907.

Irwin *see also* **McNaughton**
>   The Irwins of Fermanagh and Donegal. Ir.Gen. 1(1941) 278–83.
>   The Irwins of Roxborough, Co. Roscommon and Streamstown, Co. Sligo.
>   Ir.Gen. 1(1937) 19–24, 51–56.
>   The Irwin family of Altmore, Pomeroy (Co.Tyrone). Family Links 1
>   (7)(1983)17–20.

Ivey
>   Pedigree of Ivey Family of Cork: IGRS Library (Leader Collection).

Ivory
>   The Ivory Family of New Ross. JRSAI 80 (1950) 242–61.

Jackson
>   The Jacksons of Ireland. Ancestor 7 (1903) 67–70
>   The Family of Jackson of Wooldale in the Co. of Cork. Gen. N.S. 37(1920)
>   29–33.
>   Pedigree of Jackson Family of Cork: IGRS Library (Leader Collection).
>   Pedigrees of Atkinson, Beck, Chambers, Cole, Jackson, and Pilleys or Pil-
>   lows. LDS Mf. 1279354.

Jacob *see also* **Rothwell**
>   Historical and genealogical narration of the families of Jacob. A. H. Jacob
>   and J. H. Glascott. Dublin, 1875.
>   Pedigree of Jacob Family of Cork: IGRS Library (Leader Collection).
>   History of the families of Jacob of Bridgewater, Tiverton & Southern Ireland.
>   H. W. Jacob. Taunton, 1929.
>   Genealogies of Esmond, Codd, Jacob, and Redmond. GO Mf. 279.
>   The Dublin family of Jacob. Dublin Hist.Rec. 2(4) (1940) 134-140.
>   Notes on the family of Jacob; being supplementary to A.W. Jacob's 'A His-
>   tory of the Families of Jacob'. Albert W. Jacob. NLI Ms 27,455.

Jagoe
>   Large Pedigree Book for Jagoe Family. IGRS Library (Leader Collection).

Jamison or **Jameson** *see also* **Carlile**

Copies of census returns for the Jamison family for 1851; NAI Mf. 5249/32.

Pedigree of Jameson Family of Cork: IGRS Library (Leader Collection).

Jameson of the Still (Wexford). Wexford Gentry Vol. 2 (see abbreviations).

Jeffcott *see* **Bernard**

Jeffereys

Pedigree of Jeffereys Family of Cork: IGRS Library (Leader Collection).

Jellett

The Pooles of Mayfield. R. ffolliott. Dublin: Hodges Figgis (1958). (Re: Jellett of Tullyard, Co. Down & Dublin).

"Great trees from little saplings grow": genealogical narrative ...the Jellett families from William Jellett (b.1632) & Katherine Morgan, his wife ... to the present era, 1931. Cora S. Gould. New York: Bartlett Orr Press, 1931. (LDS Lib. 929.2415 J393g).

Jennings *see* **Ashmur**

Jephson or **Jepson**

The English settlement in Ireland under the Jephson family. JCHAS 12 (1906) 1–26.

Anglo-Irish miscellany. Maurice Denham Jephson. Dublin: Figgis, 1964. (LDS Lib. 929.2415 J462j) (Ref. to Norreys, Dannett, Denham, Boyle, Dreaver, Preston).

Mallow Castle and the Jephson family. Mallow Field Club J. 3 (1985) 42-54.

Pedigree of Jepson Family of Cork: IGRS Library (Leader Collection).

Jermyn

Pedigree of Jermyn Family of Cork: IGRS Library (Leader Collection).

Johnston or **Johnson** *see also* **Ashmur, Acheson, Woods**

The Johnstons of Correnney, Co. Fermanagh. Ir.Gen. 1 (1941) 321.

Pedigree of Johnston Family of Cork: IGRS Library (Leader Collection).

Johnsons – lineal descendants of Ui Neill. N. Munster Antiq. J. 17(1975) 55-62.

Jolly

A Portarlington settler and his descendants. M. A. Jolly. London, 1935.

Jones

The Jones family in Ireland. Robert Leach. Yonkers, N.Y., 1866.

Pedigree of Jones Family of Cork: IGRS Library (Leader Collection).

Jordan

Pedigree of Jordan Family of Cork: IGRS Library (Leader Collection).

Joyce *see also* **Murphy**

The Joyces of Merview. Ir. Gen. 9 (1) (1994) 89–113; 9 (2) (1995); 10(2) (1999).

Joyce country. William D. Joyce. Worcester, Mass.: Butterfly Press, 1988. (LDS Lib. 929.2415 J851j).

Judd
> Pedigree of Judd family of Cork: IGRS Library (Leader Collection).

Juman
> Pedigree of Juman Family of Cork: IGRS Library (Leader Collection).

O'Kane *or* **Kane**
> Some account of the sept of the O'Cathains of Ciannachta Glinne-Geimhin. Now the O'Kanes of the Co. of Londonderry. Ulster J. Arch. 3 (1855) 1–8, 265–72; 4 (1856) 139–48.
>
> O'Mullen, O'Kane and O'Mellan. The Ulster clans. T. H. Mullin & J. E. Mullan. Belfast, 1966.
>
> Kane family history: Descendants of Thomas Kane (1820-1900) & Agnes Ann Mitchell (1824- 1863). (Armagh to Canada). Mitchell, Ont.: E. Bingham, 1988. (LDS Ms 929.271 A1 no. 296).
>
> The Kane family descended from Richard Kane of Co. Longford & Co. Dublin, Ireland. LDS Mf. 1279253 Item 3.

Kavanagh or **Cavenagh** *see also* **Rothwell**
> The fall of the Clan Kavanagh. JRSAI 12(1873) 282–305.
>
> The family of the MacMurrough Kavanaghs. Carloviana 1 (3) (1954) 13–16.
>
> The Kavanaghs. Ir. Gen. 5(1977) 435–447; 6 (1978) 573–580.
>
> Kavanagh Papers (Borris, Co. Carlow). Anal. Hib. 25: 15–30.
>
> Some Kavanaghs of the County Kildare. JCKAS 5 (6) (1908) 462-463.
>
> Historical Reminiscences of O'Byrnes, O'Tooles, O'Kavanaghs & Other Chieftains. O'Byrne, G. London: 1843.
>
> Col. Charles Cavenagh (of Carrickduff, Carlow) in 'King James' IAL' (Notes on family members pre-1700).
>
> A Carlow emigrant to Australia. Carloviana 34 (1986/7) 15-19. (Martin Kavanagh of Monmore, Co Carlow).
>
> Kavanagh of Borris. Wexford Gentry Vol. 1 (see abbreviations).

MacKay *see* **MacKee**

Keane *see* **Teape**

Keaney
> Copies of 1841 census returns of Keaney family. NAI Mf. 5248(6).

Kearney
> Lt. Patrick Kearney (of Tipperary & elsewhere) in 'King James' IAL' (Notes on family members pre-1747).
>
> Clann Ceithearnaigh. JGAHS 23 (1948) p. 70- (Kearne or Kearney family).

Keating
> Records of the Keating family. Thos. Matthews. N.d.
>
> The early Keatings. Ir.Gen. 6 (1976).
>
> Pedigree of Keating Family of Cork: IGRS Library (Leader Collection).
>
> Nicholastown Castle and its owners. J. F. McCarthy. Clonmel, 1 (1954) 64–7.

MacKee *see also* **Orr**

   The book of McKee. Raymond W. McKee. Dublin, 1959.

   A history of the descendants of David McKee, with a sketch of the early
      McKees. James McKee. Philadelphia, 1872.

O'Keefe

   Capt. Art O'Keefe (of Glenfriacan, Co.Cork) in 'King James' IAL' (Notes on
      family members pre-1766).

   O'Keefe/O'Caoimh in 'Family Names of Co. Cork' (see abbrevs.) (Notes on
      family origins and members up to 1700).

Keevil

   Pedigree of Keevil family of Cork: IGRS Library (Leader Collection).

Keily

   Large Pedigree book for Keily Family. IGRS Library (Leader Collection).

Kell or **Kells** *see also* **Pearson**

   The Kells and Philpotts in Mallow, 1749. JCHAS 15 (1909) 95–8.

   Pedigree of Kells Family of Cork: IGRS Library (Leader Collection).

Kelleher

   Pedigree of Kelleher Family of Cork: IGRS Library (Leader Collection).

Kellett *see also* **Rothwell**

   Pedigree of Kellet Family of Cork: IGRS Library (Leader Collection).

Kelly or **O'Kelly** *see also* **O'Mullally**, **Riordan**

   Pedigree of Kelly Family of Cork: IGRS Library (Leader Collection).

   The O'Kellys of Gallagh, counts of the Holy Roman Empire. JGAHS 3 (1903–
      04) 180–5.

   Notes on the family of O'Kelly. JGAHS 4 (1905–06) 92–6.

   The pedigree of Maria Anna O'Kelly, countess of Marcolini. JGAHS 4 (1905–
      06) 108–10.

   Notes on the O'Kelly family. JGAHS 16 (1934–35) 140–3.

   Memorial religieux de la famille O'Kelly, originaire d'Irlande. Brussels, 1875.

   Tribes and customs of Hy Many. John O'Donovan. Dublin: Irish Archaeo-
      logical Soc. 1844. Appendix A, 97–129.

   That Kelly family [the Kellys of Philadelphia]. John McCallum. New York,
      1957.

   Capt. Denis Kelly (of Screen, Galway) in 'King James' IAL' (Notes on fam-
      ily members pre-1747).

   History of the name O'Kelly. J.D. Williams. Cork: Mercier Press, 1977.

   The Kelly connection: Gleanings about Kelly families in Ireland & abroad;
      especially …S.Roscommon & N. Galway area. Athlone: Irish Connec-
      tions Family Res. Gp. & Soc. 1995. LDS Lib. 929.2415 K295kc.

   Ainsworth miscellany . Misc. genealogical records: Kelly deaths…. GO Ms.
      no. 622, LDS Mf.257819.

   Memoirs of the Countess Turquet de al Boisserie (nee Matilda O'Kelly) 1865-

1956. Typscript in NLI (Call no. Ir 9292 k8) (Kelly of Newtown, Galway).

Kemmis

A short account of the family of Kemmis in Ireland. JCKAS 12 (1935–45) 144–69.

MacKenna

The MacKennas of Truagh. C. E. Swezey. Huntingdon: N.Y., 1972. (LDS Lib. 929.2415 M199a).

Origins of the McKennas with a history of the sept. Anthony Mathews. Author Published: Dublin 1972 (LDS Lib. 929.2415 M196m)

Emyvale - McKenna Country. Seamus McCluskey. N.p., 1996.

Notes on the MacKennas of Truagh. Clogher Record 8 (2) (1974) 221.

Kenneally or **Keaneally**

Pedigree of Keaneally Family of Cork: IGRS Library (Leader Collection).

Kennedy or **O'Kennedy** *see also* **Guinness**, **Lowry**

A family of Kennedy of Clogher and Londonderry c. 1600–1938. F. M. E. Kennedy. Taunton, 1938.

Pedigree of Kennedy Family of Cork: IGRS Library (Leader Collection).

Records of the four Tipperary Septs. Martin Callanan. JAG Publishing, Galway 1938. (ISBN 0952660806).

The decline of the O'Kennedys of Ormond. Tipp.Hist.J. 7 (1994) 129-141.

Kenney or **Kenny**

Pedigree of the Kenney family of Kilclogher, Co. Galway. J. C. F. Kenney. Dublin, 1868.

History of Kenny, Lysaght, O'Loghlen, and related Clare families. NLI ms. 2109–2110.

Pedigree of Kenny Family of Cork: IGRS Library (Leader Collection).

As the crow flies over rough terrain: incorporating the diary 1827/1828 & more of a divine.Ed. James G. Kenny. Ballymena, Antrim: J.G. Kenny. 1988. (LDS 929.2415 K399k). (Ref to Magill, Gault, Montgomery, Beattie).

MacKenzie *see* **MacCormick, Fitzgerald, Guinness**

Keogh or **McKeogh**

McKeoghs of Moyfinn. J. Old Athlone Soc. 1 (4) (1974/75) 234–37; 2 (5) (1978) 56–70.

Pedigree of Keogh Family of Cork: IGRS Library (Leader Collection).

O'Keohane

The Keohanes of West Cork. Newsletter of the Keohanes of W. Cork Soc. 1 (1993).

Kerdiff

The Kerdiffs of Kerdiffstown, Co. Kildare. JCKAS 7 (3) (1913) 182-6.

Kerin

> Pedigree of Kerin Family of Cork: IGRS Library (Leader Collection).

Kernan

> Notes on the descendants of John Kernan of Ned, Co. Cavan. J. D. Kernan.
> Englewood, N.J. 1969.
>
> Kernan of Ned, Co. Cavan. Ir. Gen. 4 (4) (1971) 323–30.
>
> The Kernan Family. Clogher Record 1 (2) (1954) 64.
>
> More on the Kernans of Enniskillen: Randal Kernan (1775 - c.1844) & oth-
> ers. Clogher Record 10 (1) (1979) 23.

Kerr

> The Gabriel and George Kerr families and descendants. H. Carl Mayhue,
> Quebec, pr. pr., 1976.

Keyburn

> Pedigree of Keyburn Family of Cork: IGRS Library (Leader Collection).

McKibbin *see* **Orr**

Kidd

> Pedigree of Kidd Family of Cork: IGRS Library (Leader Collection).

Kingan *see* **Darbyshire**

King *see also* **O'Halloran**

> Pedigree of King Family of Cork: IGRS Library (Leader Collection).
>
> The Kings of King House: the story of the descendants of Sir John King of
> Boyle and their estates at Mitchelstown, Rockingham and Newcastle.
> Anthony L. King-Harman. Pr.pr. Bedford 1996.

Kingsbury

> Kingsbury of Dublin. Pedigree in 'Swanzy Notebooks'. RCB Library, Dub-
> lin.

Kingston

> The Kingston family in Co. Cork. D. Trimble. 1929.
>
> Pedigree of Kingston Family of Cork: IGRS Library (Leader Collection).
>
> Kingston (Cinnseaman) in 'Family Names of Co. Cork' (see abbrevs.) (Notes
> on origins & members in Co.Cork).
>
> The Origins of Co. Cork Kingstons. JCHAS 76 (1981) 75–99.

MacKinley *see also* **Moore**

> The McKinleys of Conagher, Co. Antrim, and their Descendants, with notes
> about the President of the United States. Ulster J. Arch. 2nd ser. 3 (1897)
> 167–70.

Kinsella *see also* **Ireton**

> Kinsella, the Irish connection (Ballyfad, Wexford). Comp. by P. & D. Des
> Jardins. LDS Lib. 929.2415 A1 no. 67.

Kirby or **O'Kirby**

> Irish chiefs and leaders. Rev. Paul Walsh. Ch. xviii. Dublin, 1960.
>
> Pedigree of Kirby Family of Cork: IGRS Library (Leader Collection).

Kirkpatrick

Chronicles of the Kirkpatrick family. Alexander Kirkpatrick. London, n.d.

Kirwan

Capt. Patrick Kirwan (of Cregg, Galway) in 'King James' IAL' (Notes on family members pre-1779).

McKitrick

The McKitricks and Roots of Ulster Scots. Frederick L. McKitrick. Pr.pr. Baltimore 1979.

Knagges

Pedigree of Knagges Family of Cork: IGRS Library (Leader Collection).

Knaresborough *see* **Archdeacon**

Knox

Notes on some of the Ranfurly Knoxes. A. K. Windsor: Oxley & Son 1950. (LDS Lib. 929.2415 K77k).

Andrew Knox, Bishop of Raphoe and some of his descendants. James Hempton; Derry. N.d.

Lacy *see also* **De Lacy, O'Halloran**

The roll of the house of Lacy. E. de Lacy-Bellingarri. Baltimore, 1928. (NLI Call No. Ir 9292 L1).

Lieut. John Lacy (of Kilmallock, Limerick) in 'King James' IAL' (Notes on family pre-1792).

Lahee

Pedigree of Lahee Family of Cork: IGRS Library (Leader Collection).

Lally *see also* **O'Mullally.**

A sept of O'Maolale (or Lally) of Hy-Maine. JGAHS 4 (1905–06) 198–209.

Capt. James Lally (of Tuam, Co Galway) in 'King James' IAL' (Notes on family members pre-1792).

Lamb

Pedigree of Lamb Family of Cork: IGRS Library (Leader Collection).

Lambert *see also* **McNamara**

Notes on the lineage of Lambert of Brookhill, Co. Mayo. Ir.Gen. 3(10)(1965) 372–79.

Lambert of Wexford. The Past 2 (1921) 129–38.

Lambert of Carnagh. Wexford Gentry Vol. 1 (see abbreviations).

The Lamberts of Athenry: a book on the Lambert families of Castle Lambert & Castle Ellen, Co. Galway. Finbarr O'Regan. Athenry, Ireland; 1999.

Lane *see also* **Lyons**

An old corporation relic. JCHAS 21 (1915) 80–2.

Pedigree of Lane Family of Cork: IGRS Library (Leader Collection).

Langham

Hay days, fair-days & not so good old days: a Fermanagh estate ...of the

Langham family 1890-1918. W. A. Maguire. Belfast: Friar's Bush Press 1986. (LDS Lib. 929.2415 L264m) (ref to Maguire & Tennent families of Tempo).

Langrishe

'A Refutation' (Re Hercules Langrishe) JRSAI 27 (1897) 434-6; & 40 (1910) 262.

Langton *see also* **Archdeacon**

Memorials of the Family of Langton of Kilkenny. JRSAI 8 (1864) 59–108.

Langtrey

Pedigree of Langtrey Family of Cork: IGRS Library (Leader Collection).

Lappan

Pedigree of Lappan Family of Cork: IGRS Library (Leader Collection).

Larkin

Profile of the Larkin Family: 1787–1983. Irish Family Links 2(2)(1984) 26–28.

Pedigree of Larkin Family of Cork: IGRS Library (Leader Collection).

La Touche

The La Touche family of Harristown, Co. Kildare. JCKAS 7 (1912–14) 33–40.

Genealogy of the De La Touche family seated in France …and … in Ireland, 1690–95. Sir A. B. Stransham. London, Mitchell & Hughes,1882. (LDS Lib. 929.2415 A1 no. 10).

Plantation of Renown. The Story of the La Touche Family of Harristown … Co. Kildare. R. Dunlop. N.p. 1970.

Ruskin & Harristown. JCKAS 14 (2) (1966/7) 152-162. (deals with LaTouche family of Harristown).

Lattimore

References to people & families named Lattimore (& variations) in Carrickfergus, Co.Antrim (c.1666 to c.1950) R. Cameron . Antrim, 1982. (LDS Lib. 929.2415 A1 no. 23).

Lattin

The Lattin & Mansfield families in the Co. Kildare. JCKAS 3 (3) (1899–1902) 186–90.

Notices of the family of Lattin. JRSAI 18 (1887) 183–8.

MacLaughlin or **McLoughlin**

The MacLaughlins of Clan Owen. J. P. Brown. W.J. Schofield: Boston, 1879.

The McLaughlin family of Inishowen JRSAI 45 (1915) 124, 216, 286-7; 53 (1923) 50.

Laurence *see* **Netterville, Lawrence**

Lavallin

History of the Lavallins. JCHAS 30 (1925) 10–15, 75–83; 31 (1926) 36–43, 53–9.

Lawder
>The Lawders of Bass and their descendants. C. A. B. Lawder. Belfast 1914.

Law or **Lawe**
>Lawe of Leixlip. JCKAS 6 (3) (1909–11) 730–39.
>Law Family of Dublin: Pedigree. JAPMD 11 (1921–25) 444.

Lawless *see also* **Archdeacon**
>The Lawless Family. Reportorium Novum 1 (2) (1956) 344–50.
>Pedigree of Lawless Family of Cork: IGRS Library (Leader Collection).
>The Lawless Family (includes MacEnally). Mrs. D. E. Lawless. Waverley, Iowa: pr. pr. 1971.
>Capt. Walter Lawless (of Kilkenny) in 'King James' IAL' (Notes on family members pre-1700).

Lawrence
>The Lawrence Connection. J. Gen. Soc. I. 1(2) 2000 59-63.

Lawson *see* **MacNair**

Leader
>Pedigree of Leader Family of Cork: IGRS Library (Leader Collection).

Leahey or **Leahy**
>Pedigree of Leahey Family of Cork: IGRS Library (Leader Collection).
>Leahy in 'Family Names of Co. Cork' (see abbrevs.) (Notes on origins & members in Co.Cork).

Leary or **O'Leary**
>A notebook of family history of the Leary family of Co. Monaghan. John L. Martin (Inc. extracts of wills, parish registers, census and land records relating to the Leary family) (LDS Lib. 929.2415 L479mj).
>Pedigree of O'Leary Family of Cork: IGRS Library (Leader Collection).
>O'Leary, O'Laoire in 'Family Names of Co. Cork' (see abbrevs.) (Notes on origins & members in Co.Cork).

Leddin
>O'Brien and Leddin Families. Irish Family History 4 (1988) 80-82.

Ledlie
>Joseph Ledlie and William Moody, their background and descendants. Pittsburgh, 1961.

Lee, Leech
>An Irish medical family: Mac An Leagha. In 'Irish men of learning' Rev. Paul Walsh. ch. xiv. Dublin, 1947.

Lees
>John and Edward Lees; Secretaries of the Irish Post Office (1774-1831). Dublin Hist. Rec. 8(3 &4) (1953) 139-150.

Leeson
>The Milltown Leesons; arch-rebels of the ascendancy. Ir.Gen. 4 (1968) 14–16.

Provisional history of the Leeson family, Earls of Milltown ... to 1964. Francis
Leeson. (LDS Lib.929.2415 L518L.

The Milltown Leeson Family. Genealogists Mag. 16 (5) (Mar 1970).

Le Fanu

Memoir of the Le Fanu family. T. P. Le Fanu. Manchester, 1945.

Lefroy or **Loffroy**

Notes and documents relating to .... Lefroy (or Loffroy) of Carrickglass, Co.
Longford. by 'A Cadet' (Sir J. H. Lefroy) pr.pr. Woolwich 1868. (NLI
Call No. Ir 9292 I18).

Loffroy of Cambray: a supplement. Jeffry A. P. Lefroy. Worcester and London, pr. pr., 1961.

Leicester *see* **Lyster**

Leigh

Lt. Samuel Leigh (of Kildare) in 'King James' IAL' (Family information pre-
1689).

Leigh of Rosegarland (Wexford). Wexford Gentry Vol. 2 (see abbreviations).

Lenox-Conyngham *see* **Conyngham**

Le Poer Trench

Memoir of the Le Poer Trench family. Richard, 2nd Earl of Clancarthy. Dublin: Hodges & Foster, 1874. (LDS Lib. 929.2415 L558c.

Leslie

The Leslies of Tarbert, Co. Kerry, and their forbears. P. L. Pielou. Dublin,
Brindley's 1935.

Of Glaslough in the kingdom of Oriel, and of noted men that have dwelt
there. Seymour Leslie. Glaslough: Donagh Press. 1913.

The Leslies of Balquhain. JCHAS 3 (1897) 302–3.

Brief Genealogies of the Families Corry, Crawford, Auchinleck, Dane,
Rampain, and Leslie. in 'The History of 2 Ulster Manors'. Earl of Belmore,
London/Dublin, 1903.

Finding My Leslie Ancestors. Ulster Gen. & Hist. Guild 19 (1996).

Lett *see also* **Archdeacon**

Records of the Lett Family in Ireland. Katherine Lucy Lett. 1925.

Levinge *see also* **Lyons**

Historical notes on the Levinge family, Baronets of Ireland 1005 - 1853. J. C.
Lyons. Ledestown, 1853.

Jottings for early history of the Levinge family. Sir Richard G. A. Levinge.
Dublin: pr.pr. by Brown and Nolan, 1873 & 1877. (NLI Call no. 9292 L
15: (LDS Lib. 929.2415 L578L).

Levinge of Clomahon. Wexford Gentry Vol. 1 (see abbreviations).

Lewis

Pedigree of Lewis Family of Cork: IGRS Library (Leader Collection).

Lighton
> Romance of the House of Lighton. Dublin Hist.Rec. 7(3) (1945) 112-119.

Limerick or **Limrick**
> The Family of Limrick of Schull, Co. Cork. H.L. Denny 1909. Also in JCHAS 13: 120–27.
> Pedigree of Limrick Family of Cork: IGRS Library (Leader Collection).

Lindesay or **Lindsay**
> The Lindesays of Loughry, Co. Tyrone: a genealogical history. Ernest H. Godfrey. London: H.H.Greaves, 1949. (LDS Lib. 929.2415 L645).
> Pedigree Books for Lindsey Family of Cork: IGRS Library (Leader Collection).
> The Lindsay memoirs. A record of the Lisnacrieve and Belfast branch of the Lindsay family during the last two hundred years. J. C. Lindsay and J. A. Lindsay. Belfast, 1884.

Linley *see* **Sheridan**

Lloyd *see* **Ferrar**, **Wilde**
> Genealogical notes on the Lloyd family in Co. Waterford. A. R. Lloyd (n.d.).
> Pedigree of Lloyd Family of Cork: IGRS Library (Leader Collection).
> Notes on the Lloyd Family of Ardnagowen, Co. Roscommon. JAPMD 6 (1904–06) 403.

O'Lochlainn *see* **O'Loughlin**

Locke
> The Lockes of Athgoe. Reportorium Novum 1 (1) (1955) 76–79.

Lockhart
> Boyds & Lockharts of Donegal. Comp. by James W, Devitt. (LDS Lib. 929.2415 B692d (refs to Adair, Busby, Dean, Devitt, Given, Long, McBride, Morrow, Nesbitt).

Lodge
> The Lodge Book: Sir Oliver Lodge's record of the Lodge family (Inc. marriage licence bonds, deeds, wills, Notes, letters & pedigrees). GO Ms. no. 611, (LDS Mf.257819).

Loffroy *see* **Lefroy**

Loftus *see also* **Kelly (Ainsworth misc)**, **Moore**, **Ely**
> Loftus Family Record. JCHAS. 2 (1896) 491–92.
> Loftus Papers (Cos. Kilkenny and Wexford). Anal. Hib. 25: 31–55.
> The Loftuses of Mount Loftus. Old Kilkenny Review, 23 (1971) p.23-34.

Logan
> Logan: A Directory of the Descendants of Andrew and Lydia Logan of Albany NY and Abbeville, S. Carolina. Richard K. Logan. Heritage Books, USA 1994.

O'Loghlen
> History of Kenny, Lysaght, O'Loghlen, and related Clare families. NLI ms. 2109–2110.

Lombard

The Lombards. Mallow Field Club J. 10 (1992) (Early history of Italian banker family in Ireland).

Londonderry

The Londonderrys, a family portrait. H. Montgomery Hyde London: Hamish Hamilton, 1979. (ISBN: 0241101530). (LDS Lib. 929.2415 L846h; Ref to Stewart, Vane, Vane-Tempest).

Long *see also* **Boyd**

The Longs of Muskerry and Kinalea. JCHAS 51 (1946) 1–9.

Pedigree of Long Family of Cork: IGRS Library (Leader Collection).

Long in 'Family Names of Co. Cork' (see abbrevs.) (Notes on origins & members in Co.Cork).

The Longs or Langs of Daars, near Bodenstown (Co. Kildare). JCKAS 5(1) (1906) p 62-63.

Longfield

Longfield Papers. (Longueville, Co. Cork.) Anal. Hib. 115: 135–42.

Longfields of Kilbride and a link with Swift. JCKAS 15 (1971) p.29-37.

Lordan or **Lordon**

Pedigree of Lordon Family of Cork: IGRS Library (Leader Collection).

O'Lorkan or **Larkin**

Lough Lorkan and the O'Lorkans. Seanchas Ardmhacha 3 (2) (1959) 261–7.

McLoughlin *see* **McLaughlin**

O'Loughlin or **O'Loghlen** *see also* **Kenny**

Short history of the Ó Lochlainn clan. É. Ó Lochlainn. Ballyvaughan, Co.Clare, 1995. (LDS Lib. 929.2415 A1 no. 85).

Loughrea

Pedigree of Loughrea Family of Cork: IGRS Library (Leader Collection).

Lovekin

Pedigree of Lovekin Family of Cork: IGRS Library (Leader Collection).

Lowry *see also* **Corry**

Thomas Kennedy Lowry, Isabella Moody: ancestors and descendants (Co. Down). Margaret L.A.Williams. (LDS Lib. 929.2415 L956w) (Refs to Hamilton, Kennedy and Ray families).

Lowther

Lowthers in Ireland in the 17th century. Sir Edmund Bewley. Kendal, 1902.

Lucas

Pedigree of Lucas Family of Cork: IGRS Library (Leader Collection).

Lucett

Pedigree of Lucett Family of Cork: IGRS Library (Leader Collection).

Lundy

Pedigree of Lundy Family of Cork: IGRS Library (Leader Collection).

Luttrel

The Luttrels of Luttrelstown. JCHAS 27 (1921) 65–9.

Col. Henry Luttrell (of Luttrellstown, Co. Dublin) in 'King James' IAL' (Notes on family members pre-1829).

Lydon or **Lyden** *see* **O'Halloran**

Lynch *see also* **Darcy, McNamara, Murphy**

Genealogical memoranda relating to the family of Lynch. London, 1883.

Lynch record, containing biographical sketches of men of the name Lynch, 16th century to 20th century. E. C. Lynch. New York: William J. Histen, 1925. (LDS Lib. 929.2415 L991L).

Account of the Lynch Family & of the Memorable Events of the Town of Galway. JGAHS 8 (1913–14) 76–93 (Inc. Deeds/Pedigrees of French of Rahasane and Monivea).

An old Lynch manuscript (continued). JGAHS 8 (4) (1913–14) 207-226.

An old Lynch manuscript (continued). JGAHS 9 (2) (1915–16) 79-107.

Lynch in 'Family Names of Co. Cork' (see abbrevs.) (Notes on origins & members in Co.Cork).

Pedigree of Lynch of Lavally, County Galway. JGAHS 10 (1917–18) 66–69.

Various Lynch officers in 'King James' IAL' (Notes on family members pre-1747).

Lyne

Dr. Dermot Lyne, An Irish Catholic landowner under the Penal Laws. JKAHS 8 (1975) 45–72.

Lynskey

Pedigree of Lynskey Family of Cork: IGRS Library (Leader Collection).

Lyons

Lyons family of Westmeath. (LDS Mf. 1279285).

Historical notice etc., of the family of Lyons and its connexions. John C. Lyons pr.pr. Ledestown. 1853. (LDS Lib. 929.2415 A1 no. 35) (refs to Auchmuty, Degennes, Fraser, Levinge, Nesbitt & Widman).

Lyons, Lane, (O')Lyne in 'Family Names of Co. Cork' (see abbrevs.) (Notes on origins & members in Co.Cork).

Lysaght or **MacLysaght**

Our Story. William Ignatius MacLysaght. Limerick, 1979.

Short study of a transplanted family in the 17th century (McLysaght). E. MacLysaght. Dublin: Browne & Nolan, 1935. (LDS Lib. 929.2415 M226ml (Ref to Arthur, O'Brien, White).

History of Kenny, Lysaght, O'Loghlen, and related Clare families. NLI ms. 2109–2110.

Lt. William Lysaght (of Clare) in 'King James' IAL' (Notes on family pre-1780).

Lyster or **Leicester**

Memorials of an ancient house. H. Lyster Denny. Edinburgh, 1913.

Lyster pioneers of lower Canada and the West: the Story of the Lysters of the old Queen's County. Ellinor Lyster Eswyn. Qualicum Beach, B.C., Canada, 1984.

Lt. Thomas Leicester (of Laois) in 'King James' IAL' (Notes on family members pre-1700).

M: *For all Mc or Mac names please look at the alphabetic entry for the part of the name after the Mc/Mac e.g. for McCann see Cann etc.)*

Mackey *see* **Pearson**

Macoboy

Pedigree of Macoboy Family of Cork: IGRS Library (Leader Collection).

Macraith

Islandmagrath (Co. Clare) and the Macraith family, The Other Clare 21 (1997) p.16.

Macutchen *see* **Rothwell**

Madden, Madan or **O'Madden**

The O'Maddens of Hy Many: some pages from the history of a distinguished family. T. M. Madden. Pr.pr Dublin, 1899. (NLI Call No. Ir 9292 m256).

The O'Maddens of Silanchia, or Siol Anmchadha, and their descendants, from the Milesian invasion of Ireland to the present time. JGAHS 1 (1900–01) 184–95; 2 (1902) 21–3.

The Madan family and Maddens in Ireland and England. F. Madan. London, 1933.

Pedigree of Madden Family of Cork: IGRS Library (Leader Collection).

The Co. Cork Ancestry of the Maddens of Australia. Ir. Anc. 16 (1) 14–20.

Lt Col. Edward Madden (of Galway) in 'King James' IAL' (Notes on family members pre-1700).

Madill *see* **Ireton**

Magan

Magan, William. Umma-More. The Story of an Irish Family. History of the Magan family of Umma, near Ballymore, Co. Westmeath, from ca. 1590. Salisbury: Element Books, 1983.

Papers (e.g., deeds, leases, and pedigrees) relating to Magan of Emoe et al. Longford/Westmeath Library; RIA (Upton Papers), and (LDS Mf. 101011).

The story of Ireland: A history of an ancient family & their country. William Magan. Shaftesbury: Element 2000. (ISBN 1862047286).

Magawly

Magawlys of Calry. J. Old Athlone Soc. 1 (2) (1970/71) 61–73; 1 (3) (1972/73) 147–60; 1(4) (1974/5) 265-6.

Magee

The Magees of Belfast and Dublin. F. J. Bigger. Belfast, 1916.

Magennis *see also* **Guinness**

The Magennises of Clanconnell. D.D.Atkinson. Ulster J. Arch., 2nd ser., 1 (1895) 30–2.

Magennis of Iveagh. JRSAI 62 (1932) 96–102.

Notes on the family of Magennis, formerly lords of Iveagh, Newry and Mourne. E. F. Danne. Salt Lake City, 1878.

Pedigree of the Magennis (Guinness) family of New Zealand and of Dublin. Richard Linn. Christchurch, N.Z., 1897.

Mageoghan

The Mageoghans. Riocht na Midhe 4 (3) (1969) 63–86.

Maghlin *see* **O'Shaughnessy**

Magill *see* **Kenny**

Magrath *see also* **McGrath**

Capt. Redmond Magrath (of Clare) in 'King James' IAL' (Notes on family pre-1700).

Maguire *see also* **Ashmur, MacGuire, Langham**

The Maguires of Fermanagh. An t'Athair P. Ua Duinnin; Dublin: Gill, 1917.

Pedigree of Maguire Family of Cork. IGRS Library (Leader Collection).

Clan Maguire of Fermanagh. Belfast: Maguire Clan Society, 1992. (LDS Lib. 929.2415 A1 no. 78).

The Maguires: Princes of Fermanagh and Barons of Enniskillen. Familia 2 (6) (1990).

The lands of the Maguires of Tempo in the seventeenth century. Clogher Record 12 (3) (1987) 305.

A Maguire family in France. Clogher Record 5 (2) (1964) 222-226.

Maher *see also* **Meagher**

Maher of Ballinkeele (Wexford). Wexford Gentry Vol. 2 (see abbreviations).

Mahon

Mahon Papers (Castlegar, Co. Galway). Anal. Hib. 25: 77–93.

Mahon of Strokestown, Co. Roscommon. Ir. Anc. 10 (2) (1978) 77–80.

Nicholas Mahon and Seventeenth-Century Roscommon. Ir. Gen. 3 (6) (1963) 228–35.

MacMahon *see also* **McNamara**

Some MacMahon wills from Clogher Diocese. Clogher Record 14 (1) (1991) p.27-36.

Pedigree of McMahon Family of Cork: IGRS Library (Leader Collection).

Col. Art McMahon (of Monaghan) in 'King James' IAL' (Notes on family members pre-1700).

The MacMahons of Monaghan. (1500-1593) Clogher Record 1 (3) (1955) 22-38

The MacMahons of Monaghan. (1593-1603) Clogher Record 1 (4) (1956) 85-107.

The MacMahons of Monaghan (1603-1640). Clogher Record 2 (1) (1958) 148-169.

The MacMahons of Monaghan [1641]. Clogher Record 2 (3) (1959) 490-502

The MacMahons of Monaghan (1642-1654). Clogher Record 4 (3) (1962) 190-194

Sir Brian and Lady Mary MacMahon Clogher Record 15 (3) (1996) 133-144 A McMahon family of Clones. Clogher Record 2 (3) (1959) 514.

The McMahons of Lisoarty, Clones. Clogher Record 12 (3) (1987) 389.

Colla Dubh MacMahon, his ancestors & descendants. Clogher Record 8 (2) (1974) 194.

French McMahons. Old Limerick J. 25 (1989) 105-112.

Mahony or O'Mahony

The O Mahony journal: organ of the O'Mahony Records Society. Bray, Co. Wicklow Pub, from 1971 -?.

History of the O'Mahony Septs of Kinelmeky & Ivagha. JCHAS 12(1906)183–95; 13(1907)27–36,73–80,105–15, 182–92; 14 (1908) 12–21,74–81, 127–41,189–99; 15(1909) 7–18, 63–75,118–26,184–96; 16 (1910) 9–24, 97–113.

The Distribution of the O'Mahoneys in County Cork. O'Mahoney J. 16 (1993).

Three Kerry families: O'Mahony, Conway & Spotswood. S. T. MacCarthy. Folkestone 1923. (LDS Lib. 929.2415 M279m).

Pedigree of O'Mahoney/Mahoney Family of Cork: IGRS Library (Leader Collection).

(O')Mahoney, Mahony, Mathuna in 'Family Names of Co. Cork' (see abbrevs.) (Notes on origins & members in Co.Cork).

The Mahonys of Kerry. JKAHS (New Series)4 (1917–18) 171–90, 223–35.

Capt. John Mahony in 'King James' IAL' (Notes on family members pre-1700).

Mahoney of Killamon. Old Limerick J. 25 (1989) 11-13.

O'Mahoney Extractions From 1901 Census of Ireland. O'Mahoney J. 16 (1993).

O'Mahoneys Around Dunmanusboy, Cork. O'Mahoney J. 16 (1993).

Malcolmson *see* Barcroft
O'Malley

O'Malley journal, 1997. Galway: O'Malley Clan Association, 1997. (LDS Lib. 929.2415 Om1omj).

Genealogy of the O'Malleys of the Owals. Philadelphia, 1913. (NLI 9292 o21).

Note on the O'Malley Lordship at the Close of the 16th Century. JGAHS 24 (1950–51) 27–57.

O'Malleys Between 1607 and 1725. JGAHS 25(1952) 32–46.

O'Malley: people and places. Sheila Mulloy. Whitegate, Co. Clare: Ballinakella Press, 1988. (ISBN: 0946538204) (LDS Lib. 929.2415 Om1m).

O'Malley Papers (Co. Mayo). Anal. Hib. 25: 185–202.

The last O'Malley Chief & his descendants. Cathair na Mart 19 (1999) 148–166.

Malone

Malones of Westmeath. Gaelic Gleanings 1(1) (1981) 9–12; 1(2)46–48; 1(3)81–84; 1(4)127–30; 2(1) (1982)9–10.

Maloney *see* **Moloney, Donnelly**

Mangan *see* **Mongan.**

Mannion *see* **Murphy**

Mansfield

The Lattin and Mansfield Families, in the Co. Kildare. JCKAS 3 (1899–1902) 186–90.

Mansfield Papers (Co. Kildare). Anal. Hib. 20: 92–125.

Mansfield – Bakers-Mallow-Melbourne Geelong. Mallow Field Club J. 12 (1994) (Mansfield family).

MacManus

Genealogical memoranda relating to the Sotheron family and the sept MacManus. C. Sotheran. 1871–73.

Where rests our Genesis: an historical note on ...clan McManus of North Roscommon. . . . Comp. by Rose, Peter and Michael McManus. Durham: McManus Family History Society, 1997. (LDS Lib. 929.2415 M227wr).

O'Maolconaire or **O'Maelconaire** *see* **O'Mulconry**

Mapowder

Pedigree of Mapowder Family of Cork: IGRS Library (Leader Collection).

Mara *see* **Meara**

Marisco

The family of Marisco. IRSAI 61 (1931) 22–38, 89–112, 62 (1932) 50–74.

Markham

Markham of Nunstown and Callinafercy, Co. Kerry. Ir. Anc. 16 (2) (1984) 60.

The Marmion family in Ireland and in general . Chevalier William F. K. Marmion, Lord of Duhallow. St. Lazarus Press, Cork 1997. (ISBN 0953130304).

Marshal

The Marshal Pedigree. JRSAI 43 (1913) 1–29.

Martin or **Martyn** *see also* **Ashmur, McNamara, Orr, O'Shaughnessy**

Genealogy of the family of Martin of Ballinahinch Castle. GO pedigree & notes. A. E. S. Martin. Winnipeg, 1890.

Genealogy of the Martins of Ross. Seymour Clarke. Inverness: Northern Chronicle, 1910. (LDS Lib. 929.2415 M363c).

Pedigree of Martin/Martyn Family of Cork: IGRS Library (Leader Collection).

The Martin family. Comp. by George Castor Martin. Frankford: Martin & Allardyce, 1911. (LDS Lib. 929.2415 M363m).

Copies of census returns for Martin family for the year 1841. NAI Mf. 5248 (13).

Martin family Bible data (Ulster): Armagh Co. Museum Ms. P8: (LDS Mf.1279356).

Martins of Irish birth, married in Victoria, Australia. Irish Family History 7 (1991) 30-32.

Marum

The Parish of Aharney and the Marum Family. Old Kilkenny Review 3 (1976) p. 169-174.

Mason *see* Switzer

Massy or Massey

Genealogical account of the Massy family. Dublin, 1890.

Pedigree of Massey Family of Cork: IGRS Library (Leader Collection).

Mathew or Matthew(s)

Genealogy of the Earls of Landaff of Thomastown, Co. Tipperary. n.d. [1945?].

Father Mathew's family: the Mathews in Tipperary. Capuchin Annual (1957) 143–52.

The Mathews of Bonnetstown, County Kilkenny. Old Kilkenny Review 4 (2) (1990) p. 767-769.

Maude

History of some of the ancestors and descendants of Sir Robert Maude, Bt. Francis Maude. London, 1881.

The Maude family. Francis Maude. London, 1903.

Maunsell or Mounsell

History of the Maunsell or Mansel family. R. G. Maunsell. Cork. 1903.

Pedigree of Maunsell Family of Cork: IGRS Library (Leader Collection).

The history of the family of Maunsell. E. P. Statham. 3 vols. London, 1917.

The Maunsell family of Islandmagrath (Co. Clare). The Other Clare 21 (1997) p. 68.

John Mounsell Will, 1637. Genealogists Mag. 16 (3) (Sep 1969) (re Mounsell family).

Maxwell *see also* Hutchinson

Seize Quartiers connected with royal descents of Henry Maxwell, 7th Lord Farnham. Henry Maxwell. Cavan, 1850.

Farnham descents from Henry III and subsequent Kings of England. (3 Parts) Henry Maxwell, 7th Lord Farnham. Henry Maxwell. Cavan, 1860.

Pedigree of Maxwell Family of Cork: IGRS Library (Leader Collection).

The annals of one branch of the Maxwell family in Ulster. William George

Maxwell. Sussex, 1957. & supplement of additions and corrections, 1958.

The Maxwell family – Descendants of John & Ann Maxwell (1701-1894). Henry D. Maxwell. Pennsylvania. 1895.

Maxwell-Barry of Newtownbarry (Wexford). Wexford Gentry Vol. 2 (see abbreviations).

Mayberry

Large Pedigree Book for Mayberry Family. IGRS Library (Leader Collection).

Maynard

The Maynards of Curriglas, Co. Cork. (ex Notes & Queries). JCHAS 22 (1960) 107–8, 164.

Pedigree of Maynard Family of Cork: IGRS Library (Leader Collection).

Mayne

Erskine Mayne: the rise and fall of a famous Belfast Bookselling dynasty. Familia 12 (1996) pp. 75-78.

Meade or Meagh

The Meades of Inishannon. J. A. Meade. Victoria, B.C., Acme Press 1956. (LDS Lib. 929.2415 M461mj) (ref to DeCourcy).

The Meades of Meaghstown Castle & Tissaxon, 1300-1766. John A. Meade. Victoria, B.C: Acme Press 1953. (LDSLib. 929.2415 M461m) (Ref to De Courcy, Galwey, Roche & variant spellings Meagh and Mede).

The Pooles of Mayfield. R. ffolliott. Dublin: Hodges Figgis (1958). (Re Meagh or Meade of Buttevant, Ballintober & Ballymartle:1341 to 1750's).

Andrew Meade of Ireland & Virginia: His ancestors & descendants. P. Hamilton Baskerville (Pub.1921) reprinted Heritage Books, USA. 1997.

Meagh *see* Meade

O'Meagher or Meagher *see also* Blake, O'Kennedy

Historical notices of the O'Meaghers of Ikerrin. J. C. O'Meagher. London, 1887. (LDS Lib. 929.2415 Om2o).

The Meaghers. Norine Meagher. Transcript in NLI 1980.

Records of the four Tipperary Septs. Martin Callanan. JAG Publishing, Galway 1938. (ISBN 0952660806).

O'Meagher, Meagher and Maher—and their dispersal in Tipperary. Tipp.Hist.J. 6 (1993) p. 160-166.

Meagher's – Maher's of Killane, Co. Tipperary and their descendants in Australia 1806-1898. Betty Bates. Bairnsdale, Victoria. 1998. (ISBN 0646358111).

Meara, Mara or O'Meara

Major Francis Meara (Toomavara, Co Tipperary) in 'King James' IAL' (Family line pre-1790).

The O'Mearas of Lissinisky. Tipp.Hist.J. 9 (1996) p.117-135.

Meehans or **O'Meehans**

The O'Meehans of Leitrim, Tipperary, Laois & Clare. (LDS Lib. 929.2415 A1 no. 75).

O'Melaghlin

Burke, Sir B. The O'Melaghlins, Kings of Meath in Viscissitudes of Families, vol. 2. London, 1883: p. 336–51.

Melance

Copies of census returns for the Melance family for 1831; NAI Mf. 5247 (3).

O'Mellan *see* **O'Mullan.**

Mellett

The Mellett sept of South Mayo. S. Mayo Family Res. J. 9 (1996) 22-25.

Mercer

The Mercer chronicle: an epitome of family history. E. S. Mercer. Pr.pr. 1866.

Meredith *see* **Tweedy**

Merrick

Pedigree of Merrick Family of Cork: IGRS Library (Leader Collection).

Merry

The Waterford Merrys. JW&SEIAS 16 (1913) 30–35.

Metcalfe

Pedigree of Metcalfe Family of Cork: IGRS Library (Leader Collection).

MacMillan

The MacMillans & their septs. Somerled MacMillan. Glasgow: K. & R. Davidson, 1952. (LDS Lib. 929.2415 M288m).

Miller

All worlds possible: the domain of the Millers of Coolybrown. Patrick J. O'Connor. Midleton, Co. Cork: Litho Press. (ISBN: 0951218441). (LDS Lib. 929.2415 M612op).

Millikin *see* **Bernard**

Mills

Notes on the Mills Family of Headford, Co. Galway and Roscommon. JAPMD 10: 241.

Milner-Barry

Pedigree of Milner-Barry Family of Cork: IGRS Library (Leader Collection).

Minchin *see* **Ferrar**

Minehan

On Looking back: Fragments of a family history. M.J. Minehan. NLI Ms 27, 653. (Minehans in Irl, Australia & NZ).

Mitchell *see also* **Ashmur**

Pedigree of Mitchell Family of Cork: IGRS Library (Leader Collection).

Moat

Copies of census returns for Moat family for the years 1821, 1831, 1841, 1851; NAI Mf. 5246 (6); 5247 (1); 5248 (14, 35, 37); 5249 (5).

Molloy or **O'Molloy**

Irish chiefs and leaders. Rev. Paul Walsh. Chs. xv–xvii. Dublin, 1960.

The Molloy family of Kells. Ir.Gen. 3 (1961) 187–9.

O'Molloys of Fircall. Riocht na Midhe 5(3) (1973) 14–45.

Moloney *see* **Donnelly**

Molyneux *see also* **Swift**

An account of the family and descendants of Thomas Molyneux. Capel Molyneux. Evesham, 1820.

Pedigree of Molyneux of Castle Dillon, Co. Armagh. Sir T. Phillips. Evesham, 1819.

The Molyneux family. Dublin Hist. Rec. 16 (1960) 9–15.

Family of Molyneux. Irish Builder. April 1, 1887, p. 101-102.

Monck

The Moncks and Charleville House. A Wicklow Family in the 19th Century. Elizabeth Batt. Dublin: Blackwater, 1979. (LDS Lib. 929.2415 M743b) (Ref to Brooke, Clancarty, Cole, McClintock, Royse, Trench).

Monckton

Monckton of Co. Limerick. Ir. Anc. 4 (1) (1972) 15–21.

Mongan or **Mongon**

Mongon family records: Pedigrees of Thomas Mongon, 1716. GO Ms. no. 516; LDS Mf.257821.

Monroe

Foulis Castle and the Monroes of Lower Iveagh. Horace Monroe. London, 1929.

Montgomery *see also* **Kenny**, **Boyd**, **Willoughby**

The making of the Montgomery manuscripts. Familia 2 (2) 1986 pp. 23-29.

The origin and history of the Montgomerys. Count Gabriel de Montgomery. London, 1948.

The Montgomery manuscripts (1603–1706) compiled from family papers by W. Montgomery. Ed. G. Hill. Belfast, Cleeland & Dargan 1869. (LDS Lib. 929.2415 M767m).

A genealogical history of the family of Montgomery of Scotland … of Mount Alexander and Grey Abbey in Ireland. Mrs. E. O'Reilly. N.p. 1842. (NLI Ir 9292 m24).

A family history of Montgomery of Ballyleck, Co. Monaghan, now of Beaulieu, Co. Louth. G. S. M. Belfast, 1887.

The Montgomerys, the Sinclairs and Drumbeg House. Donegal Ann. 44 (1992) p.51-62.

Montgomery of Alamcin and the Montgomerys of Moville. Donegal Ann. 47 (1995) p.9-23.

Montmorency

Les Montmorency de France et d'Irlande. Paris, 1828.

Moody *see also* **Lowry**

Joseph Ledlie and William Moody, their background and descendants. Pittsburgh, 1961.

Moone

The Moone Family of Doon (Co. Limerick). Irish Family History 2 (1986) 71–81.

Mooney

Pedigree of Mooney Family of Cork: IGRS Library (Leader Collection).

Moore *see also* **Acheson**

The family of Moore. Countess of Drogheda. Dublin, 1906.

The Moores of Moore Hall. Joseph Hone. London: Jonathan Cape, 1939. (LDS Lib. 929.2415 M781h).

The Anglo-Norman Moores in Ireland. Gen., N.S. 33(1916) 1–8.

The Moores of the city of Drogheda. Gen., N.S. 33(1916)127–8.

Notes on the Moore Family, Tinraheen, Co. Wexford. JAPMD 9: 189; 10: 252.

Moore of Mooremount. Pedigree in 'Swanzy Notebooks'. RCB Library, Dublin.

Moore of Moyne Hall. Pedigree in 'Swanzy Notebooks'. RCB Library, Dublin.

Moore of Tullyvin. Pedigree in 'Swanzy Notebooks'. RCB Library, Dublin.

Moore of Rutland Square, Dublin. Pedigree in 'Swanzy Notebooks'. RCB Library, Dublin.

The Moore Family of Brize Castle, Co. Mayo. JRSAI 31 (1901) 434-435.

Sir Thomas More: his descendants in the male line: the Moores of Moorehall, Co. Mayo. JRSAI 36(1906) 224–30.

The Moores of Ardee. CLAHJ 7(4) (1932) p. 472-484.

Pedigree of Moore Family of Cork: IGRS Library (Leader Collection).

History and genealogy of Moore Family of Fayette Co., Pennsylvania. Rogan H. Moore. Heritage Books, USA 1999.

History of the Moore family. Compiled by Anne, Countess of Drogheda. Belfast: W. & G. Baird, 1902. (LDS Lib. 929.2415 M781d) (Refs to Clifford, Loftus & Ponsonby).

Grandfather's box: an Irish family history (Moore: Co. Antrim). Kate J. Harkness. Isle of Wight: 1993. (LDS Lib. 929.2415 M781hk).

Moores and Hanlons of the Creeslough, Donegal area. compiled by James W. Devitt. (LDS Lib. 929.2415 M787d) (Refs to Alcorn, Algoe, Campbell, Devitt, Hay, McKinley, Stewart, Wilkinson, Wilson).

Moorhouse

A Moorhouse Family of Dublin, Carlow, and Kildare. Ir. Anc. 9 (1) (1977) 15–18.

Moran

The Morans and the Mulveys of South Leitrim. Ardagh and Clonmacnois
Antiq. J. 1 (3) (1932) 14–19.

The O'Moran septs. Ir.Gen. 4 (1970). 167–73; (1971) 267–76.

O'Morchoe

O'Morchoe of Oulartleigh. Wexford Gentry Vol. 1 (see abbreviations).

More or **O'More**

Notes on an Old Pedigree of the O'More Family of Leix. JRSAI 35(1905)
53–59.

Historical Notes on the O'Mores & Their Territory of Leix, to the End of the
16th Century. JCKAS 6 (1909–11) 1–88.

The O'More Family of Balyna in the Co. Kildare, ca. 1774. JCKAS 9 (1918–
21) 227–91, 318–30.

Sir Thomas More; Descendants in the Male Line: The Moores of Moorehall,
Co. Mayo. JRSAI 36 (1906) 224–30.

Morgan

Families of Hodges and Morgan of Old Abbey, Co. Limerick. Ir. Anc. 11 (2)
(1979) 77–84.

Pedigree of Morgan Family of Cork: IGRS Library (Leader Collection).

The Pooles of Mayfield. Rosemary ffolliott. Dublin: Hodges Figgis (1958).
(Deals with Morgans of Tivoli, Cork:1800 to 1950's).

The Morgan family of 'Niddrie': History of a group of related Irish-Austral
ian families. Richard Morgan. Essendon Richard Spillane 190. (ISBN
0731683951) (NLI Ir 9292 m73).

Morgill

Pedigree of Morgill Family of Cork: IGRS Library (Leader Collection).

Moriarty or **O'Moriarty**

The O'Moriarty family. J. King. in 'History of Co. Kerry' 265–79. Dublin,
1910.

Morris *see also* **McNamara**

Morris of Ballybeggan and Castle Morris, Co. Kerry. The Marquis of Ruvigny
and Raineval. Pr.pr. 1904.

Memoirs of my family: together with some researches into the early history
of the Morris families of Tipperary, Galway and Mayo. E. M. Chapman.
Pr.pr. London 1928. (NLI Call No. 9292 m13).

Pedigree of Morris Family of Cork: IGRS Library (Leader Collection).

The Pooles of Mayfield. R. ffolliott. Dublin: Hodges Figgis (1958). (Re: Morris
of Castle Salem & Benduff, Cork).

Capts. Harvey & Redmond Morris (of Kilkenny & Offaly) in 'King James'
IAL' (Notes on family origins pre-1700).

Henry Morris: Family papers. CLAHJ I (4) (1907) p. 65-72. (with mention of
Blake family).

Origin & distribution of the surname Morris in Ireland. Andrew J. Morris. Fort Collins, Colo: 1984. (LDS Lib. 929.2415 A1 no. 40.

The family background of Henry Morris. Clogher Record 8 (3) (1975) 259.

Morrison *see also* **Murphy**

The Pooles of Mayfield. Rosemary ffolliott. Dublin: Hodges Figgis (1958). (re Morrisons of Tivoli, Cork City).

Morrow *see* **Boyd**

Morton

Pedigree of Morton Family of Cork: IGRS Library (Leader Collection).

Mosman *see* **Ireton**

Moulton *see* **Rothwell**

Mounsell *see* **Maunsell**

Moutray

Moutray of Seafield & Roscobie, now of Favour Royal, Co. Tyrone: an historical and genealogical memoir of the family in Scotland, England, Ireland and America. Marquis de Ruvigny and Raineval London: Elliot Stock, 1902

Mowbray *see* **Stinson**

Mulcahy

The Widow Mulcahy: from Golden Vale to Goulborn Valley. Old Limerick J. 23 (1988) 125-128.

Mulconry or **O'Mulconry**

The learned family of Ó Maelconaire. in: 'Irish Men of Learning'. Paul Walsh; Three Candles, Dublin (1947) (A family line from 1314-1900).

The O'Maolconaire Family. JGAHS 20 (1942–43) 82–88; & 29 (1940–41) 118–46.

Ballymulconry and the Mulconrys (Co. Roscommon). M.J.Connellan. Dublin.

Mulhern

Pedigree of Mulhern Family of Cork: IGRS Library (Leader Collection).

Mulholland

Mulholland: hereditary keepers of Clogh Columcille. JRSAI 30 (1930) 47, 49, 51, 52

O'Mullally or **Lally**

History of O'Mullally and Lally clans (800–1940 AD). by Dennis P. O'Mullally. Chicago: pr.pr. 1942 (NLI Call no. Ir 9292 o19: (LDS Lib. 929.2415 Om8o) (Refs to MacDavitt, Dawson), MacFirbis [Forbes], O'Kelly, O'Neill).

Mullan or **O'Mullan**

O'Mullen, O'Kane and O'Mellan. The Ulster clans T. H. Mullin and J. E. Mullan. Belfast, 1966.

Roots in Ulster soil. T. H. Mullin (Refs to: Mullan; Barbour of Argarvan ;

Black of Kildress & Cookstown: Black of Doons; Black of Drumsurn; Forsythes; Wallace; Brown of Ballinaloob; Henderson; Hendersons of Ann St.; Holdom & Anderson) Belfast: BNL Printing Co.:1968. (LDS Lib. 929.2415 M911m).

O'Mullane

The O'Mullanes and Whitechurch. JCHAS 48 (1953) 20–21.

The O'Mullanes. JCHAS 48 (1953) 97.

Pedigree of O'Mullane Family of Cork: IGRS Library (Leader Collection).

Catherine O'Mullane: Mrs. O'Connell, mother of Daniel O'Connell, the Liberator. Ir.Gen. 2 (1953) 311–16.

McMullen

Pedigree of McMullen Family of Cork: IGRS Library (Leader Collection).

Mulligan *see* Cleland

Mulloy or Molloy

Capts. 'Greene' & William Mulloy (of Hughstown, Roscommon) in 'King James' IAL' (Notes on family pre-1700).

Mulock

The family of Mulock. Sir Edmund Bewley. Dublin, 1905.

O'Mulryan or Mulryan *see* Ryan

Mulvey

The Morans and the Mulveys of South Leitrim. Ardagh & Clonmacnois Antiq. J. 1 (3) (1932) 14–19.

Murphy *see also* Devlin

Genealogy of a North Louth family. CLAHJ 18(2) (1974) p.105-109. (family of Pat Murphy 1750).

Murphys of Muskerry. JCHAS 219 (1969) 1–19.

Murphy of Gragara and Castle Annaghs. Old Kilkenny Review. 20 (1968) p.54-61.

Pedigree of Murphy Family of Cork: IGRS Library (Leader Collection).

Murphy, O'Murchu in 'Family Names of Co. Cork' (see abbrevs.) (Notes on origins & members in Co.Cork).

Eight generations (Progenitors of John F. Vickers & Agnes M. Murphy). D.C. Vickers. Manchester: Pr.pr. 1996. (LDS Lib. 929.2415 V663v) (Refs to Mannion (Co. Galway), Lynch (Galway), Tyrell (Sligo), Joyce (Mayo) & Greenall, Harrison, Atkins, Morrison, Casey, Kellett, Ward, Carruthers, Hassard, Nuttall, Davis).

Brief Outline of the history of the family of John Blackwell (1800-85) & Elizabeth Biggs Murphy (1805-88). Ir.Am. Gen.(1979) 247-252. Also Pub. by Authors Ontario 1878. (NLI Call No. Ir 9291 p3).

Murray or McMurray

Pedigree of McMurray Family of Cork: IGRS Library (Leader Collection).

McMurtry

A guide to Irish McMurtry history & genealogy. Richard K. McMurtry. (LDS Lib. 929.2415 A1 no. 9).

Musters *see* **Wandesforde**

Myers or **Meyers**

Pedigree of Meyers/Myers Family of Cork: IGRS Library (Leader Collection).

Myhills

Predecessors and Successors of the Myhills of Killarney (Kilkenny). Old Kilkenny Review (1995) 94.

Myles

Large Pedigree Book for Myles Family. IGRS Library (Leader Collection).

MacNaghten *see* **McNaughton**

Nagle

The Nagles of Mount Nagle, Annakissy (Co. Cork). Ir.Gen. 2 (11) (1954) 337–48.

The Nagles of Mount Nagle (Co. Cork) & later of Jamestown and Dunower, Barts. Ir.Gen. 2 (12) (1955) 377–89.

The Nagles of Garnavilla. Ir.Gen. 3 (1956) 17–24.

The Nagles of Ballygriffin, and Nano Nagle. Ir.Gen. 3 (1957) 67–73.

Capt. Francis Nagle (of Cork) in 'King James' IAL' (Notes on family members pre-1747).

Nagle, Nangle, DeNogla in 'Family Names of Co. Cork' (see abbrevs.) (Notes on origins & members in Co.Cork)

Nano and the Nagles. Mallow Field Club J. 5 (1987).

MacNair

McNair Genealogies. Compiled by A.A. Macnair. Gloucester: 1981. (LDS Lib. 929.2415 M231m) (Refs to Cutting, Irvine, Jehne, Lawson, Rudge, Williamson).

Nally or **McNally**

Pedigree of McNally Family of Cork: IGRS Library (Leader Collection).

The Nallys of Balla (Co Mayo). S. Mayo Family Res. J. 5 (1992) 52-56.

MacNamara

The MacNamara name. E. J. McAuliffe. Other Clare 5(1981) 23. (Reprint from Irish Herald. San Francisco).

The story of an Irish sept. N. MacNamara. London, 1896.

Histoire d'un sept irlandais: Les Macnamara. Eugene Forgues. Paris, 1901.

The pedigree of John McNamara sq. (Co. Clare). R. W. Twigge. 1908. (NLI Call No. Ir 9292 m19).

Capt John MacNamara (of Tulla, Co Clare) in 'King James' IAL' (Notes on family members pre-1747).

The Macnamaras of Doolin and Ennistymon (Co. Clare). Dal gCais 11 (1993) p. 10-19.

Pedigrees of Co. Clare, Galway and Limerick families (Inc. McNamara, Taylor, Burnell, Martin, Morris, Fitzgerald, D'Arcy, Lynch, Geigan, Butler, Lambert, Blake-Forster, Creagh, Blackall, O'Shaughnessy, MacMahon, Wilson, England, O'Fahy, Hickey, Baker, Flanagan). (GO Ms. no. 520; LDS Mf.257821).

Nangle

Ballysax and the Nangle family. JCKAS 6 (1909–11) 96–100.

A short account of the Nangle Family. F.E. Nangle & J.F.T. Nangle. Pr.pr.. Ardglass, Co. Down, 1986. (LDS Lib. 929.2415 A1 no. 71).

Capts. Walter & Geo. Nangle (of Westmeath) in 'King James' IAL' (Notes on family pre-1700).

Nash

Genealogies of the Nash and allied families. Typescript: Edward F. Nash. Florida 1968. (NLI Ir 9292 n3).

Pedigree of Nash Family of Cork: IGRS Library (Leader Collection).

McNaughten or **McNaughton**

Family quest (McNaughten). Angus D. MacNaughten. (LDS Lib. 929.2415 M232m. (Ref to Irwin, Riddel Walker, Woodley & Corric).

Gleanings in Family History from the Antrim Coast: The MacNaghtens and MacNeills. Ulster J. Arch. 8, 1st ser. (1860) 127–44.

MacNeale *see* **McNeill**

Neary

In search of a Louth family, the Nearys. CLAHJ 15(1968) 239–50.

MacNeill or **McNeale** *see also* **Stewart**

Copies of census returns for the McNeil family for the year 1821; NAI Mf.5446 (4).

Gleanings in Family History from the Antrim Coast, The MacNaghtens & MacNeills. Ulster J. Arch. 8, (1860) 127–44.

Material for a MacNeale pedigree. Ir.Gen. 1(1942) 327–33.

The McNeills of Cushendun and the McNeiles of Ballycastle. The Glynns 1 (1973).

Neill and O'Neill *see also* **Gower, O'Hagan, O'Hanlon, O'Mullally**

Neills of Bangor. Ian Wilson. Pub. by the author, 1982.

The O'Neills of Ulster: their history and genealogy. Thomas Mathews. Dublin, 1907.

The will and family of Hugh O'Neill, Earl of Tyrone ed. Rev. Paul Walsh. Dublin, 1930.

Irish chiefs and leaders. Rev. Paul Walsh. Chs. xi–xii. Dublin, 1960.

The O'Neills in Spain. Micheline Walsh. (O'Donnell lecture). Dublin, 1960.

The O'Neills of County Cork. Germaine C. Grady. Genealogical Pub. Co., Baltimore, 1999

Pedigree of O'Neill Family of Cork: IGRS Library (Leader Collection).

The Clan Nial or Neil in Ireland, 279-1030 AD. M. Westacott. Sydney: Westworth Books 1970.

Gleann an Óir: History of the O'Neill family of Ballyneale, Co. Tipperary. (In Irish). Eoghan Ó Néill. Dublin: 1988.

O'Neill: people and places. Sean O'Neill. Whitegate, Clare: Ballinakella Press, 1991. (LDS Lib. 929.2415 On2o

The O'Neills of Leinster: an investigation into the origins of the O'Neills of Moyacomb. Seán Ó Néill. Belfast: Irish Heritage Association, 1992.

The son of Sir Phelim O'Neill. Seanchas Ardmhacha 1(2) (1954) 132-150. (Genealogy of family pre-1700).

Black Hugh O'Neill (1610-1660). Seanchas Ardmhacha 6(2) (1972) 287-296. (O'Neill descendants in Spain).

The O'Neills of the Fews. Seanchas Ardmhacha 7(1) (1973) 1-64 (history to 1650's); 7(2) (1974) 263-315 (Genealogy of descendants in Spain); 8(2) 1977 386-413 (Genealogies of O'Neills of Anagad, Drumbee, Carran, Dorsey and Ummerican in Tyrone).

Abstracts of some Neale and O'Neill wills, administrations, and marriage licence bonds from Diocese of Ferns. Ir.Anc. 11(1) (1979) 27-30.

Hugo O'Neill's Ancestry. Irish Heritage Links 3 (7) (1989) 12-22.

Neilson

The Neilsons of Rademon and Down: Educators and Gaelic Scholars. Familia 2 (4) (1988).

Nelligan or **Neligan**

Pedigree of Nelligan Family of Cork: IGRS Library (Leader Collection).

Nesbitt *see also* **Ashmur, Boyd, Lyons**

History of family of Nisbet or Nesbitt in Scotland & Ireland. A.Nesbitt. Pr.pr. Torquay, 1898 (NLI Call No. Ir 9292 n1).

History of the Nesbitt family: sometime resident in the townland of Corglass, parish of Ematris, County Monaghan, Ireland. compiled by Robert Nesbitt. Belfast: M'Caw, Stevenson & Orr, 1930. (LDS Lib. 929.2415 N367n (Refs to Coburn, Greer, Henry, Shannon, Swann, Thornton).

Nesbitt of Woodhill. Pedigree in 'Swanzy Notebooks'. RCB Library, Dublin.

Netterville *see also* **Blakeney**

Richard Netterville (of Dowth, Co. Meath) in 'King James' IAL' (Notes on family members pre-1700).

Netterville peerage: case on behalf of Arthur J. Netterville of Cruicerath, Co. Meath, claiming to be Viscount Netterville of Douth. London: C.F. Hodgson, 1867. (LDS Lib. 929.2415 N387n (Ref to Laurence, MacEvoy).

Nevil

> The Pooles of Mayfield. Rosemary ffolliott. Dublin: Hodges Figgis (1958).
> (Re: Nevils of England, Wicklow & Cork).

Nevins

> The Nevins Family 1800–1840. Decies 37 (1988) 9–19.

Newenham

> Pedigree of Newenham Family of Cork: IGRS Library (Leader Collection).

Nicholson

> Pedigree of Nicholson Family of Cork: IGRS Library (Leader Collection).

Nihell

> Nihell of Co. Clare and Co. Limerick. Ir. Gen. 4 (5) (1972) 496–506.

Nixon

> Families of French of Belturbet & Nixon of Fermanagh & descendants. H.B.
> Swanzy. Dublin: Alex.Thom 1908.

Noble

> Noble of Co. Monaghan. Pedigree in 'Swanzy Notebooks'. RCB Library,
> Dublin.
>
> Capt. John Noble (of Kildare) in 'King James' IAL' (Family line pre-1689).

Nolan or **Nowlan**

> Pedigree of Nowlan/Nolan Family of Cork: IGRS Library (Leader Collec-
> tion).
>
> The Nolans & Costelloes of Listowel, Limerick & Calgary. Old Limerick J.
> 27 (1990) 13-19 (mainly Nolan).

Noonan

> Noonan, Nunan in 'Family Names of Co. Cork' (see abbrevs.) (Notes on ori-
> gins & members in Co.Cork).

Norreys *see* **Jephson**

Norton *see* **Wandesforde**

Notter

> Genealogical info on Notter families of Co. Cork, 1690-1880. Ms. (LDS
> Lib.929.2415 A1 no. 5).
>
> Pedigree of Notter Family of Cork: IGRS Library (Leader Collection).

Nottingham

> Nottinghams of Ballyowen. Reportorium Novum 1 (2) 1956: 323–24.

Nugent *see also* **Kelly (Ainsworth Misc.), & Skelly.**

> Historical sketch of the Nugent family. J. C. Lyons, Ladestown, 1853.
>
> Nugent Papers. [Mount Nugent, Co. Cavan]. Anal.Hib. 20, 126–215.
>
> Nugent & Rochfort families (biographies, property & pedigrees). Longford/
> Westmeath Library & LDS Mf.1279285.
>
> Colonel Thomas Nugent, Earl of Westmeath, in 'King James' IAL' (Notes on
> family members pre-1779).

Nunn

Nunn of Castlebridge. Wexford Gentry Vol. 1 (see abbreviations).

Nuttall

The Nuttalls of Co. Kildare. JCKAS 8 (1915–17) 180–84.

O: *For all O' names please look at the alphabetic entry for the part of the name after the O, e.g. for O'Connor see Connor etc.*

Obins

Obins of Castleobins. Pedigree in 'Swanzy Notebooks'. RCB Library, Dublin.

Odell

The family of Odell. Ir. Anc. 1 (2) (1969) 114–44; 3 (1) (1971) 41–8.

The Odells of Carriglea. Ardmore J. 3 (1986) 44 -59.

Odlum

Odlums of Offaly. Irish Family History 5 (1989) 71–79.

Oliver

The Olivers of Cloghanadfoy and their descendants. J. R. Oliver. London, 1904.

Pedigree of Oliver Family of Cork: IGRS Library (Leader Collection).

Olney

Pedigree of Olney Family of Cork: IGRS Library (Leader Collection).

Ormsby

Pedigree of the family of Ormsby, formerly of Lincolnshire, now of Ireland. J. F. Fuller. London, 1886.

The Ormsbys of Tobervaddy (Co. Mayo). Ir.Gen. 1(1941) 284–6.

Orpen

The Orpen family: being an account of the life and writing of Richard Orpen of Killowen, Co. Kerry, together with some researches into the early history of his forbears. G. H. Orpen. Frome, 1930.

Orr

Ulster pedigrees: descendants of James Orr & Janet McClement, who emigrated from Scotland to N. Ireland ca. 1607. Ray A Jones. San Francisco: F. A. Jones, 1977. (LDS Lib. 929.2415 Or7j) (Ref to McConnell, McKee, McKibbin or McKibben, Martin, Patterson, Stewart).

Osborne

The genealogy of Lucius O'Brien and Thomas Osborne. JCHAS 3 (1897) 11–21.

McOstrich

Pedigree of McOstrich Family of Cork: IGRS Library (Leader Collection).

Otway

Papers concerning the history of the Otway family 1790-1984. NLI Ms 27,815. (also Otway Ruthven).

Ouseley

The name and family of Ouseley. JRSAI 40 (1910) 132–46; 355.

Genealogy of the Ouseley family (1486-1896). 9 pages compiled by Richard Kelly. (LDS Lib. 929.2415 A1 no. 24).

Ovens

Ovens of Fermanagh. Pedigree in 'Swanzy Notebooks'. RCB Library.

Owen *see also* **Tweedy**

Owen & Perrin family history: being an account of the family of Owen of Rathdowney, and related family of Perrin of Wicklow ... Hugh Owen; pr.pr. Chichester 1981.

Owgan

Pedigree of Owgan Family of Cork: IGRS Library (Leader Collection).

Oxburgh

Col Heward Oxburgh (of Ballybritt, Offaly) in 'King James' IAL' (Notes on family members pre-1700).

Pakenham or **Packenham**

The Packenham family of Tullynally Castle. Hugh O'Donnell. Typescript copy at Longford/Westmeath Library, 1984; (LDS Lib. 929.2415 A1 no. 2).

Longford Papers. [Co. Westmeath]. Anal.Hib., 20, 109–27.

Palliser *see* **Codd**

Palmer

Genealogical and historical account of the Palmer family of Kenmare, Co. Kerry. A. H. Palmer. 1872.

Account of the Palmer family of Rahan, Co. Kildare. T. Prince. New York: Temple Prince 1903.

Pedigree of Palmer Family of Cork: IGRS Library (Leader Collection).

Two Kildare Palmers. JCKAS 14 (1966-67) p.168.

Genealogical record of the descendants of John & Mary Palmer, PA, especially through ... James Trimble. Lewis Palmer. Lippicott & Co., Philadelphia 1875.

Parke

Genealogy of the Parke family. 1720-1920. by John P. Wallace. Pr.pr. 1920. (Donegal).

Parker

Pedigree of Parker Family of Cork: IGRS Library (Leader Collection).

The Parkers of Tuamgraney(Co. Clare). Sliabh Aughty 5 (1994) p. 21-23.

Parkinson

Some notes on the Parkinson family (Louth). CLAHJ 10(3) (1943) p. 255-6.

Parnell

Parnell and the Parnells: a historical sketch. R. Johnston. Dublin and London, 1888.

The Parnell sisters. Dublin Hist. Rec. 21 (1966/7) 14-27. (Family of Charles
S. Parnell).

Parr

Parr of Co. Cavan. Pedigree in 'Swanzy Notebooks'. RCB Library, Dublin.

Parsons

Pedigree of Parsons Family of Cork: IGRS Library (Leader Collection).

Notes on families and individuals of the name of Parsons. Richard Parsons.
London, 1903.

Parsons of Monkstown, Birr and Newcastle-upon-Tyne. Dun Laoghaire J. 8
(1999) 57-60.

Patterson *see also* **Orr**

Edmund and Margaret (Leamy) Patterson and their descendants. Betty
Patterson, Madison, Wisconsin, pr. pr., 1979.

Some family notes. W. H. Patterson. Belfast, 1911.

Payton, Peyton or **Patton** *see also* **Colhoun**

Notes on the O'Peatains of Donegal, Mayo, and Roscommon. Ir. Gen. 4 (4)
(1971) 303–07.

The Pattons and Dills of Springfield. Donegal Ann. 11 (1) (1974) 33-40.

Bible records of Peyton, Powell, Shaw, Crymble, Cunningham & related families. (GO Ms. no. 519; LDS Mf.257821).

Pearson or **Pierson**

Pierson (Pearson) family records in Co.Armagh: Inc. wills of John Mackey of
Keneonin Parish, Jacob Pearson of Muloughletra (Kilmore), David Kell
of Cormagh (Loughgall), William Allen & George Wickliff of Coragh,
Joseph Pearson of Drumard. Armagh Co. Museum Ms. M9: LDS
Mf.1279356.

Pedigree of Pearson Family of Cork: IGRS Library (Leader Collection).

Peebles

Pedigrees of … Peebles et al. LDS mf. 1279327.

Pemberton

Pemberton of Dublin. Ir. Anc. 11 (1) (1979) 14–26.

Penn

Pedigree of Penn Family of Cork: IGRS Library (Leader Collection).

Admiral Penn, William Penn, and Their Descendants in Co. Cork. JCHAS 14
(1908) 105–14, 177–89.

Pennefather

Pedigree of Pennefather Family of Cork: IGRS Library (Leader Collection).

Pennington

Pedigree of Pennington Family of Cork: IGRS Library (Leader Collection).

Penrose

The Penroses of Woodhill. JCHAS 85 (1980) 79-98.

Pedigree of Penrose Family of Cork: IGRS Library (Leader Collection).

The Penrose family of Helston, Cornwall & Wheldrake, Yorkshire & Co.
Wicklow, Ireland. Charles C. Penrose. New York 1975.

Pentheny

Memoir of the ancient family of Pentheny, or De Pentheny, of the Co. Meath.
Dublin, 1821.

Peppard

The Peppards of Cappagh, Co. Limerick. Ir. Anc. 16 (2) (1984) 68–70.

Pedigree of Peppard Family of Cork: IGRS Library (Leader Collection).

Percival *see* **Rothwell**

Percy

Percy of Co. Wicklow. Pedigree in 'Swanzy Notebooks'. RCB Library, Dublin.

Deeds, leases & pedigrees of Percy..et al. Longford/Westmeath Library; RIA
(Upton Papers); & LDS mf. 101011.

Notes on the Percy family of Ballylinny, Co. Antrim. By Jon Neill. (LDS Lib.
929.2415 A1 no. 76).

Perrin *see* **Owen**

Perrott

Pedigree of Perrott Family of Cork: IGRS Library (Leader Collection).

Perrott of Co. Cavan. Pedigree in 'Swanzy Notebooks'. RCB Library, Dublin.

Perry

Pedigree of Perry Family of Cork: IGRS Library (Leader Collection).

Pettapiece *see* **Switzer**

Petty *see* **Fitzmaurice**

Peyton *see* **Payton**

Phaire or **Phair** *see also* **Fair**

Colonel Robert Phaire, Regicide. His ancestry, history, and descendants.
JCHAS 29 (1924) 76–80; 30 (1925) 20–6; 31 (1926) 31–6; 32 (1927) 24–
32.

Pedigree of Phayre/Phair Family of Cork: IGRS Library (Leader Collection).

Phillips *see also* **Swift**

Lt. Col. James Phillips (of Clonmore, Mayo) in 'King James' IAL' (Notes on
family up to 1828).

Pedigree of Phillips Family of Cork: IGRS Library (Leader Collection).

The Phillips Families of Ulster and South Carolina. Familia 2 (4) (1988).

Philpotts or **Philpot** *see also* **Kell**

Pedigree Book for Philpot Family of Cork: IGRS Library (Leader Collection).

Phipps *see* **Guinness**

Pierce

Pierce Family of Offaly. Irish Family History 8 (1992) 78–83.

Pierse or **Piers**

Piers of Tristernagh. Riocht na Midhe 7 (4) (1980/81) 52–76.

The origin of the Pierse family of Co. Kerry. JKAHS (New Series)5 (1972) p.14-32.

Pierson *see* **Pearson**

Pilkington

Harland's history of the Pilkingtons, from the Saxon times to the present time. 2nd ed. Dublin, 1886.

Pilleys or **Pillows**

Pedigrees of Atkinson, Beck, Chambers, Cole, Jackson, and Pilleys or Pillows. (LDS mf. 1279354.

Pim *see* **Goodbody**

Piphoe *see* **Travers**

Place *see* **Barry**

Pleasant

Thomas Pleasant (1729-1818). Dublin Hist. Rec. 6(4) (1944) 121-132.

Plunkett *see also* **Blake**

The ancestry of St. Oliver Plunkett, a genealogical puzzle. Ir.Gen. 5(1977) 428–430.

The Plunkett family of Loughcrew. Riocht na Midhe 1 (4)(1958) 49–53.

Plunkett of Loughcrew. Ir. Gen. 5(4) (1977) 422–27.

The house of Louth in the seventeenth and eighteenth centuries. CLAHJ 17 (1966) 67–84.

Plunkett Papers. [Co. Dublin]. Anal. Hib. 25, 203–14.

The Plunketts of Dunsoghly. Reportorium Novum 1 (2) (1956) 330–36.

Plunketts of Portmarnock. Reportorium Novum 2 (1) (1958) 106–08.

Capt Lord Dunsany (Plunkett) (of Co. Louth) in 'King James' IAL' (Notes on family members pre-1747).

New light on the family of Blessed Oliver Plunkett. Seanchas Ardmhacha 3(2) (1959) 385-388 (Spanish relatives and other notes from 1683).

Family and Literary papers of Geraldine Plunkett Dillon. NLI Ms Collection List 43. (20 Folders of materials including Plunkett family papers, books etc.).

Pockrick, Poekrich, or **Pockrich**

Pockrick of Co. Monaghan. Pedigree in 'Swanzy Notebooks'. RCB Library, Dublin.

Richard Poekrich. Dublin Hist. Rec. 10(1) (1948) 17-32.

Poe

Origin and early history of the family of Poe, with full pedigrees of the Irish branch. Edmund Bewley. Dublin: University Press 1906 (200 copies only). (LDS Lib. 929.2415 P752b).

Pollexfen *see* **Yeates**

Pollock

The family of Pollock of Newry & descendants. A. S. Hartigan. Folkestone, n.d.

Pomeroy

Pedigree of Pomeroy Family of Cork: IGRS Library (Leader Collection)

Ponsonby *see also* **Moore**

Bishopscourt and its owners. JCKAS 8 (1915–17) 3–29. (Ponsonby family).

The Ponsonby family. Sir John Ponsonby. London: Medici Society, 1929. (LDS Lib. 929.2415 P775p).

Two Ponsonby letters. Old Kilkenny Review 4 (5) (1993) p. 1181-1185.

The Ponsonbys and Fiddown Church. Old Kilkenny Review, 19 (1967) p.41-44.

Poole

The Pooles of Mayfield and other Irish families. Rosemary ffolliott. Dublin, Dublin: Hodges Figgis, 1958. (LDS Lib. 929.2415 P785f).

Popham

Pedigree Books (2) for Popham Family of Cork: IGRS Library (Leader Collection).

Porter

Rev. James Porter (1735-1798). Donegal Ann. 8(1) (1969) 7-15.

Potter

Potters of Ardee. CLAHJ 18 (2) (1974) 165–70.

Potterton *see* **Waldron**

Powell *see also* **McClintock, Payton**

Pedigree of Powell Family of Cork: IGRS Library (Leader Collection).

The Powells of Templederry, Co. Tipperary. Gateway to the Past 1 (3) 134–139.

Power *see also* **Blake**

The Powers of Clashmore, Co. Waterford. JCHAS 47 (1924) 121–22.

An historical memoir of the family of Poher, Poer or Power. by Gabriel O'C. Redmond. Dublin: Irish Builder 1891. (LDS Lib. 929.2415 P871p.

Notes and pedigrees relating to the family of Poher, Poer or Power. Edmund, 17th Lord Power. Clonmel, n.d.

Patrick, Margaret, Jeffery, Ellen Power and their descendants. Betty Patterson, Madison, Wisconsin, pr. pr. 1980.

Power Papers. [Kilsheelan, Co. Tipperary]. Anal. Hib. 25: 57–75.

Lt. Col. John Power (of Waterford) in 'King James' IAL' (Notes on family members pre-1700).

Power-O'Shee Papers (Gardenmorris, Co. Waterford). Anal. Hib. 20: 216–58.

Power of Edermine. Wexford Gentry Vol. 1 (see abbreviations).

Poyntz

Poyntz family of Ulster Province: Armagh Co. Museum Ms. N8: LDS Mf.1279356.

Pratt

Pratt family records: an account of the Pratts of Youghal and Castlemartyr, Co. Cork. Millom: P.C.Dickinson, 1931. (LDS Lib. 929.2415 P888p).

The family of Pratt of Gawsworth and Carrigrohane, Co. Cork. John Pratt. 1925.

Prendergast *see also* **O'Shaughnessy**

The Prendergast Family: notes collected for John P. Prendergast. Kings Inn Library, Dublin. (Tipperary & Waterford).

Preston *see also* **Jephson**

Pedigree of Preston Family of Cork: IGRS Library (Leader Collection).

Gormanston Papers. Anal. Hib. 25, 149–83.

The Gormanston Register, ed. Mills and MacEnery, Dublin 1916.

Col. Jenico Preston (of Gormanston, Co. Meath) in 'King James' IAL' (Notes on family members pre-1700).

Priestly

Pedigree of Priestly Family of Cork: IGRS Library (Leader Collection).

Pritchard

Pedigree of Pritchard Family of Cork: IGRS Library (Leader Collection).

Prunty *see* **Brunty**

Pulvertaft

Pedigree of Pulvertaft Family of Cork: IGRS Library (Leader Collection).

Punch

The Punch family. Ir.Gen. 3 (1961) 210–16.

Pedigree of Punch Family of Cork: IGRS Library (Leader Collection).

Pons to Punch. Ir. Anc. 2 (1) (1970) 2–18.

Purcell *see also* **Blake, Ireton**

Family papers belonging to Purcells of Loughmoe, Co. Tipperary. N. Munster Antiq. J. 3 (1914) 124–29, 191–203.

Pedigree of Purcell Family of Cork: IGRS Library (Leader Collection).

Col. Nicholas Purcell (of Loughmow, Co Tippperary) in 'King James' IAL' (Notes on family members pre-1700).

The last of the Purcells of Loughmoe. JW&SEIAS 4 (1898) 110-119.

Purdon

Pedigree of Purdon Family of Cork: IGRS Library (Leader Collection)

Puxley

Puxleys of Dunboy, Co. Cork. Irish Family History 5 (1989) 7–16.

Pyne

Pedigree Book for Pyne Family of Cork: IGRS Library (Leader Collection).

The Pynes of Co. Cork. Ir. Gen. 6 (6) (1985) 696–710; 7 (1) (1986) 31–50; 7 (2) (1987) 229–244.

Quain

The Quains of Mallow. Mallow Field Club J. 8 (1990).

Quigley

Fr. James Quigley. Seanchas Ardmhacha 5(2) (1970) 247-168. (Refs to Quigley of Kilmore, Co Armagh 1700-1800)

MacQuillan or **McQuillin**

Lords of the Route. Edmund Curtis. Proc. R.I.A., 44 (1938) 99–113.

The MacQuillins of the Route. Ulster J. Arch. 9, pp 57–70.

The Clan of the MacQuillins of Antrim. Ulster J.Arch. 8,1st ser.(1860)251–68.

The fate of the McQuillans (Antrim). Familia 13 (1997) pp. 36–50.

Capt. Ross McQuillan (of Antrim) in 'King James' IAL' (Notes on family members pre-1700).

The Enigma of the Battle of Orra and the Fate of the MacQuillans. Familia 2 (13) 1997.

Quinn or **O'Quinn** *see also* **Devlin, O'Hagan**

Quinn of Newry. Pedigree in 'Swanzy Notebooks'. RCB Library, Dublin.

Capt. Thady Quinn (of Limerick) in 'King James' IAL' (Notes on family pre-1700).

Rabbitt

Pedigree of Rabbitt Family of Cork: IGRS Library (Leader Collection).

Macraith

Islandmagrath (Co. Clare) and the Macraith family. The Other Clare 21 (1997) p.16.

Radcliffe

Pedigree of Radcliffe Family of Cork: IGRS Library (Leader Collection).

Radcliffe family of Ireland. Armagh Co. Museum Ms.P7: LDS Mf.1279356.

Radley

Pedigree of Radley Family of Cork: IGRS Library (Leader Collection).

Rae *see* **Rea**

Raggett *see* **Archdeacon**

Raines

Pedigree of Raines Family of Cork: IGRS Library (Leader Collection).

Ram

Ram of Ramsfort. Wexford Gentry Vol. 1 (see abbreviations).

Ramadge

Some notes on the Ramadge family. Clogher Record 10 (1) (1979) 154.

Rampain

Brief Genealogies of Rampain et al, in 'The History of 2 Ulster Manors'. Earl of Belmore, London/Dublin, 1903.

McRannal *see* **Reynolds**

Rathborne

An early Dublin candlemaker: history of the family of Rathborne. Dublin Hist. Rec.14 (1957) 66–73.

Ray *see* **Lowry**

Raycroft

Pedigree of Raycroft Family of Cork: IGRS Library (Leader Collection).

Rea or **Rhea**

Samuel Rea 1725–1811: his heritage and descendants. H. O. Rea. Dungannon, pr. pr., 1960.

The Rea Genealogy. J. Harris Rea, pr. pr. Banbridge, 1972. (LDS Lib. 929.2415 R22r).

Rea/Rae of Ballynahinch, Holywood and allied families. Osbourne, M. J.: Univ. of California, 1980.

Descendants of Rev. Joseph Rhea of Ireland. Edward F. Foley. Heritage Books, USA, 1996.

Descendants of Matthew "The Rebel" Rhea of Scotland & Ireland. Edward Foley. Heritage Books, USA, 2000.

Reade

The Reades of Cos. Tipperary and Kilkenny. Ir. Gen. 8 (1) (1990) 15–44; 8 (3) 336–364.

Pedigree of Reade Family of Cork: IGRS Library (Leader Collection).

Richard Reade, Lord Chancellor of Ireland. Genealogists Mag. 14 (3) (Sep 1962).

Real

Tracing Real family Ancestors. Gateway to the Past 1 (2) (1994) 97-99.

My Real Ancestors. Gateway to the Past 1 (3) (1994) 114-119.

Reardon *see* **Riordan**

Redmond

Military and political memoirs of the Redmond family. JCHAS 27(1921) 22–35, 73–8; 28(1922) 1–11. 81–9; 29(1924) 19–28, 87–93; 30(1925) 34–40, 96–9.

Pedigree of Redmond Family of Cork: IGRS Library (Leader Collection).

Genealogies of Esmond, Codd, Jacob, and Redmond. GO mf. 279.

Redmond of The Hall. Wexford Gentry Vol. 1 (see abbreviations).

Regan, Reagan and O'Regan

The O'Regans of Carbery. JCHAS 63 (1958) 18–22.

Pedigree of Reagan Family of Cork: IGRS Library (Leader Collection).

(O')Regan, O'Riagain in 'Family Names of Co. Cork' (see abbrevs.) (Notes on origins & members in Co.Cork).

The Stonemason O'Regans. Mallow Field Club J. 11 (1993).

Ronald Reagan & the Isle of Destiny. Matthew J. Culligan. 1982. ISBN 0806348682.

Reilly or **O'Reilly** *see also* **Kelly (Ainsworth misc).**
> The O'Reillys of Templemills, Celbridge with a note on the history of the clann Ui Raghallaigh in general. Compiled by E. O'H. Dundrum, Co. Dublin, 1941.
> The origin of the surname O'Reilly. Anthony Mathews, Dublin, 1970.
> Poems on the O'Reillys ed. James Carney. Dublin, 1950.
> A genealogical history of the O'Reillys: written in the 18th century. Written by Eóghan Ó Raghallaigh in the 18th c. & ed. by James Carney. Dublin: Pub. by an Cumann Sheanchais Bhreifne 1959. (LDS Lib. 929.2415 Or3c).
> Irish chiefs and leaders. Rev. Paul Walsh. Chs. vii, viii. Dublin. 1960.
> O'Reilly, formerly of Baltrasna, Co. Meath. In Visitation of Ireland, Crisp, F. A., ed. Vol. 4. Privately printed, 1911.
> Copies of census returns of the Reilly family, Co. Longford, 1851. NAI M 5349 (65).
> A Genealogical History of the O'Reilly's. (written in the eighteenth century) Eoghan O'Raghallaigh and incorporating the earlier work of Dr. Fitzsimons, Vicar-General of the Diocese of Kilmore. Dublin, 1959.
> The Descendants of Col. Miles O'Reilly in Co. Leitrim (1650–1830) from Tradition. Breifne 2 (1) (1962) 15–19.
> The line of Colonel John O'Reilly. Breifne, 2 (5) (1962) 84–105.
> The O'Reilly's of East Breifne, circa 1250–1450. Breifne 8 (2) (1991) 155–180.
> The O Reillys and MacQuaids of Lisdoagh. Breifne 8 (2)(1991) p.182-206.
> The O'Reilly's of Corlattylannan and Their Relations. Breifne 8 (4) (1994) 489–495.
> Thomas O'Reilly (1830-72) of Lurgan and Atlanta, Georgia, U.S.A. Breifne 8 (1995) 607-15.
> Col. Edmund O'Reilly (of Ballinacargy, Cavan) in 'King James' IAL' (Notes on family members pre-1794).

Rentoul
> A record of the family and lineage of Alexander Rentoul. E. Rentoul. Belfast, 1890.

Reynell
> Pedigree of Reynell Family of Cork: IGRS Library (Leader Collection).

Reynolds
> Some Co. Leitrim wills and leases. Breifne, I, 2, 3 (1960–66). (Inc. Reynolds wills).
> Notes on the MacRannals of Leitrim and their country: being introductory to a diary of James Reynolds, Lough Scur, Co. Leitrim, for the years 1658–1660. JRSAI 35(1905) 139–51.
> Capt. Edward Reynolds (of Leitrim) in 'King James' IAL' (Notes on family members pre-1700).

Reynolds family of Donegal. JRSAI 40 (1940) 239-140.

Rice

Edmund Rice 1762-1844. Daire Keogh. Dublin: Four Courts Press 1994. (ISBN: 1851822119).

Pedigree of Rice Family of Cork: IGRS Library (Leader Collection).

Capt John Rice: in 'King James' IAL' (Notes on various Rice families pre-1700).

The Rice Family of Mallow in Australia. Mallow Field Club J. 14 (1996).

Richards

Pedigree of Richards Family of Cork: IGRS Library (Leader Collection).

Richards of Solsboro, Monksgrange & Ardamine. Wexford Gentry Vol. 2 (see abbreviations).

Richardson

Six Generations of Friends in Ireland 1655-1890. Jane M. Richardson. London 1895.

James Nicholson Richardson of Bessbrook. Charlotte F. Smith. London 1925.

Richardson of Somerset. Pedigree in 'Swanzy Notebooks'. RCB Library, Dublin.

Riddel *see* **McNaughton**

Riggs

Pedigree Book for Riggs Family of Cork: IGRS Library (Leader Collection).

Ringrose *see* **O'Shaughnessy**

(O') Riordan or **Reardon**

Pedigree of Riordan Family of Cork: IGRS Library (Leader Collection).

(O')Riordan, Rearden in 'Family Names of Co. Cork' (see abbrevs.) (Notes on origins & members in Co.Cork).

Reardon family history: William J Reardon and Bridget Murray, Co. Tipperary and … Wisconsin. B.R. Childs. Evanston, Ill. 1991. NLI Ir 9292 r16. (refs to Reardon, Kelly and O'Keefe families).

Rivers

The Rivers Family of Co. Waterford. Decies 12 (1979) 32–61.

Robbins

Robbins family of Ballyduff and Firgrove, Kilkenny. Old Kilkenny Review (1994) 122.

Roberts

A Roberts family, quondam Quakers of Queen's Co. E. J. Adeir Impey. London, 1939.

Pedigree of Roberts Family of Cork: IGRS Library (Leader Collection).

The Roberts family of Waterford. JW&SEIAS 2(1896) 98–103; 190-191.

Some account of the Roberts family of Kilmoney. JCHAS 24 (1929) 107–10.

Robertson *see* **McClintock**

Robinson

Robinson of Killogeenaghan; a Westmeath Quaker Family. Ir. Anc. 14 (1) (1982) 1–5.

Pedigree of Robinson Family of Cork: IGRS Library (Leader Collection).

The Robinsons of North Kildare: 300 years of family history. James Robinson. Dublin: McRobin Publications, 1997 (ISBN: 095301150X). (LDS Lib. 929.2415 R56rn.

Roche or **Roch** *see also* **Meade**

The Roches, Lords of Fermoy. JCHAS 38(1933)86–91; 39(1934)38–40,57–68; 40(1935)37–42,63–73; 41(1936)2–28,78–84; 42(1937)40–52.

The pedigree of Sir Boyle Roche. Ir.Gen. 2 (1950) 240–4.

Roches of Newcastlewest, Co. Limerick. Ir.Gen. 2 (1950) 244–5.

Pedigree of Roche Family of Cork: IGRS Library (Leader Collection).

Roche Papers [Co. Cork]. Anal. Hib. 15: 143–52.

Capt John Roch (Fermoy, Co Cork) in 'King James' IAL' (Family line pre-1712).

(De) Roche in 'Family Names of Co. Cork' (see abbrevs.) (Notes on origins & members in Co.Cork).

The Roches of Wexford. JOWS 2 (1969) 39-48.

The Roches of Annakisha. Mallow Field Club J. 14 (1996).

Rochford

A Cork Branch of the Rochford Family. JCHAS 21 (1915) 112–20.

Pedigree of Rochford Family of Cork: IGRS Library (Leader Collection).

The Rochfords of Tulla (Co. Clare) and Australia, 1798 to 1920, Sliabh Aughty Vol.3, p.11-12.

Notes on the history of the family of Rochfort or Rochefort with genealogies of the principal Irish branches. R. Rochfort Forlong. Oxford: 1890. NLI Ir 9292 r4.

Rochfort

Nugent and Rochfort families (biographies, property & pedigrees). Longford/Westmeath Library & LDS Mf.1279285.

Roden

PRONI: Twenty-one volumes (approx 2000 docs.)of papers & correspondence of Roden family. Newcastle, Co. Down.

Roe

Pedigree of Roe Family of Cork: IGRS Library (Leader Collection).

Rogers

Rogers of Lota and Ashgrove. JCHAS 72 (1967) 75–80. (Late eighteenth to mid-nineteenth century. Cork).

Rogers of Co. Monaghan. Pedigree in 'Swanzy Notebooks'. RCB Library, Dublin.

Rolt

Large Pedigree Book for Rolt Family. IGRS Library (Leader Collection).

Ronayne or **Ronan**

Some Desmond incidents and notes on the Ronayne family. JCHAS 23 (1917)
104–7.

Notes on the Family of Ronayne, or Ronan, of Cos. Cork and Waterford.
JCHAS 22 (1916) 56–63, 109–14, 178–85; 23 (1917) 93–104, 142–52.
(Also in 1 Vol.: Rev. F W Knight. Messrs Guy & Co. Cork: 1917).

Pedigree of Ronayne Family of Cork: IGRS Library (Leader Collection).

Across the Threshold: A Ronan family History, from Kilkenny to Victoria.
M. Ronan. Victoria: Macron Pub. (ISBN: 0646159003).

Rooney

Pedigree of Rooney Family of Cork: IGRS Library (Leader Collection).

MacRory or **Rory**

The Past: MacRorys of Duneane, Castle-Dawson, Limavady and Belfast. R.
A. MacRory. Belfast 1881.

A history of the Clanna Rory or Rudricians. Richard F. Cronnelly. Pr.pr. Dublin 1864. (NLI Call No. Ir 9292 r1).

Rosborough

Later history of the family of Rosborough of Mullinagoan, Co. Fermanagh.
H. B. Swanzy. Pr.pr. 1897.

Rose

Rose family documents ; Turner notes (abstracts from Quaker registers, Eustace
Street, Dublin; Lurgan & Lisburn Parish registers) ; Verner notes. Armagh
Co. Museum Ms. P8: LDS Mf.1279356.

James, H. E. The Rose-Cleland Family. The author, 1984.

Ross

Remembrance and research. Harrison Ross. Privately pr., 1938.

Rosseter or **Rossiter**

The Rosseters of Rathmacknee Castle (Co. Wexford), 1169–1881. Past 5 (1949)
103–16; 6 (1950) 13–44.

Rothe *see also* **Archdeacon**

The Family of Rothe of Kilkenny. JRSAI 17 (1886) 501–37, 620–54.

The Rothes of Kilkenny. Old Kilkenny Review 2 (1949) 7-13.

The Rothes in Irish and French history. Old Kilkenny Review 20 (1968) 45-
53.

Rothwell

Family register of the Rothwells (Kells, Co. Meath) comp. by Caroline F.
Rothwell. (LDS Lib. 929.2415 A1 no. 68) (Refs to Thomson, Kellett,
Alison).

Rothwell: the origin, heraldry and history of name. Daniel Rothwell. Great
Britain: C.D. Rothwell, 1994 (ISBN: 0952197707). (LDS Lib. 929.2415

R746r. (Ref to Kavanagh, Percival, Jacob, Power, Deacon, Moulton, Macutchen).

O'Rourke

Documents and materials for the history of the O'Rourke family. Danzig, 1925.

The origin of the surname O'Rourke. Anthony Mathews. Dublin, 1970.

Ensign Con O'Rourke (of Leitrim) in 'King James' IAL' (Notes on family members pre-1700).

O Ruairc (O'Rourke) of Breifne, Betty McDermot. Manorhamilton: Drumlin Pubs. 1990. (LDS Lib. 929.2415 Or9mb).

Roy *see* **Allen – Allens of Ulster**

Royse *see also* **Monck**

An Irish Rudd family 1760-1988: progeny of Gordon Arthur Rudd & Alicia Wellwood, Rathsarn Parish, Queens Co., Ireland. Norman N. Rudd. Chula Vista, Calif.: Rudd Family Research Assoc., 1992.

Ruddock

Pedigree of Ruddock Family of Cork: IGRS Library (Leader Collection).

Rudge *see* **MacNair**

Rudkin

The Rudkins of the Co. Carlow. Sir Edward Bewley. Exeter, 1905. see also Gen., N.S., 21 (1905) 145–62.

Rumley

The Rumley Family of Cork. JCHAS 7 (1901) 127.

Runnett or Runnell

Possible origin of Runnett family of Sessiamagroll. Duiche Neill 5 (1990) 133-143; & 6 (1991) 52-75.

Ruskin

Ruskin and Harristown. JCKAS 14 (1966-67) p.152-162.

Russell

Pedigree of Russell Family of Cork: IGRS Library (Leader Collection).

Capt. Bartholomew Russell (of Dublin) in 'King James' IAL' (Notes on family pre-1700).

Rutter

Pedigree of Rutter Family of Cork: IGRS Library (Leader Collection).

Ruttledge

The Ruttledge Families of Co. Mayo. Ir. Gen. 7 (3) 433–453.

Rutherford *see* **Allen – Allens of Ulster**

Ruxton

The Ruxtons of Ardee. CLAHJ 23(4) (1996) p.387-392.

Ryall

Pedigree of Ryall Family of Cork: IGRS Library (Leader Collection).

Ryan, Mulryan or **O'Mulryan**

The family of O'Mulryan in Spain. Ir.Gen. 3 (1961) 195–7.

O'Ryan of Mallorca. Ir.Gen. 3 (1962) 266–9.

Records of the four Tipperary Septs. Martin Callanan. JAG Publishing, Galway 1938. (ISBN 0952660806).

Census Returns Relating to Ryan family (1851) NAI Mf. 5249 (66, 67).

Gen. W.A.C. Ryan: The Cuban Martyr (Birr, Co. Offaly). Irish Sword 8 (31) (1967) 115-119.

Capt. Teigue Ryan (of Clare) in 'King James' IAL' (Notes on family members pre-1789).

The Ryan and Terry Families in Spain. Ir. Gen. 10(2) (1999) 245-249.

Ryder

Pedigree of Ryder Family of Cork: IGRS Library (Leader Collection).

Rye

Pedigree of Rye Family of Cork: IGRS Library (Leader Collection).

Ryland

Pedigree of Ryland of Dungarvan and Waterford. JRSAI 15 (1881) 562–65.

Sadleir

Pedigree of Sadleir Family of Cork: IGRS Library (Leader Collection).

St. Lawrence

Notes on the St. Lawrences, lords of Howth, from 12th to 16th century. JRSAI 37(1907) 349–59.

St. Leger or **St. Ledger**

St. Leger 'Doneraile Papers'. Anal.Hib. 15, 333–62; 20, 56–91.

Pedigree of St. Ledger Family of Cork: IGRS Library (Leader Collection).

The St. Legers and Doneraile. Mallow Field Club J. 16 (1998).

The lady Freemason (Elizabeth St Leger 1695-1775). Mallow Field Club J. 3 (1985) 150-153.

Sall or **Salle**

A History of the Sall(e) family of Cashel. Ir Gen.10(2) 1999.

Sanders

Pedigree of Sanders Family of Cork: IGRS Library (Leader Collection).

Sandys

Some notes for a history of the Sandys family of Great Britain and Ireland. C. Vivian and T. M. Sandys. 1909.

Sankey

Memorials of the Sankeys of England and Ireland 1207–1880. Sankey Best-Gardner. Swansea, pr. pr., 1880.

Sarsfield

Dr. Caulfield's records of the Sarsfield family of the County Cork. JCHAS 21 (1915) 82–91, 131–36.

The Sarsfields of Co. Clare. N. Munster Antiq. J. 3 (1914–15) 92–107, 170–90, 328–43.

Pedigree of Sarsfield Family of Cork: IGRS Library (Leader Collection).

The family of Sarsfield. Herald & Genealogist, 2 (1865) 205–15.

Patrick Sarsfield, Earl of Lucan, with an Account of His Family and Their Connection with Lucan and Tully. JCKAS 4 (1903–05) 114–47.

Patrick Sarsfield (of Lucan, Co. Dublin) in 'King James' IAL' (Notes on family members pre-1700).

Saunders
The Family of Saunders of Saunders Grove, Co. Wicklow. JCKAS 9 (1918–22) 125–33.

Saunderson
Saunderson of Castle Saunderson. H. Saunderson. London: Butler & Tanner, 1936. (LDS Lib. 929.2415 Sa87.

Savage
The ancient and noble family of the Savages of the Ards: with sketches of English and American branches. Ed. G. F. Savage-Armstrong. London: Marcus Ward, 1888. (LDS Lib. 929.2415 Sa92s.

Genealogical history of Savage family in Ulster.G. F. Savage-Armstrong. Chiswick Press, London: 1906. (NLI Ir 9292 s1).

Capt. Roland Savage (of Ards, Co Down) in 'King James' IAL' (Notes on family members pre-1700).

Savile *see* Hargreaves
Scanlan
Scanlan of the barony of Upper Connello, Co. Limerick. Ir. Anc. 4 (2) (1972)71–80.

Scarborough
Pedigree of Scarborough Family of Cork: IGRS Library (Leader Collection).

Scott
Duncan Scott (c.1796-1823) of Aberfeldy & Kilkeel & descendants of his son Duncan Scott (1823-1898) of Derryoge. Winnifred P. Pierce. Ann Arbor, Mich: W.P.Pierce,1988. (LDS Lib. 929.2415 Sco83p. (Ref to O'Neill, McCann).

Pedigree of Scott Family of Cork: IGRS Library (Leader Collection).

Scully
Scully tombstones on the Rock of Cashel. Ir Gen.10(2) 1999.

Scurlock
The Scurlocks of Rathcredan. Reportorium Novum 1 (1) (1955) 79–80.

Sealy
Pedigree of Sealy Family of Cork: IGRS Library (Leader Collection).

Seaver
History of the Seaver (or Sievers) family: formerly of Heath Hall in Co. Armagh. George Seaver. Dundalk: Dundalgan Press 1950 (only 250 copies)

(NLI Call No. 9292 s12; LDS Lib. 929.2415 Se19a).

Seaver family of Co. Armagh: Armagh Co. Museum. Ms. N8: LDS Mf.1279356.

Segrave or Seagrave

The Segrave family, 1066 to 1935. C. W. Segrave. London, 1936.

Segrave Papers. [Cabra, Co. Dublin]. Anal.Hib. 15, 384–8.

Segraves of Cabra. Reportorium Novum 1 (2) (1956) 324–28.

Seagrave Family. (Ireland & Eng.) Genealogists Mag. 7 (11) (Sept 1937).

Seymour

Seymour of County Galway. Irish Family History 14 (1998).

Shackleton

The Annals of Ballytore. Mary Leadbeater (vol. 1 of the Leadbeater Papers). London, 1862.

The Shackletons and Ballitore. Carloviana, (Old series) 1 (4) (1951) 161–6.

The Shackleton Letters: 1726-55. JCKAS 9(1) (1918) 70-79. (Ballitore, Co Kildare).

The Shackleton Letters: 1763-83. JCKAS 9(2) (1919) 134-177 . (Ballitore, Co Kildare).

Letters and papers of the Shackleton family of Ballitore (Co. Kildare). Fennell collection in the Friends Historical Library, Donnybrook, Dublin.

The Shackletons of Ballitore, 1580-1987. Jonathon Shackleton. Ltd. Ed. of 100 copies of genealogical tables. (LDS Lib. 929.2415 Sh11sj).

The Shackletons. Bernice C. Shackleton. Kansas: 1972.

Shaen

Pedigree of Shaen Family of Cork: IGRS Library (Leader Collection).

Shannon *see also* Forster, Nesbitt

Pedigree of Shannon Family of Cork: IGRS Library (Leader Collection).

(O')Shaughnessy *see also* McNamara

O'Shaughnessy of Gort (1543–1783) tabular pedigree. JGAHS 7 (1911–12) 53.

The story of an Irish property. R. S. Rait. Oxford, 1908.

Tribes and customs of Hy Fiachra. John O'Donovan. Dublin: Irish Archaeological Soc. 1844. Appendix B, 372–91.

The O'Shaughnessys of Munster: the people and their stories. John P. M. Feheney. Mardyke, Cork: Iverus Pubs, 1996. (ISBN: 0952205955). (LDS Lib. 929.2415 Os4fj).

Pedigree of O'Shaughnessy Family of Cork: IGRS Library (Leader Collection).

Limerick O'Shaughnessy's. Irish Family History 9 (1993) 10–16.

Capt Roger Shaughnessy (of Clanricarde, Galway) in 'King James' IAL' (Notes on family pre-1700).

The O'Shaughnessy Woods. N. Munster Antiq. J. 6(3) (1951) 83-90 (Appendix with notes on families involved in a land issue: Prendergast, Butler, Maghlin, Taylor, Martyn & Ringrose- 1500-1800).

Shaw *see also* **Payton**

Some notes on the Shaw family of Monkstown Castle. JCHAS 37 (1932) 93–5.

Concluding notes on the Shaw family of Monkstown Castle. JCHAS 40 (1935) 53–4.

Shears

Pedigree of Shears Family of Cork: IGRS Library (Leader Collection).

Shee or **Shea (O'Shee** or **O'Shea)** *see also* **Archdeacon, Power**

The Shee family of Garrandarragh. Old Kilkenny Review 4 (5) (1993) p. 1208-1214.

Capt. Thomas Shee (Merchant of Kilkenny City) in 'King James' IAL' (Notes on family members pre-1747).

Sheehan *see also* **Ireton**

Sheehan, Sheahan, O'Siochain in 'Family Names of Co. Cork' (see abbrevs.) (Notes on origins & members in Co.Cork).

Getting to know my gg grandfather Bernard Sheehan 1800 – 1868. Irish Family History 15 (1999).

(Mac) Sheehy

The MacSheehys of Connelloe, Co. Limerick. Ir. Gen. 4 (1970) 560–577.

Sheppard

Pedigree of Sheppard Family of Cork: IGRS Library (Leader Collection).

Sheridan *see also* **Gower**

Some account of the Sheridan family. Ancestor, 9 (1904) 1–5.

The genealogy of the Sheridans. Ir.Gen. 3 (1960, 1962) 162–9, 217–20, 274–6.

Sheridan's sisters; Sheridan's sons. W. Frazer Rae. Temple Bar, 45–63, 407–26. London, 1899.

The lives of the Sheridans. Percy Fitzgerals. London: Richard Bentley & Son, 1866. (LDS Lib. 929.2415 Sh53f. (Ref. to Brinsley, Callender, Chamberlaine, Linley).

Sherlock

Distinguished Waterford families. I: Sherlock. JW&SEIAS 9(1906)120–8,171–5; 10(1907) 42–4, 171–3.

Notes on the Family of Sherlock: from State Papers & Official Docs. JCKAS 2(1896–99) 33–47; 6(1909–11) 155–59.

The family of Sherlock. JCKAS 6 (2) (1909–11) 155–9.

Pedigree of Sherlock Family of Cork: IGRS Library (Leader Collection)

Notes on the pedigree of Sherlock of Mitchelstown, Co. Cork. JCHAS 12 (1906) 50–51.

Sherlock of Butlerstown, Co. Waterford. Ir.Gen. 4 (1969) 131–41.

Capt. Christopher Sherlock (of Littlerath, Waterford) in 'King James' IAL' (Notes on family pre-1700).

Capt. Thomas Sherlock (of Blackhall, Co Kildare) in 'King James' IAL' (Notes on family members pre-1703).

Shields

Irish origins of the Shields family. John Edgar Shields. Gathersburg, Md.: Shields, 1975. (LDS Lib. 929.2415 Sh61a.

Shirley

Stemmata Shirleiana, or annals of the Shirley family. E. P. Shirley. London, 1873.

Shirley Papers. [Lough Fea, Co. Monaghan]. Anal.Hib. 259–78.

Shortall or Shortill *see also* **Switzer**

Ballylarkin & the Shortall family. Old Kilkenny Review, 17 (1965) p. 5-8.

Shortis

Pedigree of Shortis Family of Cork: IGRS Library (Leader Collection).

Sibthorpe

Pedigree of Sibthorpe Family of Cork: IGRS Library (Leader Collection).

Siggins

Genealogical gleanings of Siggins & other Pennsylvania families. Emma Siggins White. Kansas City, Missouri. 1918.

Sinclair

The Sinclair genealogy. C. T. McCready. Dublin 1867.

Genealogy of the Sinclairs of Ulster. Sir John Sinclair. 1810.

The Montgomerys, the Sinclairs and Drumbeg House. Donegal Ann. 44 (1992) p.51-62.

Singleton *see* **Donnelly**

Sinnett, Sinnot *see also* **Synnott**

Sinnet genealogy . . . records of Sinnets, Sinnotts, etc. in Ireland and America. C. N. Sinnett. Concord, N.H., 1910.

Sirr

A genealogical history of the family of Sirr of Dublin. London, 1903.

The Sirr family and freemasonry. Harry Sirr. Margate: pr.pr. 1906. (LDS Lib. 929.2415 Si79s.

Sitlington

The Sitlington Family of Dunagorr, Co. Antrim. Ulster J. Arch. 15 (1909) 161–72.

Skelly

Some notes on Drogheda (Co.Louth) families of Carroll, Clinton, McGovern & Skelly. J.Old Drogheda Soc.11 (1998).

Notes on the Skellys of Drogheda and Nugents of St. Croix. J. Gen. Soc. I.2(1) (2001) 22-26.

Skerrett

Some records of the Skerrett family. JGAHS 15 (1931–33) p. 33–72.

Skiddy

The Skiddy family and Skiddy's Castle. JCHAS 29 (1893) 128–9.

Skrine *see* **Devereux**

Slacke

Records of the Slacke family in Ireland. Helen A. Crofton. 1900–02. (LDS Lib. 929.2415 Sl11c.

Sloane

Ancestors and descendants of Alexander Sloane, Killyleagh, Co. Down in Ireland. L.H. Altpeter. The author, 1986.

Pedigree of Sloane Family of Cork: IGRS Library (Leader Collection).

Smillie *see also* **Smyly**

Elder, L. C. The Smillies of Ballynahinch: a genealogy. The author, 1985.

Smith *see also* **O'Gowan & Hargreaves**

The chronicles of a puritan family in Ireland (Smith of Glasshouse). G. N. Nuttal-Smith from notes collected by R. Wm. Smith. Oxford: University Press, 1923. (LDS Lib. 929.2415 Sm51n.

Narrative Pedigree of the Family of Smith of Co. Offaly. Nuttall-Smith, G. N. 1921. GO Ms. 556.

Pedigrees of ...... & Smith. (LDS Mf.1279327.

Pedigree of Smith Family of King's Co. and Co. Tipperary 1666–1881. JAPMD 8 (1910–12) 208.

Pedigree of Smith/Smythe Family of Cork: IGRS Library (Leader Collection).

Smith of Co. Louth & Co. Down. Pedigree in 'Swanzy Notebooks'. RCB Library, Dublin.

Entries from Family Bible of Stirling Smith of Rush, Co. Dublin. Ir.Anc. 11(1) (1979) 3.

Smithwick

The Smithwick family. Old Kilkenny Review, 12 (1960) p. 21-24.

Smyly *see* **Gerrard**

Smye

Pedigree of Smye Family of Cork: IGRS Library (Leader Collection).

Smyth *see also* **Smith**

Genealogia dell' antica e nobile famiglia Smyth di Ballynatray nella Contea di Waterford in Irlanda. Estratta dagli antichi dal fu Cavaliere William Betham. Lucca, 1868.

Smyth Papers. [Drumcree, Co. Westmeath]. Anal. Hib. (20) 279–301.

The Smyths of Damma. Old Kilkenny Review, 4 (1) (1989) p. 614-621.

Snowe or Snow

Pedigree of Snowe Family of Cork: IGRS Library (Leader Collection).

Snows of Larkfield. JW&SEIAS 10(1) (1907) 261-2.

Somerville

The descent of the Somervilles of Drishane, Co. Cork. Ir. Gen. 5(1979) 704–
709.

The Somervilles and Their Connections in Cork. JCHAS 47 (1942) 30–33.

Records of the Somerville family of Castlehaven and Drishane, from 1174 to
1904 compiled. E. E. Somerville and Boyle Townshend Somerville. Cork,
1940.

The Pooles of Mayfield. R. ffolliott. Dublin: Hodges Figgis (1958). (Re:
Somervilles of Cork: 1690s to 1830's).

The Edith Somerville Archive in Drishane: catalogue & evaluative essay. Otto
Rauchbauer et al. Dublin: Irish Manuscripts Comm. 1994. (ISBN:
1874280053). (refs to Somerville and Coghill families).

Sotheron *see* **MacManus**

Southwell

The Southwells. JCHAS 18 (1912) 141–49.

Spearman

Pedigree of Spearman Family of Cork: IGRS Library (Leader Collection).

Spedding

Spedding family, & short accounts of families allied by marriage [Deey,
Brownrigg]. J. C. D. Spedding. Pr.pr. Dublin. 1909.

The Spedding family of Windgates. (7 p. manuscript & pedigree chart) NAI
Ms 4886.

Speer

Genealogy of the Speer family of Co. Donegal. Ms. (119 leaves) (LDS Lib.
929.2415 Sp32s.

Spenser

Spenser's pedigree. W. Devereux. JCHAS 15 (1909) 101–2; see also 11 (1905)
196.

Memorials of Edmund Spenser, the poet, and his descendants in the county of
Cork. JCHAS 14 (1908) 39–43.

The family and descendants of Edmund Spenser. W. H. Welply. JCHAS 28
(1922) 22–23, 49–61.

Lt Peregrine or Hugoline Spencer (of Rinney, Cork) in 'King James' IAL'
(Notes on family members pre-1700).

Splaine

Pedigree of Splaine Family of Cork: IGRS Library (Leader Collection).

Spotswood *see* **O'Mahony**

Spread

Pedigree of Spread Family of Cork: IGRS Library (Leader Collection).

Spread of Co. Cork. Ir. Anc. 2 (2) (1970) 102–11.

Stack

Pedigree of Stack Family of Cork: IGRS Library (Leader Collection).

Stafford

Staffords: From Wexford to Lanark Co. Canada. J. Gen. Soc. I. 1(1) (2000) 3-7.

Staker *see* **Wallace**

Stamers

Notes on the Stamers Family. JCHAS 3 (1897) 152–53, 193–94, 232, 304.

Standish

A History of the Standish Family in Ireland, Ontario & Alberta. J.R. Houston. Toronto:1979 (ISBN 0920830021).

Stapleton

The Stapletons of Drom, alias Font-Forte, Co. Tipperary. Rita C. Ryan-Hackett. Dublin: 1995 (ISBN: 095268500 0) (LDS Lib. 929.2415 St27r.

Staunton or **Stanton** *see also* **Blakeney**

Cornet Patrick Staunton (of Great Island, Cork) in 'King James' IAL' (Notes on family pre-1700).

Pedigree of Stanton Family of Cork: IGRS Library (Leader Collection).

Stawell

A Quantock family. G. D. Stewart. Taunton, 1910.

Pedigree of Stawell Family of Cork: IGRS Library (Leader Collection).

Steel

History as destiny in the James Steel Family from County Monaghan to Westmoreland Co. Familia 12 (1996) 52-74

Stevenson *see* **MacCormick**

Steward *see also* **Stewart**

Steward Family Papers (1671–1720). PRONI DOD 459; LDS Mf. 247311.

Stewart or **Steward** *see also* **Londonderry, Moore, Orr, Steward**

The Stewarts of Ballintoy: with notices of other families of the district in the 17th century. Ulster J. Arch. 6(1900) 17–23, 78–89, 143–61, 218–23. 7 (1901) 9–17. Also published by George Hill; Coleraine 1865.

The Stewarts of Ballintoy: with notices of other families of the district. George Hill. Ballycastle: Impact - Amergin, 1976. (LDS Lib. 929.2415 St49h. (Refs to Boyd, Dunlop, Fullerton, Hill, M'Neill, O'Hara).

Notes on the Stewart Family of Co. Antrim. JAPMD 7 (1907–09) 701.

Pedigree of Stewart/Steward Families of Cork: IGRS Library (Leader Collection).

Geographical index of Stewarts in Western Ulster, 1610-1900. Mary Stewart Kyritsis. (LDS Lib. 929.2415 St49k (Listing of Irish Stewart families by counties & baronies).

Stinson

Extracts from records of Drumholm Parish, Co Donegal (1695-1900) Stinson,

Mowbray, Cockburn, Thompson, & Taylor families: & Drumcree Parish in Co. Armagh, Ireland: Creany, O'Connell & Higgins families D.W. & H.S. Stinson. (LDS Lib. 929.2415 A1 no. 28).

Stirling

Stirlings in Scotland, Ulster and America. Familia 12 (1996) pp. 75-82.

Stoker

Pedigree of Stoker Family of Cork: IGRS Library (Leader Collection).

Stokes

The Stokes family. J. King. History of Co. Kerry, 192–9. Dublin, 1910.

Pedigree of Stokes Family of Cork: IGRS Library (Leader Collection).

A Stokes family of Dublin. A G Stokes. Melbourne 1986.

Stoney

Some old annals of the Stoney family. Major Stoney. London 1879.

Stopford

Stopford of Courtown. Wexford Gentry Vol. 1 (see abbreviations).

Stothard

Stothard of Co. Down. Pedigree in 'Swanzy Notebooks'. RCB Library, Dublin.

Stranaghan

Stranaghan family, Co. Down 1800–1950. N.P., 1990.

Strange

Pedigree of Strange Family of Cork: IGRS Library (Leader Collection).

Stout

The old Youghal family of Stout. JCHAS 23 (1917) 19–29.

Stuart

Genealogical & historical sketch of the Stuarts of the house of Castlestuart in Ireland. A.G. Stuart. Edinburgh: Blackwood, 1854. (LDS Lib. 929.2415 St92s).

Studdert

The Studdert family. R. H. Studdert. Dublin, 1960.

The Studderts of Kilkishen. The Other Clare 4 (1980) p. 32-34.

(O) Sullivan *see also* **Walsh, Kelly (Ainsworth misc.)**

The MacFinin Duibh O'Sullivans. JKAHS (New Series) 9 (1976) 32–67.

Materials for a history of the family of John Sullivan of Berwick, New England & O'Sullivans of Ardea. Gertrude E. Meredith. Pr.pr. Cambridge: Mass. 1893. (NLI Call No. Ir 9292 s7: LDS Lib. 929.2415 Su54m).

The Sullivans: a notable 19th century Kilkenny family. Old Kilkenny Review 16 (1954) 23–32.

A family chronicle derived from the notes and letters selected by Lady Grey. Ed. Gertrude Lyster. London, 1908.

(O') Sullivan in 'Family Names of Co. Cork' (see abbrevs.) (Notes on origins & members in Co.Cork).

Pedigree of Sullivan Family of Cork: IGRS Library (Leader Collection).

History of the O'Sullivans. JCHAS 4 (1898) 120–31, 207–12, 255–78.

Selections from The Zoilomastix of Philip O'Sullivan Beare ed. T. J. O'Donnell. Dublin 1960.

Cormick O'Sullivan: in 'King James' IAL' (Notes on Cork & Kerry family members pre-1750).

The Sullivans—A Notable 19th Century Kilkenny Family. Old Kilkenny Review, 16 (1964) p.23-32.

Bantry, Berehaven & the O'Sullivans. T. D. Sullivan. Dublin: Sealy, Bryers & Walker 1908. (LDS Lib.929.2415 Os8s.

The Sullivans: from Mallow to Killiney. Dun Laoghaire J. 7 (1998) 3-7.

Sutcliffe *see* **Switzer**

Sutton

Capt. John Sutton (of Kildare) in 'King James' IAL' (Family line pre-1689).

Capt. John Sutton (of Galway) in 'King James' IAL' (Notes on family pre-1700).

Swann *see* **Nesbitt**

Swanton

Pedigree of Swanton Family of Cork: IGRS Library (Leader Collection).

Swanzy

The Swanzys of Clontibret. Clogher Record 16 (1) (1997) 166-176.

The Swanzys of County Cavan. Clogher Record 16 (3) (1999)58-70.

Sweeney or **MacSweeney**

Leabhar Chlainne Suibhne: an account of the MacSweeney families in Ireland, with pedigree. ed. Rev. Paul Walsh. Dublin, 1920.

Irish chiefs and leaders. Rev. Paul Walsh. Ch. ix. Dublin, 1960.

Sween, clan of the battle-axe, a brief history of the MacSweeney (Mac Suibhne) galloglass. R. Mingo Sweeney. Bonshaw, Prince Edward Island, 1968. (LDS Lib. 929.2415 M249s).

Pedigree of Sweeney Family of Cork: IGRS Library (Leader Collection)

McSweeney, McSwiney in 'Family Names of Co. Cork' (see abbrevs.) (Notes on origins & members in Co.Cork).

The origins of Clann Suibhne. Donegal Ann. 42 (1990) p. 61-62.

The Rocky road to Dublin: McSweeney families of Tirconall. Seamus McManus. Talbot Press: Dublin.

McSweeney families of Tirconall. JRSAI 3(1854) 163; 19(1889) 42, 283-284; 43(1913) 103, 116; 45(1915) 223, 227, 240; 55(1925) 98; 60 (1950) 79.

Sweetman

Notes on the Sweetman family. JCKAS 3 (1899–1902) 389–90.

Swete

Pedigree of Swete Family of Cork: IGRS Library (Leader Collection)

Swift *see also* **Cope**

Notes on the Cooke, Ashe and Swift Families, all of Dublin. JAPMD 9 (1912–16) 503.

Family pedigrees, notes & letters for … Swift (primarily from Ulster in 17th & 18th centuries). Armagh Co. Museum Ms. F6: LDS Mf.1279353.

Switzer

Tipperary Switzers: descendants of John Switzer of Newpark, Co. Tipperary. Mary E. Switzer Manning, Bruce B. Peel, B. Wesley Switzer. Brantford, Ont: B.W. Switzer, 1987. (LDS Lib. 929.2415 Sw68m. (Refs to Cowan, Cowin, Doherty, Mason, Pettapiece, Shortill, Sutcliffe).

Swords

A Swords family collage. Irish Family History 3 (1987) 65-66.

Pedigree of Swords Family of Cork: IGRS Library (Leader Collection).

Edward Swords: A brief biography of a brief life. Irish Family History 5 (1989) 107-109.

Sykes

Sykes family – The Yorkshore Connection (Note). Irish Family History 3 (1987) 44.

Symes *see* **Warren**

Synan

The Synans of Doneraile. Mananaan Mac Lir. Cork, 1909.

Pedigree of Synan Family of Cork: IGRS Library (Leader Collection).

The family of Synan. Rev. J. A. Gaughan. Dublin, 1971.

Synge

The family of Synge or Sing. Pedigree tables bearing the above name. Mrs. L. M. Synge. Southampton, n.d. [1937?].

The Pooles of Mayfield. Rosemary ffolliott. Dublin: Hodges Figgis (1958). (Re: Synge of Cork).

Synott or **Synnott** *see also* **Sinnett**

Synnott (Wexford/ NJ-USA) Irish Roots. (3) 1997. p. 13.

William Synnott (Wexford) in 'King James' IAL' (Notes on family members pre-1700).

Synnott of Ballybrennan (Wexford). Wexford Gentry Vol. 2 (see abbreviations).

Taaffe

Memoirs of the family of Taaffe. Count E. F. J. Taaffe. Vienna, 1856. (LDS Lib. 929.2415 T11t).

Taaffe of Co. Louth. CLAHJ 14 (1960) 55–67.

Taggart *see also* **Tegart**

Discovering my Taggart Roots in Lecale, Co. Down. Ulster Gen. & Hist. Guild 19 (1996).

Tait

The Taits in Limerick & Melbourne. Old Limerick J. 23 (1988) 82-87.

Talbot

Genealogical memoir of the family of Talbot of Malahide, Co. Dublin. 1829.

The Talbots of Belgard. Reportorium Novum 1(1) (1955) 80–83.

Pedigree of Talbot Family of Cork: IGRS Library (Leader Collection).

Talbot de Malahide. Reportorium Novum 2(1) (1958) 96–103.

Catholic families of the Pale (inc. Talbot de Malahide). Reportorium Novum, 2 (1958) 88–108.

Richard Talbot, Capt. John Talbot (& other Talbot Family of Dublin) in 'King James' IAL' (Family line pre-1700).

Talbot of Ballytrent and Castle Talbot. Wexford Gentry Vol. 1 (see abbreviations).

Tandy

Tandy of Sion Lodge. Pedigree in 'Swanzy Notebooks'. RCB Library, Dublin.

Tandy of Drewstown. Pedigree in 'Swanzy Notebooks'. RCB Library, Dublin.

Tandy of Johnsbrook. Pedigree in 'Swanzy Notebooks'. RCB Library, Dublin.

Tanner

Pedigree of Tanner Family of Cork: IGRS Library (Leader Collection).

Tarrant

Pedigree of Tarrant Family of Cork: IGRS Library (Leader Collection).

Tartarain

Pedigree of Tartarain Family of Cork: IGRS Library (Leader Collection).

Taverner

Pedigree of Taverner Family of Cork: IGRS Library (Leader Collection).

Taylor *see also* **McNamara, O'Shaughnessy, Stinson**

Capt. John Taylor (of Dublin) in 'King James' IAL' (Notes on family pre-1700).

Pedigree of Taylor Family of Cork: IGRS Library (Leader Collection).

An Enterprising Cromwellian Family: The Taylors of Dunkerron (Kilkenny). JKAHS (New Series) 17 (1984) p.61-76.

Teape

Teape - a genealogy, with special reference to those outside the U.S. Jesse H. Day. Athens, Ohio: 1983. (LDS Lib. 929.2415 T222d (Refs to Bunce, Fugard, Huxley, Keane).

Tegart or **Taggart**

The Tegarts of Co. Cavan (1781-1972). (LDS Lib. 929.2415 A1 no. 4.

Tempest *see* **Londonderry**

Tennent *see* **Langham**

Terry
> Some Spanish Terry's of Irish Origin. Ir.Gen. 10 (3) (2000) 372-373.
> Terry pedigree. JCHAS 9 (1903) 274–6.
> The Ryan and Terry Families in Spain. Ir. Gen. 10(2) (1999) 245-249.

Thompson or **Thomson** *see* **Stinson, Guinness, Rothwell**

Thornhill
> Pedigree of Thornhill Family of Cork: IGRS Library (Leader Collection).

Thornton *see* **Ireton, Nesbitt**

Thurston
> The Thurstons and Ardmore. Ardmore J. 1 (1984) 26–30; 2 (1985) 32.

Tidbury
> Pedigree of Tidbury Family of Cork: IGRS Library (Leader Collection).

Tiernan or **McTiernan/McTernan**
> The Tiernans and other families. C. B. Tiernan. Baltimore, 1901.
> Pedigree of McTernan Family of Cork: IGRS Library (Leader Collection).

Tierney
> The Tierneys and the Egmont estates. JCHAS 27 (1921) 10–14.

Tighe
> Papers (e.g., deeds, leases, and pedigrees) relating to following families: Daly;
> Dunne of Brittas; Fetherston; Hatfield of Killimor; Homan; Magan of
> Emoe; Percy; Tighe; Wilson of Piersfield. Longford/Westmeath Library
> (Upton Papers), and LDS Mf. 101011.

Tipper
> Lt. Edward Tipper (& Tipper Family of Tipperstown, Co.Kildare) in 'King
> James' IAL' (Family line pre-1689).

Tobin or **Tobyn** *see also* **Blake**
> The genealogy of Walter Tobin and his family. Ossory, 2 (1880–83) 92–5.
> ·Tobin of Caherlesk and Tobinstown. Ir.Gen. 5(1979) 760–762.
> Tobin of Kilnagranagh, Co. Tipperary. Ir. Gen. 5(4) (1977) 491–95.

Tollett
> Pedigree of Tollett Family of Cork: IGRS Library (Leader Collection).

Tomkins
> Pedigree of Tomkins Family of Cork: IGRS Library (Leader Collection).

Tone
> The Family of Tone. JCKAS 12 (1935–45) 326–29.
> Wolf Tone's House. JCKAS 14 (4) (1969) 376. (Re: residences of Tone family members).
> History of the Tone family. Frank G. Tone. Niagara Falls, NY 1944.

O'Toole & Toole
> The O'Tooles, anciently lords of Powerscourt. John O'Toole. Dublin. n.d.
> (LDS Lib. 929.2415 Ot6ot.
> Les O'Toole: notice sur le clan ou la tribu des O'Toole. La Role, 1864.

O'Byrne, G. Historical Reminiscences of O'Byrnes, O'Tooles, O'Kavanaghs and Other Irish Chieftains. London: M'Gowan, 1843.

Ensign Edward Toole (of Wicklow) in 'King James' IAL' (Notes on family pre-1700).

History of the clan O'Toole & other Leinster septs. P. L.O'Toole. Dublin: M.H.Gill, 1890. (LDS Lib. 929.2415 Ot6o).

Toomey

Toomey, Twomey in 'Family Names of Co. Cork' (see abbrevs.) (Notes on origins & members in Co.Cork).

Topp

Pedigree of Topp Family of Cork: IGRS Library (Leader Collection).

Torrens

Pedigree of Torrens Family of Cork: IGRS Library (Leader Collection)

Tottenham

The family of Tottenham. Sir Richard Tottenham. Privately pr., 1959.

Tottenham of Tottenham Green (Wexford). Wexford Gentry Vol. 2 (see abbreviations).

Towgood

Large Pedigree Book for Towgood Family. IGRS Library (Leader Collection).

Townley *see also* **Ashmur**

Two residences of the Townley family. CLAHJ 5 (4) (1924) p. 267.

Townsend or **Townshend**

An officer of the Long Parliament and his descendants being an account of the life & times of Colonel Richard Townshend of Castletown (Castle Townshend), & a chronicle of his family. R. & D. Townshend. London, 1892.

Pedigree of Townsend Family of Cork: IGRS Library (Leader Collection).

The Pooles of Mayfield. R. ffolliott. Dublin: Hodges Figgis (1958). (Re: Townsends of Derry: 1600's to late 1800's).

Genealogical history of the family of Townsend in Engand and Ireland. G. D. Daunt (1850). NLI Ms 25,529.

Tracey

Traceys of Tipperary. Irish Family History 8 (1992) 33–34.

Traill *see* **Darbyshire**

Trant

Trant family. JCKAS 5(1919) 18–26.

Trant Family. JKAHS (Old Series) 2 (1914) 237–62; 3 (1914) 20–38; 5(1919) 18–26.

The Trant family. S. T. McCarthy. Folkstone, 1924. Supplement, Folkstone, 1926. (LDS Lib. 929.2415 T688m.

The Trant family. J. King. History of Co. Kerry. 346–52. Dublin, 1911.

The Trants: an Enterprising Catholic Family in 18th Century Co. Cork. JCHAS 86 (1981) 21–29; 243-4.

Just Across the water. Ion Trant. Dovea, Co Tipperary, 1996. (ISBN 0952759519). (Trants of Dovea, Co Tipperary).

Travers *see also* **Blake**

Hollywood, Co. Wicklow: with account of owners to the commencement of 17th century. JCKAS 8 (1915–17) 185–96.

Pedigree of Travers Family of Cork: IGRS Library (Leader Collection).

Trehy

The Trehy Family (Tipperary). Irish Family History 8 (1992) 69–77.

Trench *see also* **Monck**

Memoir of the Trench family. T. R. F. Cooke-Trench. London: Spottiswoode 1897. (LDS Lib. 929.2415 T722c.

Genealogical record of the descendants of John & Mary Palmer, PA, especially through … James Trimble. Lewis Palmer. Lippicott & Co.; Philadelphia 1875.

Tressillian

Pedigree of Tressillian Family of Cork: IGRS Library (Leader Collection).

Trousdell

Pedigree of Trousdell Family of Cork: IGRS Library (Leader Collection).

Troy *see* **D'Aran**

Truman

Pedigree of Truman Family of Cork: IGRS Library (Leader Collection).

Tucker

Tucker of Petersville. Pedigree in 'Swanzy Notebooks'. RCB Library, Dublin.

Tuite

Tuite family biographies and records. Longford/Westmeath Library and LDS Mf. 1279285.

Tuke

The family of Tuke. Ir. Anc. 6 (1974) 67–72.

Tuohy

Pedigree of Tuohy Family of Cork: IGRS Library (Leader Collection).

Turner *see also* **Rose**

The Pooles of Mayfield. R. ffolliott. Dublin: Hodges Figgis (1958). (Re: Turners of Kent, Cork etc: 16th to 18th c.).

Pedigree of Turner Family of Cork: IGRS Library (Leader Collection)

Turpin

The Turpin Family of Tullamore, Co. Offaly. Ir. Anc. 16 (1) (1984) 1–5.

Turton *see* **Bernard**

Tuthill

Pedigrees of families of Tuthill and Villiers of Co. Limerick [with notes]. P. B. Tuthill. London, 1907–8.

Tweedy

The Dublin Tweedys: the story of an Irish family 1650–1882. Owen Tweedy. London: Vallentine & Mitchell, 1956. (LDS Lib. 929.2415 T916. (Refs to Owen, Bond & Meredith).

Twiss

Pedigree of Twiss Family of Cork: IGRS Library (Leader Collection).

Twomey *see* **Toomey**

Tyndall

Tyndall of Leighlin: Carlow's genius. Carloviana 2 (27) 22-27; 2(28) 23-27.

Tynte

Some notes on the Tynte family. JCHAS 9 (1903) 156–7.

Tyrrell *see also* **Murphy**

Genealogical history of the Tyrrells of Castleknock in Co. Dublin, Fertullagh in Co. Westmeath and now of Grane Castle, Co. Meath. J. H. Tyrrell. London, 1904.

The Tyrrells of Castleknock. JRSAI 76 (1946) 151–54.

Capt. Sir Edward Tyrrell (of Meath) in 'King James' IAL' (Notes on family pre-1700)

The Tyrrells of County Wexford. JOWS 7 (1978-9) p. 5-20

Kate Tyrrell, 'Lady Mariner'. John Mahon. Dublin: Basement Press 1994 (ISBN: 1855941406). (Tyrell of Arklow 1863-)

Uniacke

The Uniackes of Youghal. JCHAS 3 (1894) 113–16, 146 52, 183–91, 210–21, 232–41, 245–55.

Ussher

The Usshers of Birr. Ir. Gen. 5 (5) (1978) 606–624.

The Ussher memoirs, or genealogical memoirs of the Ussher families in Ireland. W. B. Wright. London, 1899.

Ussher Papers (Cappagh, Co. Waterford). Anal. Hib. 15: 63–78.

Uvedale

Pedigree of Uvedale Family of Cork: IGRS Library (Leader Collection)

Valentine

The Valentine Family of Donard. West Wicklow Hist. Soc. J. 2 (1983/4) 63–69; 1 (1985/6) 22–26.

Pedigree of Valentine Family of Cork: IGRS Library (Leader Collection).

Vance *see* **Cleland**

An account historical and genealogical of the family of Vance in Ireland. W. Balbirnie. Cork: Noblett 1860. (Another edition - Letchworth: Arden Press, 1908) (Refs to Balbirnie connections). (LDS Lib. 929.2415 A1 no. 11.

Vane *see also* **Londonderry**

Vaughan

A Tipperary farmer & Waterford tradesman of 2 centuries ago. JW&SEIAS 8(32) (1903) 80-89.

Venable *see* **Ferrar**

Venn

Pedigree of Venn Family of Cork: IGRS Library (Leader Collection).

Vereker

The Vereker family. Ir. Anc. (1973) 69–75.

Verling

Dr. James Roche Verling and the pedigree of the Verlings. JCHAS 22 (1916) 66–71.

Verner *see* **Rose**

Vesey-Fitzgerald

The Vesey-Fitzgerald family (Co. Clare). The Other Clare 14 (1990) p.48-51.

Vicars

Vicars of Laois and Carlow. Ir. Anc., 2 (2) (1970) 90–101.

Vickery

Vickery, Louise E., & Rice, B. Vickery of Evansville, Indiana 1850–1987: the descendants of William Warner Vickery and Elizabeth Wolfe from South-west Cork, Ireland. Evansville, Indiana, 1987: 408pp.

Vickers *see* **Murphy**

Vigors

Vigors Papers. [Burgage, Co. Carlow]. Anal. Hib. 20, 302–10.

The Vigors of Leighlinbridge. Carloviana 2 (8) (1980).

Villiers

Dromona, the memoirs of an Irish family. T. M. Mackenzie, Dublin c.1910.

Pedigree of the family of Villiers of Kilpeacon, Co. Limerick. P. B. Tuthill. London, 1907.

Pedigrees of Families of Tuthill and Villiers of Co. Limerick (with notes). Tuthill, P. B. London, 1907–08.

Vincent

The Vincent family of Limerick and Clare. Ir.Gen. 4(4) (1971) 342–8.

Pedigree of Vincent Family of Cork: IGRS Library (Leader Collection).

Vowell

Pedigree of Vowell Family of Cork: IGRS Library (Leader Collection).

Waddell

Waddell of Co. Down. Pedigree in 'Swanzy Notebooks'. RCB Library, Dublin.

Wadding *see* **Dobbyn.**

Waddy *see also* **Warren**

The Harvey-Waddy Connection. JOWS 8 (1980–81).

Wade *see* **Clarke**

Waggett

Large Pedigree Book for Waggett Family. IGRS Library (Leader Collection).

Wakeham

Pedigree of Wakeham Family of Cork: IGRS Library (Leader Collection).

Wakely

The Wakelys of Navan and Ballyburly. Riocht na Midhe 5(4) (1974) 3–19.

Walcott

Pedigree of Walcott Family of Cork: IGRS Library (Leader Collection).

Waldron

Sketches of Waldron & Hamilton history (1135-1927). Jane Waldron Patterson. Stafford: W. H. Smith, 1927. (LDS Lib. 929.2415 W147p. (Refs to Armstrong, Coats, Graham, Potterton).

Walker *see* **Ashmur, McNaughton**

Wall

The Wall Family in Ireland 1170–1970. Hubert Gallwey. Naas: Leinster Leader Co., 1970. (LDS Lib. 929.2415 W154g).

Wallace *see also* **Mullan**

Memoirs of the Staker Wallaces, with genealogy of family. by Eunice G. Brandt & William Staker Wallace. Chicago: J. S. Hyland, 1909. (LDS Lib. 929.2415 W155b).

Waller

Waller family records: includes pedigrees, notes etc on Warren, Ward, Smyly, Butler, Hamilton & related families. (GO Ms. no. 652, LDS Mf.257819).

Wallis

The Wallis Family of Drishane. JCHAS 67(1962)48–51.

Walsh or **Welsh** *see also* **Devoy**

Notes on the Norman-Welsh family of Walsh in Ireland, France and Austria. JRSAI 75 (1945) 32–44.

Nota et synopsis genealogiae comitum de Walsh aut Wallis. Ossory 2 (1880–83) 95–8.

The French branches of the family of Walsh. Gen. 17 (1900–01) 36–43, 90–9, 153–8.

The Austrian branches of the family of Walsh. Gen. 17 (1901) 217–24; 18 (1901) 79–88.

The family of Walsh from 1170 to 1690. J. Walsh. New York [1925].

A royalist family, Irish and French (1689–1789). translated from French by A. G. Murray MacGregor. Edinburgh: William Brown, 1904. (LDS Lib. 929.2415 W168t.

Pedigree of Walsh of Crannagh, Co. Roscommon. JAPMD 7 (1907–09) 700.

Pedigree of Walshe/Welsh Family of Cork: IGRS Library (Leader Collection).

A 'lost' history of the Walsh family, 1588. Eigse 30 (1997) 133-157.

Scraps of Walsh Mountain History. JW&SEIAS 10(1907) 73-87; 311-316; 12 (1909) 173-178 (pedigree).

Walsh, Welsh, Breathnach in 'Family Names of Co. Cork' (see abbrevs.) (Notes on origins & members in Co.Cork).

The Walsh family of Lower Grange, Goresbridge, Co. Kilkenny. Old Kilkenny Review 49 (1997) p. 89-106.

The lament for John MacWalter Walsh: with notes on the history of the family (1170 to 1690). J. C. Walsh. New York: Kelmscott Press, 1925. (NLI Call NO. Ir 9292 w20: LDS Lib. 929.2415 W168w).

The Walshs of Castlehowel (Kilkenny). Patrick Walsh & J. J. Walsh. Ms. (177 leaves) (LDS Lib. 929.2415 W168wc (refs to O'Sullivan & McCarthy).

History of the Walsh clan; 1170-1970. Patrick J. Walsh. Kilkenny:1970. (LDS Lib. 929.2415 W168wp.

Capts. Valentine & Peirs Walsh (of Waterford) in 'King James' IAL' (Notes on family members pre-1700).

Walter *see* **Waters.**

Wandesforde

Story of the family of Wandesforde of Kirklington & Castlecomer. Ed. by Hardy Bertram M'Call. London: 1904. (LDS Lib. 929.2415 W183m. (Refs to Bowes, Colville, Conyers, Fulthorpe, Musters, Norton).

Warburton

Memoir of the Warburton family of Garryhinch, King's Co. Dublin, 1848. 2nd ed., 1881.

Pedigree of Warburton Family of Cork: IGRS Library (Leader Collection).

Ward or **Mac an Bhaird** *see also* **Murphy**, **Waller**

The learned family of Mac an Bhaird. in: 'Irish Men of Learning'. Paul Walsh; Three Candles, Dublin (1947) (16th century & earlier references).

Pedigree of Ward Family of Cork: IGRS Library (Leader Collection).

Waring

Pedigree of Waring Family of Cork: IGRS Library (Leader Collection).

Warren

History of the Warren family (in various countries). Thomas Warren. Oxford: Gresham 1982. (ISBN 0946095019).

Pedigree of Warren Family of Cork: IGRS Library (Leader Collection).

Some Notes on the Family of Warren of Warrenstown, Co. Louth. CLAHJ 4 (1916) 26–34.

The Warren saga. Edward O'Boyle. Londonderry, n.d. [1947?]. (LDS Lib.

929.2415 W251o.

Warren family pedigrees: Warren, Gates, Cusack, Symes & related families pedigrees & genealogical records. GO Ms no. 635, (LDS Mf.257819. (Also Swan & Waddy).

Washington

The Irish Washingtons. George Washington. Boston, 1898.

Waters or Walter

The Waters or Walter Family of Cork. JCHAS 31 (1926) 7–78; 32 (1927) 17–23, 104–13; 33 (1928) 35–41; 34 (1929) 36–42, 97–105; 35(1930) 36–43, 102–13; 36 (1931) 26–38, 76–86; 37 (1932) 35–41.

Pedigree of Waters Family of Cork: IGRS Library (Leader Collection).

The Waters or Walter family of Cork. Eaton W. Waters. Cork: Guy, 1939. (LDS Lib. 929.2415 W315w).

Waters of Waterstown, Co. Wicklow. Ir.Gen. 3 (1965) 380–3.

Watkin

Pedigree of Watkin Family of Cork: IGRS Library (Leader Collection).

Watson *see also* Ashmur

Watson of Larchill [query]. JCKAS 14 (1966-67) p.233.

The Fitzwilliam, O'Brien & Watson families: History & Genealogy. Dorothy M.G. Holland. Pr.pr. St Louis 1973.

Wauchop(e)

The Ulster branch of the family of Wauchope. G. M. Wauchope. London, 1929.

Brigadier John Wauchop in Appendix to 'King James' IAL' (Notes on military career pre-1700).

Weekes

Pedigree of Weekes Family of Cork: IGRS Library (Leader Collection).

Wellesley

The Barons of Norragh, Co. Kildare 1171-1660. JRSAI 45 (1915) 84-101.

West

The Wests of Ballydugan, Co. Down; the Rock, Co. Wicklow; & Ashwood, Co. Wexford. Ulster J. Arch. 12 (1906) 135–41, 159–65.

Westropp

Pedigree of Westropp Family of Cork: IGRS Library (Leader Collection)

Whaley

Pedigrees of …Whaley et al. LDS mf. 1279327.

Wheddon

Pedigree of Wheddon Family of Cork: IGRS Library (Leader Collection).

Whelan *see* Forster, Fahy

Wherland

Pedigree of Wherland Family of Cork: IGRS Library (Leader Collection).

White *see also* **McLysaght**

The Whites of Dufferin & their connections. Ulster J. Arch. 12 (1906) 117–25, 169–74; 13 (1907) 89–95, 125–32.

Pedigree of White Family of Cork: IGRS Library (Leader Collection).

The History of the family of White of Limerick, Knockantry, Cappawhite, Lisowen, Kilmoylan etc. J. D. White. Pr.pr. Cashel 1887.(NLI Call no. Ir 9292 w10).

Capt John White (of Loyhall, Co Limerick) in 'King James' IAL' (Notes on family members pre-1747).

The Whites of Bantry: family origins. Bantry Hist. & Arch Soc. J. 2 (1994) 47-58.

Whiteside

Whiteside(s) & related surnames in Diocese marriage licence bonds, 1629-1845. Don Whiteside. Ottawa, Ont: 1985. (LDS Lib. 929.2415 A1 no. 62.

Index to Whiteside(s) births, 1864-1921. compiled by Don Whiteside. LDS Lib. 929.2415 A1 no. 64.

Index to Whiteside(s) marriages, 1845-1921. compiled by Don Whiteside. LDS Lib. 929.2415 A1 no. 63.

Whiteside(s) names in the public records 1649-1900. Compiled by Don Whiteside. (Includes Registry of Deeds, Wills & Administration Bonds, 1669 Hearth Money Rolls & Armagh Poll Book, 1753). Ms. LDS Lib. 929.2415 W588w.

Index to Whiteside(s) deaths: 1864-1921: & N. Ireland 1922-1929. compiled by Don Whiteside. Ms. LDS Lib. 929.2415 W588wd.

Whiteside/Whitsitt, etc., from selected Irish sources: Vol I: General records. by Don Whiteside LDS Lib. 929.2415 W588wdo.

Records of Whitesides in records inc. censuses, taxation, land, civil, military, directories, etc. (1659 to 1954). LDS Lib. 929.2415 W588wdo.

Whitley

The Whitleys of Enniskillen. T. Whitley Moran. Hoylake, 1962.

Whittington

Whittington family notes. Appendix to 'Old St Malachy's'. Seanchas Ardmhacha 1(2) (1955) 169-191. (single page of family info 1680-1848 – re Armagh).

Whitty

Pedigree of Whitty Family of Cork: IGRS Library (Leader Collection).

Wickham

Byrnes and Wickhams of Wexford. Irish Family History 9 (1993) 55–58.

Wickliff *see* **Pearson**

Widman *see* **Lyons**

Wilde *see also* **Elgee**

The Wildes of Merrion Square: the family of Oscar Wilde. Patrick Byrne. London & NY: Staples Press. LDS Lib. 929.2415 W644b. (Ref to Lloyd).

Wilkes

Pedigree of Wilkes Family of Cork: IGRS Library (Leader Collection).

Wilkinson *see also* **Moore**

Fragments of family history. S. P. Flory. London, 1896.

Williams

The Groves and Lappan; Monaghan county, Ireland. An account of a pilgrimage thither, in search of the genealogy of the Williams family. J. F. Williams. Saint Paul, 1889. (LDS Lib. 929.2415 W671w).

Williamson *see* **MacNair**

Willis

Pedigree of Willis Family of Cork: IGRS Library (Leader Collection).

Willoughby

Notes: Willoughbys in Fermanagh & Monaghan. Clogher Record 15 (3) (1996) 158.

Notes: Willoughbys & Willoughby-Montgomerys in the North of Ireland. Clogher Record 16 (1) (1997) 177-179.

Wilson *see also* **McNamara, Moore**

Papers (e.g., deeds, leases, & pedigrees) relating to … Wilson of Piersfield. Longford/Westmeath Library (Upton Papers) & LDS mf. 101011.

Wilsons of Upper Cavan (1818-1895) a tale of prosperity, tragedy & bankruptcy. Donegal Ann. 43 (1991) p. 99-108.

Some Wilsons of Ulster: related families and descendants. Louis Alexander Astell. LDS Lib. 929.2415 W691a.

Six Generations of Friends in Ireland 1655-1890. Jane M. Richardson. London 1895. (Wilson of Co Offaly).

Wilton

Alcock Wilton of Wexford. Irish Builder. 1888.

Wingfield

Muniments of the family of Wingfield. Viscount Powerscourt. London, 1894.

Winthrop

Some account of the early generations of the Winthrop family in Ireland. Cambridge, Mass., 1883.

Wiseman

Pedigree of Wiseman Family of Cork: IGRS Library (Leader Collection).

Wogan

Memoire historique et genealogique sur la famille de Wogan. Count Alph. O'Kelly of Galway. Paris, 1896.

Wogans of Rathcoffey. The Clongownian. 3(3) (1904) pp. 46-54.

The Wogans of Rathcoffy, Co. Kildare – a correction. JCKAS 5 (2) (1906) pp. 109-113.

Lt.-Colonel. John, & Major James, Wogan (of Kildare) in 'King James' IAL' (Family line pre-1689).

Request for information on Thomas Wogan. JRSAI 21 (1890) p 320-321.
(Gives info on Rathcoffy family).

Adventures of Edward Wogan. Frederick Maurice. London, Routledge Paul
1945.

Wogans of Rathcoffy, Co. Kildare. JRSAI 21 (1890) p 119-129.

Wolfe or **Woulfe** *see also* **Flanagan**

The Wolfe family of Co. Kildare. JCKAS 3 (1899–1902) 361–67.

Wolfes of Forenaghts, Blackhall, Baronrath, Co. Kildare, Tipperary, Cape of
Good Hope etc. R. T. Wolfe. Guildford: W. Matthew, 1893. LDS Lib.
929.2415 W832w.

Vickery of Evansville, Indiana 1850–1987: the descendants of William Warner
Vickery and Elizabeth Wolfe from Southwest Cork, Ireland. Vickery,
Louise E., & Rice, B. Evansville, Indiana, 1987: 408 pp.

Pedigree of Wolfe Family of Cork: IGRS Library (Leader Collection).

Ensign Philip Wolfe (of Kildare) in 'King James' IAL' (Family line pre-1689).

Wolverston

The Wolverstons of Stillorgan. Reportorium Novum 2(2) (1960) 243–45.

Wood or **Woods**

The family of Wood, Co. Sligo. Ir. Gen. 3 (8) (1963) 300–09; 3 (9) (1964)
364–65.

Pedigree of Woods Family of Cork: IGRS Library (Leader Collection).

William & Eliza (Johnson) Woods of Co Antrim, Ireland: Their descendants
& some allied families. J. Robt. Woods & Laurence C. Baxter. Gateway
Press: Baltimore 1984.

Woodhouse

Pedigrees of … Woodhouse et al. LDS mf. 1279327.

Woodley *see also* **McNaughton**

Pedigree of Woodley Family of Cork: IGRS Library (Leader Collection)

Wray

The Wrays of Donegal, Londonderry & Antrim. C. V. Trench. Oxford Univ.
Press, 1945; & Hodges Figgis 1946. LDS Lib. 929.2415 W924t.

Wray of Co. Monaghan. Pedigree in 'Swanzy Notebooks'. RCB Library,
Dublin.

Wright *see also* **Ashmur**

Wright of Co. Monaghan. Pedigree in 'Swanzy Notebooks'. RCB Library,
Dublin.

Wrixon

Wrixon of Co. Cork. Pedigree in 'Swanzy Notebooks'. RCB Library, Dublin.

Pedigree of Wrixon Family of Cork: IGRS Library (Leader Collection).

Wynne

The Wynnes of Sligo and Leitrim. Winston G. Jones. Manorhamilton: Drumlin Pubs, 1994 (ISBN: 1873437072). (LDS Lib. 929.2415 W992g).

Wyly *see* **Acheson**
Wyse
> Ancient & Illustrious Waterford Families: The Wyses of the Manor of St.
> John's, Waterford. JW&SEIAS 5(1899) 199–206.

Yarner
> A collection concerning the family of Yarner of Wicklow. J. C. H. N.p.,1870.
Yeats or **Yeates**
> The Yeates family and the Pollexfens of Sligo. William M. Murphy. Dublin:
> Dolmen Press, 1971. 929.2415 A1 no. 2.
Yelverton
> Pedigree of Yelverton Family of Cork: IGRS Library (Leader Collection).
Young *see also* **Gower**
> Three hundred years in Inishowen, being more particularly an account of the
> family of Young of Culdaff. Ann Isabel Young. Belfast: McCaw, Stevenson
> & Orr, 1929. LDS Lib. 929.2415 Y84y.
> The Extinct Family of Young of Newtown-O'More, Co. Kildare. JCKAS 3
> (1899–1902) 338.

Placename Index

This is **not** a comprehensive index to the places associated with the families listed in this book. The index refers only to placenames noted in the titles of the book or article cited. Some of the placenames used in these titles are the names of houses or properties and will therefore not be found in listings of townlands, parishes etc. Where possible, the county location of each placename has been provided, but it was not always possible to determine the location, usually because several places of the same name exist, and it is not clear which one is referred to.

Abbotstown (Dublin)	Falkiner
Aberfeldy (Scotland)	Scott
Achill (Mayo)	Butler
Achonry (Sligo)	O'Conor
Adamstown (Wexford)	Devereux
Aghalow (Tyrone)	Hamilton
Aharney (Kilkenny)	Marum
Altmore (Tyrone)	Irwin
America	see USA
Anagad (Tyrone)	O'Neill
Annakisha (Cork)	Roche
Annakissy (Cork)	Nagle
Annfield (Kildare)	Dexter
Antrim	Agnew, McAulay, Barcroft, Bell, Caters, MacDonald, Donnan, Macdonnell, Fulton, O'Hara, Higginson, McKinley, Lattimore, Moore, MacNaghten, MacNeill, Percy, MacQuillin, McRory, Rose, Sitlington, Stewart, Woods, Wray
Ardagh (Longford)	Fetherton
Ardagh (Cork)	O'Flynn,
Ardamine (Wexford)	Richards
Ardee (Louth)	Dawson, Hatch, Moore, Potter, Ruxton,
Ardea (Laois)	Sullivan
Ardes, Great	Hamilton
Ards (Down)	Savage
Ardfert (Kerry)	Fitzmaurice
Ardmore (Waterford)	Anson, Thurston

Ardnagowen (Roscommon)	Lloyd
Ardtully (Kerry)	MacCarthy
Argarvan	Barbour
Armagh	Acheson, Blacker, Blaney, McCann, McCone, Cust, Donaldson, McDonnell, Glasson, Halliday, Hanlon, O'Kane, Molyneux, Obins, Pearson, Richardson, Seaver, Stinson,
Artane (Dublin)	Hollywood
Ashgrove (Cork)	Rogers
Athenry (Galway)	Bermingham, Lambert
Athgoe (Dublin)	Locke
Athlone (Westmeath)	Devenish, Hynes
Athlumney (Meath)	Dowdall
Athy (Kildare)	Archbold, Fitzgerald
Atlanta (Georgia – USA)	O'Reilly
Augher (Tyrone)	Gartland
Aughrim (Galway)	Butler
Austria	Walsh
Australia	Browne, Caraher, Cardiff, D'Aran, Duffy, Forrestal, O'Halloran, Heron, Kavanagh, Mansfield, Martin, Maher, Morgan, Mulcahy, Rice, Rochford, Ronan, Tait
Balla (Mayo)	Nally
Ballea (Cork)	McCarthy
Ballinacargy (Cavan)	O'Reilly
Ballinahinch Castle (Galway)	Martin
Ballinderry (Antrim)	Higginson
Ballinderry (Derry)	McGuckin
Ballinkeele (Wexford)	Maher
Ballinrobe (Mayo)	Fair
Ballintoy (Antrim)	Stewart
Ballitore (Kildare)	Shackleton
Ballyadams (Laois)	Bowen
Ballyarthur (Wicklow)	Bayly
Ballybeggan (Kerry)	Morris
Ballybrennan (Wexford)	Synnott
Ballybrittas (Laois)	Devoy, Flynn,
Ballybritt (Offaly)	Oxburgh
Ballybur (Kilkenny)	Comerford
Ballyburly (Meath)	Wakely
Ballycarr (Clare)	Colpoys
Ballycastle (Antrim)	McNeill

Ballycuneen (Clare)	O'Halloran
Ballyduff (Kilkenny)	Robbins
Ballydugan (Down)	West
Ballyellen (Carlow)	Blackney
Ballyfad (Wexford)	Kinsella
Ballygarrett (Cork)	Curtin
Ballygriffin (Cork)	Nagle
Ballyheigue (Kerry)	Cantillon
Ballylagan (Meath)	Fleming
Ballylarkin (Kilkenny)	Shortall
Ballyleck (Monaghan)	Montgomery
Ballylinny (Antrim)	Percy
Ballymacane (Wexford)	Barrington
Ballymacone (c. Armagh)	McCone
Ballymagir (Wexford)	Devereux
Ballymore (Westmeath)	Magan
Ballymore (Wexford)	Donovan
Ballymulconry (Roscommon)	Mulconry
Ballymurray (Roscommon)	Crofton
Ballynahinch (Down)	Rea/Rae, Smillie
Ballynamalough (Kildare)	Bermingham
Ballynascullogue (Kildare)	Flatesbury
Ballynastragh (Wexford)	Esmonde
Ballyneale (Tipperary)	O'Neill
Ballyowen (Dublin)	Nottingham
Ballyporeen (Tipperary)	O'Brien
Ballyrankin (Wexford)	Devereux
Ballysax (Kildare)	Nangle
Ballyshannon (Donegal)	Connolly, Hewetson
Ballyshannon (Kildare)	Fitzgerald, Hewson
Ballytrent (Wexford)	Hughes, Talbot
Ballyvonare (Cork)	Harold
Balmagir (Wexford)	Devereux
Balmain (Australia)	Duffy
Baltimore (USA)	O'Donnell
Baltinglass (Wicklow)	Eustace, FitzEustace
Baltrasna (Meath)	O'Reilly
Balyna (Kildare)	O'More
Bandon (Cork)	Barry, Bernard
Bangor (Down)	Bradshaw, Neill
Bannow (Wexford)	Boyse
Bantry (Cork)	O'Sullivan, White

Bargy (Wexford)	Harvey
Baronrath (Kildare)	Wolfe
Bawnmore (Kilkenny)	Bellew
Beaulieu (Louth)	Montgomery
Belagh	FitzGerald
Belfast (Antrim/Down)	Bell, McCabe, Ferguson, Lindsay, Magee, Mayne, MacRory
Belleisle	Cole
Bellevue (Wexford)	Cliffe
Belmont (Galway)	Coulson, Donnelly, Crushell
Belturbet (Cavan)	French
Belvelly Castle	Hodnett
Berehaven (Cork)	O'Sullivan
Berwick (New England)	Sullivan
Bessbrook (Armagh)	Richardson
Birchgrove (Tipperary)	Birch
Birr (Offaly)	Parsons, Ryan, Ussher
Bishopscourt (Kildare)	Ponsonby
Blackhall (Kildare)	Sherlock, Wolfe
Blarney (Cork)	McCarthy
Bodenstown (Kildare)	Long
Bonnetstown (Kilkenny)	Mathew
Bonniconlon (Mayo)	O'Dowda
Boom Hall	Alexander
Borris (Carlow)	Kavanagh
Bowenscourt (Cork)	Bowen
Boyle (Roscommon)	King
Bracknagh (Offaly)	Campion
Brawney (Meath)	Brien
Brittas (Wexford)	Dunne
Brize Castle (Mayo)	Moore
Brookhill (Mayo)	Lambert
Bullingate (Wexford)	Braddell
Burgage (Carlow)	Vigors
Burrishoole (Mayo)	Butler
Butlerstown (Waterford)	Boxwell, Sherlock
Byfleet (England)	Cooper
Cabinteely (Dublin)	Barrington
Cabra (Dublin)	Segrave
Caherlesk (Kilkenny)	Hayden, Tobin
Cahermacnaughten (Clare)	O'Davoren
Cahir (Tipperary)	Butler

Cahirnane (Kerry)	Herbert
Caledon (Tyrone)	Hamilton
Calgary (Canada)	Nolan
Callan (Kilkenny)	Candler
Callinafercy (Kerry)	Markham
Calry (c Westmeath)	Magawly
Cambray (France)	Loffroy
Camolin (Wexford)	Annesley
Canada	O'Brien, Caldwell, Chadwick, Grattan, O'Kane, Lyster, Nolan, Stafford, Standish
Cape of Good Hope	Wolfe
Cappagh (Limerick)	Peppard
Cappagh (Waterford)	Ussher
Cappard (Galway)	Galbraith
Cappercullen (Limerick)	O'Grady
Carbery, West (Cork)	Cole, O'Regan
Carbury (Kildare)	Birmingham, Boylan, Colley
Cardiff (Wales)	Herbert
Cardistown (Louth)	Caraher
Carlingford (Louth)	Acheson
Carlow	Blackney, Breen, Brereton, McCall, Conwil, Cooke, Dillon, Duckett, Kavanagh, Moorhouse, O'Neill, Rudkin, Tobin, Tyndall, Vicars, Vigors
Carnagh (Wexford)	Lambert
Carolina, South (USA)	Phillips
Carran (Tyrone)	O'Neill
Carrickblacker (Armagh)	Blacker
Carrickduff (Carlow)	Cavenagh
Carrickfergus (Antrim)	Caters, Lattimore
Carrickglass (Longford)	Lefroy
Carrigcastle (Waterford)	Anthony
Carriglea (Waterford)	O'Dell
Carrigrohane (Cork)	Pratt
Cashel (Tipperary)	Butler, Sall, Scully
Castle Annaghs (Kilkenny)	Murphy
Castle-Dawson (Derry)	MacRory
Castle Dillon (Armagh)	Molyneux
Castle Ellen (Galway)	Lambert
Castle Lambert (Galway)	Lambert
Castle MacGarrett (Mayo)	Browne
Castle Morris (Kerry)	Morris
Castle Saunderson (Cavan)	Saunderson

Castle Talbot (Wexford)	Talbot
Castle Townshend (Cork)	Townshend
Castleborough (Wexford)	Carew
Castlebridge (Wexford)	Dixon, Nunn
Castlecomer (Kilkenny)	Wandesforde
Castlecoole (Fermanagh)	Corry
Castlefish (Kildare)	Fish
Castlegar (Galway)	Mahon
Castlehaven (Cork)	Somerville
Castlehowel (Kilkenny)	Walsh
Castleknock (Dublin)	Tyrrell
Castlemartin (Kildare)	Eustace
Castlemartyr (Cork)	Daly, Pratt
Castleobins (Armagh)	Obins
Castlepollard (Westmeath)	Evans
Castlestuart (Scotland)	Stuart
Castletown (Kildare)	Connolly, Dongan
Cavan	Adams, Poole, Babington, Baker, Boylan, Burrows, Colkin, French, Humphreys, Kernan, Moore, Nugent, Parr, Perrott, O'Reilly, Saunderson, Swanzy, Tegart, Wilson
Celbridge (Kildare)	O'Reilly
Charleville House (Wicklow)	Monck
Chester (England)	Clayton, Folliott
Clainsullagh (Donegal)	O'Hegerty
Clanbrasil (Galway)	Donelan
Clandeboye (Down)	Blackwood, Hamilton
Clanricarde (Galway)	Shaughnessy
Clara (Offaly)	Goodbody
Clare	Bentley, Blake-Butler, Blood, Bloxham, Borough, O'Brien, Browne, Butler, O'Callaghan, Colpoys, MacConmara, Cuffe, Darcy, O'Davoren, D'Esterre, Fahy, Finucane, FitzGibbon, O'Halloran, Huleatt, Kenney, O'Loghlen, Lysaght, Macraith, Maunsell, Magrath, O'Meehan, McNamara, Nihell, Parker, Rochford, Ryan, Sarsfield, Studdert, Vesey-Fitzgerald, Vincent
Claremorris (Mayo)	Gray
Clashmore (Waterford)	Power
Clobemon (Wexford)	De Rinzy, Dundas
Cloghanadfoy	Oliver
Cloghballymore (Galway)	French

Clogher (Tyrone)	MacCathmhaoil, Delany, Kennedy
Cloghoge (Armagh)	McCann
Cloghran (Dublin)	FitzRery
Cloghrennan (Kilkenny)	Butler
Clomahon (Wexford)	Levinge
Clonbrock (Galway)	Dillon
Clones (Monaghan)	McMahon
Clooneene Estate (Galway)	Forster
Clones (Monaghan)	Connolly
Clongowes (Kildare)	Browne
Clonleigh (Cork)	Condon
Clonmacnoise (Offaly)	Charlton
Clonmeen (Cork)	O'Callaghan
Clonmel (Tipperary)	Bagwell
Clonmore (Carlow)	McCall
Clonmore (Mayo)	Phillips
Clonoulty (Tipperary)	Browne
Clontibret (Monaghan)	Swanzy
Clonuane (Clare)	Darcy
Cloonbonny (Longford)	Davys
Coill t-Sealbhaigh (Cork)	O'Crowley
Coleraine (Derry)	Caldwell
Comber (Down)	Andrews
Conagher (Antrim)	McKinley
Connello,Upper (Limerick)	Scanlan, MacSheehy
Coolbanagher Castle (Laois)	Hartpole
Coolbawn (Wexford)	Breen
Coole Park (Galway)	Gregory
Cooloney (Sligo)	O'Hara
Coolroe (Laois)	Flynn
Coolybrown (Limerick)	Miller
Coragh (Armagh)	Pearson
Corcreevy (Tyrone)	Burnside
Corglass (Monaghan)	Nesbitt
Cork	Acheson, Adderley, Ahearne, Aher, Aitkenhead, Alcock, Aldworth, Allen, Anstis, Archer, Armstrong, Atkin, McAuliffe, Austen, Baker, Baldwin, Ball, Barnard, Barrett, Barrington, Barron, Barry, Barter, Bassett, Bateman, Beamish, Bennett, Berkley, Berry, Betson, Bettesworth, Bevan, Biggs, Blackhall, Blair, Blatchford, Blennerhassett, Boate, Bolster, Bourne, Bowden,

Cork—*contd.*

Bowen, Bradfield, Brady, Bray, Brennan, Brettridge, O'Brien, Brinkley, Britton, Broderick, Brohen, Brooks, Brotherton, Browne, Buckley, Bullen, Bunworth, Burnett, Busteed, Butt, O'Callaghan, Carbery, Cardigan, Carew, Carlisle, Casey, Cashman, Chadwick, Chartres, Cherry, Chinnery, Chivers, Christian, Claffey, Clarke, Clements, Coakley, Coane, Cogan, Coghill, Colclough, Cole, Coleman, Collis, Collins, Condon, McConnell, O'Connell, Connolly, O'Connor, Conron, Cooper, Copley, Corban, Corbet, Corker, McCormick, Cosgrove, Costello, Cotter, Courthope, Creagh, Crocket, Crofton, Crofts, Croker, Crone, Cronin, Crooke, Crosby, Cross, Crowley, Cudamore, Cuffe, Cullen, McCullagh, Curran, Curtin, McCutcheon, Dacey, Daly, Danckert, Daniels, Darcy, Darrah, Daunt, Davies, Dawson, Deane, Deady, Delany, Dennehy, Dennison, Denny, Mac Dermot, Desmond, Dobbs, Dobbin, Dogherty, MacDonogh, O'Donnell, O'Donovan, Dowden, Dowe, Dowman, Downcy, Doyle, O'Driscoll, Duffield, Duggan, Dullea, Dungan, Eagar, Earberry, Eason, Eaton, Eedy, Egan, Ellerd, Ellis, Evans, Evanson, Evatt, Everitt, Fenwick, Fitton, Fitzell, Fitzgerald, Fleetwood, O'Flynn, Foott, Fowkes, Fox, Franklin, Freeman, Freke, Fry, Fuller, Furlong, Gamble, Garde, Gardiner, Gelston, Gibbs, Gillman, Gleeson, Godkin, Godson, Gollick, Good, Goodbody, Goold, Gore, Gosnell/Gosnold, Granard, Grant, Gray, Greatrakes, Green, Gregory, Haines, Halahan, Hall, Hammet, Hare, Harman, Harmon, Harrington, Harris, Harrison, Hart, Hartland, Hawkes, Hawkins, Hawkshaw, Hayes, Hazelton, O'Hea, Healy, Heard, O'Hegarty, Henderson, Hendley, Hennessey, Henry, Heppentall, Herlihy, Heron, Herrick, Hickcy, Hickson, Hilliard, Hoare, Hobson, Holmes, Homan, Honner, Howard, Hudson, Huleatt, Hull, Humphreys, Hurley, Husscy, Ince, Ingram, Ireton, Ivey, Jackson, Jacob, Jameson, Jeffereys, Jepson, Jermyn, Jones, Jordan, Judd, Juman, Keating, O'Keefe, Keevil, Kell,

Cork—*contd.*

Kelleher, Kellet, Kelly, Keaneally, Kennedy, Kenney, Keogh, Keohane, Kerin, Keyburn, Kidd, King, Kingston, Kirby, Knagges, Lahee, Lamb, Lane, Langtrey, Lappan, Larkin, Lawless, Leader, Leahey, O'Leary, Lewis, Limrick, Long, Lordon, Loughrea, Lovekin, Lucas, Lucett, Lundy, Lynskey, Lyons, Macoboy, Madden, Maguire, McMahon, O'Mahony, Mapowder, Martin, Massey, Maunsell, Maxwell, Maynard, Meade, Merrick, Metcalfe, Milner-Barry, Mitchell, Mooney, Moore, Morgill, Morton, Mulhern, O'Mullane, McMullen, Murphy, McMurray, Meyers, Nagle, McNally, Nash, O'Neill, Nelligan, Nevil, Newenham, Nicholson, Nowlan/Nolan, Noonan, Notter, Oliver, Olney, McOstrich, Owgan, Palmer, Parker, Parsons, Pearson, Penn, Pennefather, Pennington, Penrose, Peppard, Perrott, Perry, Phayre/Phair, Philpot, Popham, Powell, Pratt, Preston, Priestly, Pritchard, Pulvertaft, Punch, Purdon, Puxley, Pyne, Quain, Rabbitt, Radcliffe, Radley, Raines, Raycroft, Reade, Redmond, O'Regan, Reagan, Reynell, Rice, Richards, Riggs, Riordan, Roberts, Robinson, Roche, Rochford, Roe, Rogers, Ronayne, Rooney, Ruddock, Rumley, Russell, Rutter, Ryall, Ryder, Rye, Sadleir, St. Leger, Sall, Sanders, Sarsfield, Scarborough, Sealy, Shaen, Shannon, Shears, Sheehan, Sheppard, Sherlock, Shortis, Sibthorpe, Sloane, Smith, Smye, Snowe, Somerville, Spearman, Spenser, Splaine, Spread, Stack, Staunton, Stawell, Stewart, Stirling, Stoker, Stokes, Strange, Stout, Sweeney, Swete, Swords, Tanner, Tarrant, Tartarain, Taverner, Taylor, Thornhill, Tidbury, McTernan, Tollett, Tomkins, Toomey, Topp, Torrens, Townshend, Travers, Tressillian, Trousdell, Truman, Tuohy, Turner, Twiss, Uvedale, Venn, Vincent, Vowell, Wakeham, Walcott, Walsh, Warburton, Ward, Waring, Warren, Waters, Watkin, Weekes, Westropp, Wherland, Whitty, Wilkes, Willis, Wiseman, Wolfe, Woods, Woodley, Wrixon, Yelverton

Corlattylannan (Cavan)   O'Reilly

Corofin (Clare)	Blood
Correnney (Fermanagh)	Johnston
Corrytanty (Monaghan?)	Carragher
Corsallagh House (Sligo)	O'Conor
Courtstown (Kilkenny)	Grace
Courtown (Wexford)	Stopford
Courtwood (Laois)	Devoy
Cradockstown (Kildare)	Allen
Crannagh (Roscommon)	Walsh
Cratloe (Clare)	O'Brien
Creeslough (Donegal)	Moore
Cregg (Galway)	Butler, Kirwan
Cruicerath (Meath)	Netterville
Culdaff (Donegal)	Young
Culvin (Westmeath)	O'Flaherty
Cumberland (England)	Bewley
Curriglas (Cork)	Maynard
Cushendun (Antrim)	McNeill
Damma (Kilkenny)	Smyth
Dangan (Kilkenny)	Butler
Decies (Waterford)	Fitzgerald
Delville (Dublin)	Delany
Delvin (Meath)	MacCoghlan
Denmark	Eskildson
Derbyshire (England)	Eyre
Derry	Allen, Ash, Boyle, Caldwell, Folliott, McGuckin, O'Kane, Kennedy, O'Mullen, MacRory, Wray
Derryoge (Down)	Scott
Derryvullan (Fermanagh)	Delany
Desertmartin (Derry)	McGuckin
Devon (England)	Cole
Donadea (Kildare)	Aylmer
Donard (Wicklow)	Valentine
Donegal	Boyd, O'Brien, Brookes, Dill, Lockhart, McColgan, Colhoun, Connolly, Crawford, Dickson, Dill, Doherty, O'Donnell, Downey, Early, McFee, O'Gormley, Hart, Harvey, O'Hegerty, Hewetson, Irwin, Knox, McLaughlin, Lockhart, Montgomery, O'Mullen, Patton, O'Peatain, Reynolds, Sinclair, Speer, Stinson, Wray, Young
Donelaong (Cork)	O'Driscoll
Doneraile (Cork)	St. Leger, Synan,

Donoughmore (Cork)	Healy
Doolin (Clare)	MacNamara
Doon (Limerick)	Moone
Doons (Tyrone)	O'Mullen
Dorsey (Tyrone)	O'Neill
Dowdstown (Louth)	Callan
Down	Acheson, Andrews, Blackwood, Bradshaw, Camac, Clayton, Cleland, Clenlow, Cossett, Henry, Jellett, Lowry, Magennis, Monroe, Montgomery, Neill, Neilson, Pollock, Quinn, Rea/Rae, Roden, Savage, Scott, Sloane, Smillie, Smith, Stothard, Stranaghan, Taggart, Waddell, West, White
Dowth (Meath)	Netterville
Drewstown (Meath)	Tandy
Drishane (Cork)	Somerville, Wallis
Drogheda (Louth)	Carroll, Clinton, McGovern, Moore, Skelly
Drom (Tipperary)	Stapleton
Dromaneen Castle	O'Callaghan
Dromiskin (Louth)	Callan
Dromlohan (Limerick)	Drew
Dromoland (Clare)	O'Brien
Dromore Castle (Clare)	O'Brien
Drumard (Armagh)	Pearson
Drumbee (Tyrone)	O'Neill
Drumbeg House (Donegal)	Montgomery, Sinclair
Drumcagh (Fermanagh)	Bredin
Drumcondra (Dublin)	Bathe
Drumcree (Westmeath)	Smyth
Drumcree (Armagh)	Stinson
Drumharsna (Galway)	French
Drumholm (Donegal)	Stinson
Drumsurn (Derry)	O'Mullen
Duagh (Kerry)	Fitzmaurice
Dublin	Acheson, Acton, Arnoldi, Ash, Barnewall, Barrington, Bathe, Bellingham, Brocas, Bury, Cooke, Cooper, Corballis, Corker, Cruise, Cusack, Delany, Denham, Dexter, Dix, Dongan, Ely, Fagan, Falkiner, Fannin, Fitzgerald, FitzRery, Fitzwilliam, Grierson, Halliday, Hargreaves, Harold, Holly-wood, Herbert, Heron, Hollywood, Holmes, Jacob, Jellett, Kane, Kingsbury, Law, Leeson, Locke, Luttrell, Magee, Magennis, Moore, Moorhouse,

Dublin—*contd.*	Nottingham, Parsons, Pemberton, Plunkett, Rathborne, Rose, St. Lawrence, Sarsfield, Scurlock, Segrave, Sirr, Smith, Stokes, Sullivan, Swift, Talbot, Taylor, Tweedy, Tyrrell, Wilde, Wolverston, Woulfe,
Duckett's Grove (Carlow)	Duckett
Dufferin (Down)	Hamilton, White
Duhallow (Cork)	MacDonogh
Duiske Abbey (Kilkenny)	Butler
Dunagorr (Antrim)	Sitlington
Dunany (Louth)	Gernon
Dunboy (Cork)	Puxley
Dunboyne (Meath)	Butler
Dunbrody (Wexford)	Etchingham
Dundonnell (Westmeath)	Dalton
Duneane (Antrim)	MacRory
Dungarvan (Waterford)	Ryland
Dungimmon (Cavan)	Boylan
Dunkerron (Kilkenny)	Taylor
Dunleer (Louth)	Foster
Dunsandle (Galway)	Daly
Dunsoghly (Dublin)	Plunkett
Edermine (Wexford)	Power
Edgeworthstown (Longford)	Edgeworth
Edmonstown Park (Dublin)	Hargreaves
Egmont estates (Cork)	Tierney
Ely House (Wexford)	Hughes
Ematris (Monaghan)	Nesbitt
Emoe (Laois?)	Magan
Emyvale (Monaghan)	McKenna
England	Bewley, Butler, Clayton, Cole, Cooper, Corker, Courthope, Davies, Dowse, Ellis, Eyre, Flood, ffolliott, Folliott, Hassard, Jacob, Madden, Maxwell, Moutray, Nevil, Ormsby, Parsons, Penrose, Pratt, Richardson, Sandys, Sankey, Savage, Steel, Sykes, Townsend
Ennis (Clare)	Cuffe
Enniskillen (Fermanagh)	Kernan, Maguire, Whitley
Ennistymon (Clare)	O'Brien, MacNamara
Erlestown (Kilkenny)	Erley
Eyre Court (Galway)	Eyre
Eyreville (Galway)	Eyre

Factory Hill (Cork)	Hoare
Fanad (Donegal)	Dill
Farnane (Waterford)	Fitzgerald
Feltrim (Dublin)	Fagan
Fermanagh	Blennerhassett, Bredin, Connolly, Corry, Delany, Downey, Fawcett, Fiddes, Frith, Mac Guire, Hamilton, Irwin, Johnston, Kernan, Langham, Maguire, Nixon, Ovens, Rosborough, Whitley, Willoughby,
Fermoy (Cork)	Dennehy, Roche
Ferns (Wexford)	O'Neill
Fernsborough (Longford)	Burrowes
Fertullagh (Westmeath)	Tyrrell
Fethard (Tipperary)	Everard
Fiddown (Kilkenny)	Ponsonby
Finuge (Kerry)	Hewson
Fircall (Meath)	O'Molloy
Firgrove (Kilkenny)	Robbins
Forenaghts (Kildare)	Wolfe
Foulis Castle (Scotland)	Monroe
Foynes (Limerick)	Fitzsimons
France	O'Brien, De la Touche, McDonnell, Hadsor, O'Hagerty, Loffroy, Maguire, McMahon, Montmorency, MacNamara, Walsh
Gallagh (Galway)	O'Kelly
Gallstown (Kilkenny)	Burke
Galway	Athy, Bellew, Bermingham, Burke, Butler, Carroll, Coulson, Crushell, Daly, Darcy, Dillon, Donelan, Donnelly, Duggan, Eyre, Forster, French, Galbraith, Gregory, O'Halloran, Hoade, Hurly, Joyce, Kelly, Kenney, Kirwan, Lacey, Lally, Lambert, Lynch, Madden, Mahon, O'Malley, Martin, Meade, Mills, Morris, MacNamara, Seymour, O'Shaughnessy, Sutton, Swanton
Gardenmorris (Waterford)	Power-O'Shee
Garnavilla (Tipperary)	Nagle
Garrandarragh (Kilkenny)	Shee
Garryhinch (Offaly)	Warburton
Gawsworth (England)	Pratt
Geelong (Australia)	Mansfield
Glanerought (Kerry)	Fitzmaurice
Glasshouse (Cork /Offaly)	Smith
Glasslough (Monaghan)	Fraser, Leslie

Glenane (Cork)	Fitzgerald
Glencolumbkille (Donegal)	O'Brien
Glendruid (Dublin)	Barrington
Glenfriacan (Cork)	O'Keefe
Glenmore (Kilkenny?)	Cardiff
Glenravel (Antrim)	Bell
Goresbridge (Kilkenny)	Walsh
Gorey (Wexford)	Doyle
Gormanston (Meath)	Preston
Gort (Galway)	Forster, O'Shaughnessy
Gragara (Kilkenny)	Murphy
Granard (Longford)	Forbes
Grane Castle (Meath)	Tyrrell
Grange, Lower (Kilkenny)	Butler
Grangemellon (Kildare)	Fitzgerald
Great Island (Cork)	Staunton
Grey Abbey (Down)	Montgomery
Gurteen	Grier
Harperstown (Wexford)	Hore
Harristown (Kildare)	Hendy, La Touche, Ruskin
Headford (Galway)	Carroll, Mills
Heath Hall (Armagh)	Seaver
Helston (Cornwall, England)	Penrose
Highfield (Cork)	Duggan
Holland	*see Netherlands*
Hollywood (Wicklow)	Travers
Holywood (Down)	Rea/Rae
Horetown (Wexford)	Goff
Hortland (Kildare)	Hort
Howth (Dublin)	St. Lawrence
Hughstown (Roscommon)	Mulloy
Hurdlestown (Clare)	Bentley
Hy Fiachra	O'Dowd, O'Heyne, O'Shaughnessy
Hy Many	Kelly, O'Madden
Idough (Kilkenny)	O'Brennan
Ikerrin (Tipperary)	O'Meagher
Illeagh	Bourke
India	Callaghan, Goodall
Indiana (USA)	Vickery
Inishbofin (Galway)	O'Halloran, Lacey
Inishowen (Donegal)	McColgan, O'Doherty, Harvey, McLaughlin
Inishannon (Cork)	Meade

Islandmagrath (Clare)	Macraith, Maunsell
Ivagha (Cork)	O'Mahony
Iveagh (Down)	Magennis, Monroe
Ivory (Kildare)	Hartpole
Jamestown (Wexford)	Gray
Jenkinstown (Kilkenny)	Bellew, Bryan
Johnsbrook (Meath)	Tandy
Johnstown (Kildare)	Flatesbury
Kells (Meath)	Molloy, Rothwell
Keneonin (Armagh)	Mackey
Kenmare (Kerry)	Palmer
Kent (England)	Courthope
Kentucky (USA)	O'Daniel, Hamilton
Kerdiffstown (Kildare)	Kerdiff
Kerry	Bernard, Blennerhassett, Browne, Cantillon, MacCarthy, Conway, Denny, Eagar, McElligott, Fitzgerald, Fitzmaurice, Fuller, O'Halloran, Herbert, Hewson, Hickie, Leslie, O'Mahony, Markham, O'Moriarty, Morris, Nolan, Orpen, Palmer, Pierse, Stokes, Sullivan, Trant
Kesh (Fermanagh)	Blennerhassett
Kilballyowen (Limerick)	O'Grady
Kilbrew (Meath)	Barnwell
Kilbride (Cavan)	Boylan
Kilbride (Kildare)	Longfield
Kilcash (Tipperary)	Butler
Kilclogher (Galway)	Kenney
Kilcor (Cork)	O'Brien
Kilcornan (Limerick)	Drew
Kilcoursey (Offaly)	Fox
Kilcronaghan (Derry)	Allen
Kilcullen (Kildare)	FitzEustace
Kildare	Acheson, Alen, Allen, Archbold, Aylmer, Bagot, Baron, Bermingham, Birmingham, Boylan, Brereton, Browne, Bulby, Burke, Colley, Connolly, O'Connor, Dexter, Dixon, Dongan, Macdonnell, Dooney, Eustace, Fish, FitzEustace, Fitzgerald, Flatesbury, Hartpole, Hendy, Henry, Hewetson, Hewson, Hort, Kavanagh, Kerdiff, Lattin, La Touche, Lawe, Loffroy, Long, Longfield, Mansfield, Moorhouse, O'More, Nangle, Noble, Nuttall, Palmer, Ponsonby, Robinson, Ruskin, Sarsfield,

Kildare—*contd.*	Shackleton, Sherlock, Spedding, Sutton, Tipper, Wogan, Wolfe, Young
Kildress (Tyrone)	O'Mullen
Kilelton (Kerry?)	Hickie
Kilfrush (Limerick)	Gubbins
Kilkea Castle (Kildare)	Dixon
Kilkeel (Down)	Scott
Kilkenny	Anderson, Archdeacon, Archer, Baron, Bathe, Bellew, Blunden, Bourchier, O'Brennan, Bryan, Burke, Butler, Candler, Cardiff, Comerford, Cowley, Dixon, Edward, Erley, Fitzgerald, Garvey, Grace, Greene, Hayden, Helsham, Hewetson, Langton, Lawless, Loftus, Marum, Mathew, Morris, Murphy, Myhill, Ponsonby, Reade, Robbins, Ronan, Rothe, Shee, Shortall, Smyth, Sullivan, Taylor, Tobin, Walsh, Wandesforde
Kilkishen (Clare)	Studdert
Killamon (Limerick)	Mahoney
Killane (Tipperary)	Maher
Killarney (Kilkenny)	Myhill
Killeen (Mayo)	O'Donnell
Killimor (Westmeath)	Hatfield
Killiney (Dublin)	Sullivan
Killogeenaghan (Westmeath)	Robinson
Killowen (Kerry)	Orpen
Killyleagh (Down)	Sloane
Killynumber (Derry)	Allen
Kilmacough	O'Hanly
Kilmacow (Kilkenny)	Greene
Kilmallock (Limerick)	Lacy
Kilmannock (Wexford)	Houghton
Kilmoney (Cork)	Roberts
Kilmore (Armagh)	Pearson, Quigley
Kilmoylan (Tipperary)	White
Kilnagranagh (Tipperary)	Tobin
Kilnamanagh (Tipperary)	O'Dwyer
Kilpeacon (Limerick)	Villiers
Kilranelagh Hse. (Wicklow)	Greene
Kilrue (Meath)	Berford
Kilsheelan (Tipperary)	Power
Kiltolla (Galway)	Darcy
Kiltra (Wexford)	Boyd

Kinalea (Cork)	Long
Kinelmeky (Cork)	O'Mahony
King's Co.	*see Offaly*
Knightstown (Meath)	Bathe
Knockantry (Limerick)	White
Knockfad (Cavan)	Humphreys
Kyle (Wexford)	Harvey
Lackagh (Kildare)	Fitzgerald
Ladysbridge (Cork)	Daly
Ladytown (Kildare)	Allen
Laois (Queen's Co.)	Baldwin, Barrington, Beale, Bowen, Byrne, Chetwood, Cosby, Dempsey, Devoy, Fitzgerald, Flynn, Hartpole, Jolly, Lyster, Leicester, Magan, O'Meehan, O'More, Owen, Roberts, Rudd, Sullivan, Vicars
Larchill	Watson
Larkfield (Waterford)	Snow
Laurelhill (Monaghan)	Griffiths
Lavally (Galway)	Lynch
Leap, The (Wexford)	Devereux
Lecale (Down)	Taggart
Legbourne (England)	Dowse
Lehana	Gray
Leighlin (Carlow)	Tyndall
Leighinbridge (Carlow)	Vigors
Leitrim	Mac Dermot, Downey, Gray, Hawksby, O'Meehan, Moran, Mulvey, O'Reilly, MacRannal, Reynolds, O'Rourke, Wynne
Leixlip (Kildare)	Lawe
Levally (Mayo)	Fair
Limavady (Derry)	Boyle, MacRory
Limerick	Barrington, Bevan, O'Brien, Drew, Ferrar, Fitzgerald, Fitzsimons, Ganley, O'Grady, Greene, Griffin, Gubbins, Hart, Lacy, Mahoney, Miller, Monckton, Morgan, MacNamara, Moone, Nihell, Nolan, Peppard, Quinn, Scanlan, O'Shaughnessy, MacSheehy, Tait, Tuthill, Villiers, Vincent, White
Lincolnshire (England)	Ormsby
Lisburn (Antrim)	Barcroft, Fulton, Rose
Lisdoagh (Cavan)	O'Reilly
Lismacue (Tipperary)	Baker
Lisnacrieve (Tyrone)	Lindsay

Lisoarty (Monaghan)	McMahon
Lisowen (Down)	White
Lissanoure (Antrim)	Macartney
Lissinisky (Tipperary)	O'Meara
Listowel (Kerry)	Nolan
Littlerath (Waterford)	Sherlock
Lixnaw (Kerry)	Fitzmaurice
Loftus hall (Wexford)	Ely
Londonderry or **Derry**	Allen, Ash, Boyle, Caldwell, Folliott, McGuckin, O'Kane, Kennedy, O'Mullen, MacRory, Wray
Longford	Bond, Barbour, Burrowes, Daly, Davys, Edgeworth, Egan, Ferrall, Fetherton, Fleming, Forbes, Geraghty, Hyde, Kane, Lefroy, Reilly
Longueville (Cork)	Longfield
Lota (Cork)	Galwey, Rogers
Lough Fea (Monaghan)	Shirley
Lough Scur (Leitrim)	Reynolds
Loughcrew (Meath)	Plunkett
Lough Eske (Donegal)	Brookes
Loughgall (Armagh)	Cope, Pearson
Loughinsholin (Derry)	Allen
Loughmoe (Tipperary)	Purcell
Loughry (Tyrone)	Lindesay
Louth	Bellew, Byrne, Cairnes, Callan, Caraher, Carroll, Chamberlain, Cliffe, Clinton, Colclough, Dawson, De Verdon, Disney, Dowdall, Fortescue, Foster, Gernon, McGovern, Hadsor, Hatch, Montgomery, Moore, Murphy, Neary, Parkinson, Plunkett, Potter, Ruxton, Skelly, Smith, Taaffe, Warren
Loyhall (Limerick)	White
Lucan (Dublin)	Fitzgerald, Sarsfield
Ludlow (England)	Davies
Lurgan (Armagh)	Blaney, O'Reilly, Rose
Luttrellstown (Dublin)	Luttrell
Luxembourg	Clancy
Lyons (Kildare)	Aylmer
Magherabeg (Donegal)	O'Hegerty
Malahide (Dublin)	Talbot
Mallow (Cork)	Barrow, Hartland, Jephson, Kell, Philpott, Mansfield, Quain, Rice, Sullivan
Manchester (England)	Corker
Marble Hill (Galway)	Burke

Marlfield House (Tipperary)	Bagwell
Martinstown (Roscommon)	Davys
Maryland (USA)	O'Daniel, Hamilton
Massachusetts (USA)	Dowse
Mayfield (Cork)	Poole, Corker, Courthope, ffolliott, Fleming, Holmes, Meade, Morgan, Morris,
Mayglass (Wexford)	Browne
Mayo	Basquill, Browne, Butler, O'Clery, O'Connor, Dolan, MacDonald, O'Dowda, Fair, Garvey, Gray, Lambert, O'Malley, Mellett, Moore, Morris, Nally, Ormsby, O'Peatain, Phillips, Ruttledge
Meaghstown Castle	Meade
Meath	Barnewall, Barnwell, Bathe, Beatagh, Berford, Brien, Butler, Cusack, Darcy, Dowdall, Draycott, Duffy, Evers, ffolliott, Fleming, Folliott, McGawley, Grierson, McKeogh, O'Melaghlins, O'Molloy, Netterville, Pentheny, Piers, Plunkett, Preston, O'Reilly, Rothwell, Tandy, Tyrrell, Wakely
Melbourne (Australia)	Heron, Mansfield, Tait
Merrion (Dublin)	Fitzwilliam
Merview (Galway)	Joyce
Mile-Cross (Down)	Bradshaw
Milltown (Dublin)	Leeson
Minnesota (USA)	Crosby
Mitchelstown (Cork)	King, Sherlock
Mocollop Castle (Cork)	Drew
Monaghan	Acheson, Blaney, Campbell, McCarron, Carson, Connolly, Corry, Dawson, Fraser, Griffiths, Harper, McKenna, Leary, Leslie, McMahon, Montgomery, Nesbitt, Noble, Pockrick, Rogers, Shirley, Steel, Swanzy, Williams, Willoughby, Wray, Wright
Monanton (Monaghan)	Carson
Monea Castle (Fermanagh)	Hamilton
Monksgrange (Wexford)	Richards
Monkstown (Dublin)	Parsons
Monkstown Castle	Shaw
Monmore (Carlow)	Kavanagh
Moore Hall (Louth)	Moore
Moorehall (Mayo)	Moore
Mooremount (Louth)	Moore
Morett Castle (Laois)	Fitzgerald

Mornington (Meath)	Draycott
Mount Alexander (Down)	Montgomery
Mount Bellew (Galway)	Bellew
Mount Falcon (Tipperary)	Falkiner
Mount Nagle (Cork)	Nagle
Mount Nugent (Cavan)	Nugent
Mountmellick (Laois)	Beale
Mourne (Down)	Magennis
Moville (Donegal)	Montgomery
Moyacomb (Wick/Carlow)	O'Neill
Moyfinn (Meath)	McKeogh
Moylurg (Leitrim)	Mac Dermot
Moyne Hall (Cavan?)	Moore
Muintir Thaidgean	Foxe
Muintuavara	O'Daly
Mullinagoan (Fermanagh)	Rosborough
Mullinahone (Tipperary)	Hackett
Murrisk (Mayo)	Garvey
Muskerry (Cork)	Long, Murphy
Navan (Meath)	Wakely
Ned (Cavan)	Kernan
Netherlands (Holland)	Bor, McDonnell
New Brunswick (USA)	Crosby
New Jersey (USA)	Synnott
New Ross (Wexford)	Dormer, Ivory
New South Wales (Australia)	D'Aran
New Zealand	Dooney, Magennis
Newcastle (Down)	Roden
Newcastle Oconyll (Limerick)	Fitzgerald
Newcastle-upon-Tyne (Eng.)	Parsons
Newgrove (Clare)	Browne
Newpark (Tipperary)	Switzer
Newry (Down/Armagh)	Acheson, Magennis, Pollock, Quinn
Newtown (Kilkenny)	Edward
Newtownbarry (Wexford)	Hall, Maxwell-Barry
Newtown-O'More (Kildare)	Young
Nicholastown Castle (Tipp)	Keating
Nizelrath (Louth)	Chamberlain
Norragh (Kildare)	Baron
Nova Scotia (Canada)	O'Brien, Caldwell
Nunstown (Kerry)	Markham
Nurney (Kildare)	Bagot, Hendy

Offaly (King's Co.) — Caldwell, Campion, Charlton, O'Connor, Coughlan, Dempsey, Fitzgerald, Fox, Goodbody, Jolly, Morris, Odlum, Oxburgh, Parsons, Pierce, Ryan, Smith, Turpin, Ussher, Warburton

Old Abbey (Limerick)	Morgan
Oldtown (Kildare)	Burke
Orior (Armagh)	O'Hanlon
Ormond (Tipperary)	O'Kennedy
Ossory (Mainly Kilkenny)	Fitzpatrick
Oulartleigh (Wexford)	O'Morchoe
Owals	O'Malley
Painstown (Carlow)	Cooke
Pennsylvania (USA)	Glasson, Moore, Siggins
Philadelphia (USA)	Fraser, Kelly
Piersfield	Wilson
Platten (Meath)	Darcy
Polehore (Wexford)	Hore
Pollacton (Carlow)	Burton
Pomeroy (Tyrone)	Irwin
Portarlington (Laois/Offaly)	Jolly
Portmarnock (Dublin)	Plunkett
Portumna (Galway)	Burke
Poulakerry (Tipperary)	Butler
Powerscourt (Wicklow)	O'Toole
Pubblebrian (Limerick)	O'Brien
Pulbawn (Mayo)	Dolan
Punchestown (Kildare)	Allen
Quartertown (Cork)	Hallinan
Quebec (Canada)	Caldwell
Querrin (Clare)	Borough
Queen's Co.	*see Laois*
Rademon (Down)	Neilson
Rahan (Kildare)	Palmer
Ramsfort (Wexford)	Ram
Raphoe (Donegal)	Knox
Rathcoffey (Kildare)	Wogan
Rathcoole (Dublin)	Fitzgerald
Rathcredan (Dublin)	Scurlock
Rathdowney (Laois)	Owen
Rathfarnham (Dublin)	Ely
Rathmacknee Castle (Wexford)	Rosseter
Rathsarn (Laois)	Rudd

Redburn House	Dunville
Richmond Harbour (Longford)	Fleming
Rine-Burren (Clare)	Fahy
Rinney (Cork)	Spencer
Rock, The (Wicklow)	West
Rockforest (Cork)	Cotter
Rockingham (Roscommon)	King
Roscobie (Tyrone)	Moutray
Roscommon	O'Connor, Crofton, Davys, Devenish, Dodwell, Flanagan, Irwin, Kelly, King, Lloyd, Mahon, McManus, Mills, Mulconry, Mulloy, O'Peatain, Walsh, Woulfe
Rosegarland (Wexford)	Leigh,
Rosmanagher (Clare)	D'Esterre
Rostellane (Cork)	Fitzgerald
Rowestown (Meath)	Barnewall
Roxborough (Roscommon)	Irwin
Rush (Dublin)	Smith
Rushen (Donegal)	McFee
St. Wolstans (Kildare)	Alen
Salterhill (Scotland)	Gordon
Santry (Dublin)	Bellingham
Saunders Grove (Wicklow)	Saunders
Scaitliffe (England)	Crossle
Schull (Cork)	Limrick
Scotland	Alexander, MacCabe, McCaughan, McClement, Conn, Macdonnell, Ellis, Gleeson, Gordon, Monroe, Montgomery, Moutray, Nesbitt, Orr, Rhea, Scott, Stirling, Stuart
Screen (Galway)	Kelly
Seafield (Tyrone)	Anthony, Moutray
Sessiamagroll (Tyrone)	Runnett
Shanhoe (Monaghan)	Carson
Sion Lodge (Waterford?)	Tandy
Sixmilecross (Tyrone)	Anderson
Skrine (Wexford)	Devereux
Slane (Meath)	Fleming
Sligo	O'Conor, McDonagh, Downey, O'Gara, O'Hara, Hawksby, Hillas, Irwin, Tyrrell, Wood, Wynne, Yeates
Solsboro (Wexford)	Richards
Somerset (England)	Richardson

Spain	Hadsor, O'Neill, Plunkett, Ryan, Terry
Spidogue (Carlow?)	Butler
Springfield (Donegal)	Dill, Patton
Stabannon (Louth)	Disney
Stameen (Louth)	Cairnes
Still, The (Wexford)	Jameson
Stillorgan (Dublin)	Wolverston
Stonebrook (Kildare)	O'Connor
Strabane (Tyrone)	Macausland
Stradbally (Laois)	Cosby
Stradbrook, (Dublin)	Acton
Stradone (Cavan)	Burrows
Streamstown (Sligo)	Irwin
Strokestown (Roscommon)	Mahon
Swinford (Mayo)	O'Connor
Tarbert (Kerry)	Leslie
Templederry (Tipperary)	Powell
Templemore (Tipperary)	Carden
Tempo (Fermanagh)	Maguire,
Thomastown (Kildare)	Acheson
Thomastown (Louth)	Bellew
Thomastown (Tipperary)	Mathew
Tinnakill Castle (Kildare)	Macdonnell
Tinraheen (Wexford)	Moore
Tintern (Wexford)	Colclough
Tipperary	Allen, Armstrong, Bagwell, Baker, Bell, Birch, Blake-Butler, O'Brien, Browne, Butler, Carden, Carroll, Cooper, O'Dwyer, Everard, Falkiner, Fennessy, Grant, Grubb, Hackett, Hayden, Kearney, (O')Kennedy, Mathew, Maher, O'Meagher, Meara, O'Meara, O'Meehan, Morris, Nagle O'Neill, Powell, Power, Purcell, Reade, Reardon, Ryan, Sall, Scully, Smith, Stapleton, Switzer, Tobin, Tracey, Trehy, Vaughan, White, Wolfe
Tipperstown (Kildare)	Tipper
Tirawley (Mayo)	O'Clery
Tirlickin (Longford)	Ferrall
Tissaxon (Galway)	Meade
Tobervaddy (Mayo)	Ormsby
Tobinstown (Carlow?)	Tobin
Tomduff (Wexford?)	Cooke

Toomavara (Tipperary)	Meara
Tottenham Green (Wexford)	Tottenham
Tralee (Kerry)	Denny
Tristernagh (Meath)	Piers
Truagh (Monaghan)	MacKenna
Tuam (Galway)	Lally
Tuamgraney (Clare)	Huleatt, Parker
Tulla (Clare)	Browne, MacNamara, Rochford
Tullamore (Offaly)	Turpin
Tullaroan (Kilkenny)	Grace
Tulliwood (Westmeath)	McGawley
Tullyard (Down)	Jellett
Tullynally Castle	Packenham
Tullyvin (Cavan)	Moore
Turvey (Dublin)	Barnewall
Tymogue (Laois)	Byrne
Tyrone	Anderson, Anthony, Burnside, Cairnes, Campbell, MacCathmhaoil, Macausland, Delany, O'Devlin, McDonnell, Gartland, O'Gormley, Hamilton, Irwin, Kennedy, Lindesay, O'Mullen, Moutray, O'Neill
Umma (Westmeath)	Magan
Ummerican (Tyrone)	O'Neill
USA	Carroll, Clancy, Colhoun, Crosby, Cudahy, O'Daniel, O'Donnell, Dowse, Early, Eskildson, Flood, Fraser, Glasson, Hamilton, Hayden, Hurley, Kelly, McKinley, Meade, Moore, Moutray, Phillips, O'Reilly, Reardon, Savage, Siggins, Sinnet, Stirling, Sullivan, Synnott, Vickery
Victoria (Austalia)	Martin, Ronan
Virginia (USA)	Colhoun, Meade
Wardstown Castle (Meath)	Folliott
Warrenstown (Louth)	Warren
Washington (USA)	Crosby
Waterford	Anson, Anthony, Bagge, Barker, Barron, Bolton, Boxwell, Connery, O'Dell, Dobbyn, Fitzgerald, Lloyd, Merry, Power, Power-O'Shee, Rivers, Roberts, Ronayne, Ryland, Sherlock, Smyth, Snow, Thurston, Ussher, Vaughan, Wadding, Walsh, Wyse
Waterstown (Wicklow)	Waters
Wells (Wexford)	Doyne

Westmeath	Dalton, Delamere, Devenish, Dillon, Evans, O'Flaherty, McGawley, Geoghegan, Halliday, Hatfield, Hynes, Lyons, Magan, Magawly, Malone, Nangle, Nugent, Robinson, Smyth, Tyrrell
Westmoreland (England)	Steel
Westport House (Mayo)	Browne
Wexford	Annesley, Barrington, Blacker, Boxwell, Boyd, Boyse, Braddell, Breen, Browne, Byrne, Carew, Cliffe, Colclough, Cooke, De Rinza, Devereux, Donovan, Dunne, Esmonde, Frayne, Furlong, Goff, Goodall, Gray, Hall, Hatchell, Hore, Ivory, Kinsella, Lambert, Levinge, Loftus, Ram, Redmond, Roche, Rosseter, Skrine, Stafford, Synnott, Tyrrell, Wickham, Wilton
Wheldrake (Yorkshire, Eng.)	Penrose
Whitechurch (Cork)	O'Mullane
Whitefort (Wexford)	Gray
Wicklow	Bayly, Byrne, Eustace, FitzEustace, Greene, O'Mahony, Monck, Nevil, Perrin, Penrose, Percy, Saunders, O'Toole, Travers, Valentine, Waters, West, Yarner
Willistown (Louth)	Bellew
Wiltshire (England)	Eyre
Windgates (Kildare?)	Spedding
Wisconsin (USA)	Reardon
Woodbrook (Wexford)	Blacker
Woodbrook (Laois)	Chetwood
Woodhill (Cork)	Nesbitt, Penrose
Wooldale (Cork)	Jackson
Yorkshire (England)	Sykes
Worcestershire (England)	ffolliott
Youghal (Cork)	Green, Pratt, Stout, Uniacke